DEALING WEED
The Allen Ahee Story

Micki Fiore

The information in this book was acquired by the author in a series of interviews. Names, dates and events are not meant to be taken as statements of fact as they are subject to the memories and interpretation of the individuals quoted.

Printed in the United States of America
First Printing, 2017

ISBN-10: 0-692-85755-9
ISBN-13: 978-0-692-85755-7

Cover design by Brad Bleich

Alibi Press
Fort Myers, Florida 33908
www.alibipress.com

DEDICATION

To friends whose loyalty lasts a lifetime.

Contents

INTRODUCTION

Allen kept his circle small. Even so, his release from prison generated buzz among friends, family and 'associates' in Tucson and Detroit. Reactions ranged from joy to fear and everything in between.

One of his contacts knew all the right people in L.A. Allen was invited to meet with the president of a major network, an executive producer and a writer. They spent time with Allen, took an interest in his story and told him 'You need to have a book written.'

It was an intriguing next step, but he wasn't sure how to take it. You don't find a lot of writers in his line of work.

His best friend in Detroit asked *my* best friend in Detroit if he knew any writers. Well yeah, he knew me. And he knew I dreamed of writing the bio of anyone in – or close to – The Outfit.

My friend called and described 'the subject' as some guy in Tucson with mafia and cartel associations. His last name was 'Ahee.' I remembered it from the jewelry store.

It would be a lot of work, so I asked about a contract.

He laughed. "We don't *do* that kinda contract." He said I could expect a call and hung up.

That felt abrupt. Was this going to kill my karma? What would I have in common with a drug dealer?

I was no angel 'in the day' but I wasn't nearly as fast as the crowd I ran with. Drugs were never my thing. Cocaine made me want to organize my closets and I HATED pot. It made me stupid and fuzzy.

Now I distrust OTC meds and *loathe* the pharmaceutical industry. From morally bankrupt Martin Shkreli to the nation's rage over price hikes on life-saving EpiPens … talk about drug cartels.

I was convincing myself it was going to be OK. If all that's legal, how bad could this Ahee be?

Allen called a few days later. He was a little arrogant, but his word choices and speech patterns took me back to East Detroit.

There's a lot to be said for having roots in southeast Michigan, knowing the same places and living through the same history-making events.

Some of us are humble descendants of bootleggers and smugglers. That rugged generation defied ridiculous laws and put their lives on the line to shelter, clothe and feed their families.

Our grandfathers married sassy dames and built comfortable homes with materials purchased from illegal profits. Our parents took baby steps on floors hammered into place by their scarred and cigarette-stained hands.

As a small child I rested my chin on the kitchen table and listened *enthralled* as Grandpa told tales of midnight runs and near misses. Sometimes he had to flip his boat – load and all – and swim for his life.

Allen's family was not nearly so humble. He was raised in a fine three-story house by ambitious Lebanese parents with a Sicilian connection as thick as blood.

Everything Allen learned and the contacts he possessed helped fuel his rise in illegal enterprise.

Alcohol vs. marijuana – the comparison is irresistible. More families are broken by booze than weed.

I asked him if marijuana in our time reminds him of prohibition in our grandparents' day.

He responded, "All the fucking time."

I was in.

Allen asked me to let him talk about his experiences in no particular order; he said questions would interrupt his train of thought. I could ask anything when he was finished.

I could ask, but he wouldn't always answer.

Where details were needed, public sources were researched, quoted and acknowledged.

DEALING WEED
The Allen Ahee Story

Micki Fiore

1 The Third Generation

Allen's grandfather didn't leave Lebanon; *he fled*.

James Ahee was born in Zahlé, in the eastern foothills of Mount Sannine in the Beqaa valley – an area still famous for its bread and wine.

When the railroad came through in the late 1800s, the town became an important trade route between Beirut and Damascus. It also grew to be politically significant, which may have had something to do with his urgent departure.

"Supposedly my grandfather ended up killing a policeman, so he had to leave. He and his brother got on a boat and came to Detroit. He was 15 or 16, came without a penny in his pocket. They sold towels from door to door.

"He and his brother married two sisters and they were cousins; their last name was Ahee too. I cannot even tell you how many cousins I have."

Other family members followed. "Some of them moved out west when Arizona was just a territory – before it was even a state."

Those early choices helped the Ahees grow strong roots in communities from southeast Michigan to Tucson, Arizona and the California coast.

While many immigrants came to Detroit for factory jobs and a steady paycheck, James was determined to make it on his own. Along the way he established a close friendship with Pietro 'Peter' Corrado.

Allen says "The Lebanese and Italian people always got along really well in Detroit. There's not any other city in the country like that. They raised their families together."

Peter was Sicilian, so he and James had much in common – Mediterranean customs, devotion to family and love of cooking.

Peter married Petrina Zerilli – daughter of Anthony and Rosalie Zerilli of Terrasini, Sicily. Petrina's brother was the legendary Joseph ('Uno') Zerilli – a.k.a. 'The Motor City Godfather.'

According to author Scott M. Burnstein, "Through the years, Zerilli would build a reputation second to none in the nation's underworld." (*Motor City Mafia* 'A Century of Organized Crime in Detroit')

1

In 1914 James had enough money to open Paramount – the first pita bread bakery in the country.

Peter and his associates were doing well too; but they were about to do MUCH better. Detroit enacted the Damon act in 1917 – nearly three years before Prohibition hit the rest of the country. It gave The Outfit a head start. They were ready with sources, transport and venues to meet the anticipated demand.

Public response was *tremendous;* nothing felt quite as good as being bad. Speakeasies sprang up as the doors of traditional drinking establishments were shackled shut.

Fringed flappers in short, sassy dresses powdered their knees, smoked, drank and shimmied with pleasure at the naughtiness of it.

Peter ran all of the booze and gambling in Detroit and Toledo. The press dubbed him 'Machine Gun Pete' – after his favorite firearm. It was an appropriate tool for a dangerous business.

After centuries of oppression, the Sicilians were masters of retaliation. "The Mafia, a network of organized-crime groups based in Italy and America, evolved over centuries in Sicily, an island ruled until the mid-19th century by a long line of foreign invaders. Sicilians banded together in groups to protect themselves and carry out their own justice." (*Origins of the Mafia* from History.com)

The friend who involved me in writing Allen's story is a history buff and long-time friend of the Corrado family's second generation. He knew both of Machine Gun Pete's sons. I refer to him as 'A.S.' (for 'anonymous source') throughout.

A.S. explained "When armies headed north to invade Rome, they moved through Sicily because it was the path of least resistance. It's such a beautiful place, some men stayed and intermarried; that's why the Sicilians look different. Their children had mixed blood as far back as the Moors.

"The northern Italians considered Sicilian children 'mixed bloods' – not true Italians. When they braced for invasion, they didn't bother protecting the Sicilians.

"As survival became increasingly difficult, the Sicilians responded with violence and it became a way of life. When they came to the United States, they did a lot of good things; but they also continued to do *their thing.*"

And few Sicilian families 'did it' better than the Detroit Mob.

Some say Detroit was the strongest, most organized crime family in the country. The 100% rule stood; everybody in Detroit was Sicilian.

The Outfit was in the perfect place at the right time. About 75% of all of the alcohol that entered the United States came through Detroit. Southeast Michigan's waterways form a discreet, accessible border between the United States and Canada.

Opportunities for driving or navigating a boat to or near Detroit were easy, as Lake Huron flows through the St. Clair River to the Detroit River and Lake Erie beyond.

Joseph Kennedy heard bootlegging was easier in Detroit than anywhere else because of the river. He wanted to come down, but 'they' assured him if he was anywhere near Detroit – or in that part of Canada – bad things would happen to him. 'Under no circumstances could he work here; it would be very unhealthy.'

Civilians weren't welcome either, but they took their chances. Like my grandfather, they smuggled product across the river by boat – or waited for winter and drove it across.

Others – including my grandmother's father – made and sold their own hooch. Without quality control, some of it caused blindness, paralysis and even death. Urban myth has it that when one wary buyer submitted a sample to a lab for analysis, the chemist informed him "Your horse has diabetes."

The Corrados prospered before, during and after the Prohibition. Mafia expert Nick Pileggi (author of *Wiseguy* and co-writer of the screenplay for the Academy Award winning *Goodfellas*) has been quoted as saying "After Prohibition, they stopped fighting internally, inter-married and put their dirty money into legitimate businesses. Meanwhile, the nation's other families were out there killing each other."

Burnstein offers details. "At the end of 1931, the modern Detroit Mafia family was born, led by Angelo Meli, Joseph Zerilli, William 'Black Bill' Tocco, John Priziola, and Pete Licavoli.

"Getting his start in the local underworld as a gunman for the River Gang, Corrado, also known as 'Pete the Enforcer,' was Joe Zerilli's brother-in-law and was named a captain in the Detroit crime family in the 1930s."
(*Motor City Mafia* 'A Century of Organized Crime in Detroit')

DEALING WEED

The Ahees did well too; *initially.* Profits from James' bakery put him in a position to buy some of the best property in Grosse Pointe.

Allen grumbled "Then the depression came and they couldn't keep up with the taxes. They lost all of it."

As if being born into that level of wealth might have changed the path he chose. *I don't think so.*

Allen's grandfather weathered the storms of that generation and taught his sons to run the family business. It would be his legacy.

"My dad had two older brothers, one was Louie and one was Joe. They all worked the bakery as kids. My dad started working at the bakery at 7 or 8. He had to stand on milk crates just to get on the counter to bake bread. It was labor intensive back then.

"My grandfather had heart problems. When doctors told him the climate in Tucson would prolong his life, he went there on his own, didn't feel the need to take his family.

"His brother's son Sol lived there. He kept an eye on my grandfather while my dad took care of the bakery.

"My mother's family came to Detroit in the 1920s. They left her with her grandparents in Lebanon while they came to America to get situated. She grew up speaking French and English. By the time her parents sent for her at ten, she could speak both languages without an accent.

"Her whole family was Muslim and – back then – all of the Muslim Lebanese lived in Dearborn around Dix Avenue. That's where my mom grew up.

"She never smoked, never drank, never did anything. She was tiny, real light skinned with shoulder length hair. You wouldn't think she was Middle Eastern if you saw her at all."

He laughed. "Some people come out light and some come out dark.

"Her father was a big muckety muck, he had done a lot of political stuff and was friends with the mayor. "I remember my mom telling me when she was 14 or 15 she wanted a driver's license.

"She couldn't drive for shit, but her father went to the mayor and they gave her one. They didn't make her take a test or anything.

"Her parents had her betrothed to some guy at 16. Back then they did it that way.

"He was older and had money – owned a grocery store in downtown Detroit.

4

"He was very good to her. They bought a big three-story house in the area; it had extra lots on each side so the neighbors wouldn't be too close.

"They must have done OK. She was able to buy the village where she was born in the Middle East. The people that lived there were all her family. She never wanted them to be displaced. We still own some of the land. None of my family would ever sell it.

"She had her first baby at 16; she had five children by the time her husband died of cancer.

"When my parents met, she was in her late 30s – ten years older than my dad. She always looked nice, dressed nice and had all the high fashion stuff.

"She had tons of gold bracelets; it must be an Arab thing for women to wear those, six or seven solid gold bracelets at a time. Family in the jewelry business brought it back from other countries and she could buy it wholesale.

"My father had grown up tall, with dark, wavy hair. He was a dead ringer for the old Hollywood heartthrob Cesar Romero. He had the bakery and all the Lebanese people in Detroit and Dearborn knew who my grandfather was; they knew the name.

"One day my dad delivered bread to her grocery store. He said when he walked in she was trying to smoke a cigarette to be cool.

"He took it out of her mouth and threw it away. He said 'Don't smoke. It doesn't look good on you.'

"He told me 'I went in there and met her and that was pretty much it.'

"My dad was a swinging bachelor before they met, but he realized she was a good person and that's what it's all about. Her name was Dorothy, but he called her DeeBee. It was a love story."

A thirty year-old Catholic bachelor meets a Muslim widow with a houseful of kids – some younger, some nearly grown. The odds weren't good. Worse yet, "A Muslim marrying a Catholic was unheard of in those days. *It just didn't happen.*

"So in 1956 they ran away, drove to Kentucky and got married." Alfred found himself a newlywed father of five. He moved into her house. He was happy, everybody was happy.

"My family wasn't like devout Muslims. There was never not Christmas. They all had it even before I was born.

David and Elaine were older, so it wasn't like they needed a father figure at that point in their lives. Midge was in her late teens, Nadra a little younger.

"Cindy was young when her real father died, so she viewed my dad as her father."

The following year was a time of mixed emotions for both families. When Machine Gun Pete died the torch was passed to Dominic, his eldest son. And Alfred and DeeBee delivered – and nearly lost – their first son.

"When I was born, my dad came in and looked at me. He said I was the ugliest thing in the world – blue or purple or something. But my sister Elaine saw me and she was like in love with me. She was 19 or 20 and there's this baby brother born with a collapsed lung.

"Doctors said I wouldn't live – or if I did, I wouldn't be able to use my right side.

"That night my dad went to church and made a vow; if I lived he'd take me to the Anointing of the Sick procession in Gary, Indiana.

"The church had a piece of the cross Jesus was crucified on. And the guy that makes the vow has to carry the invalid on his shoulders in a procession for a mile.

"At the time my dad was smoking a pack of Pall Malls a day – so he was in no condition to do it."

But he never forgot it needed to be done.

"Elaine married Ronnie shortly after I was born, but she continued to think of me as one of her own. Ronnie was Muslim and our families were already connected before they got together.

"Once I learned to talk I never shut up. And I was walking pretty early, before I was one.

"In home movies I'd be jumping around like a little monkey, smiling and joking. I would run around and play games, slide down bannisters.

"One day a vacuum salesman comes to our house and my mom lets him in. I'm running along the top of one couch and jumping from the top of one to the other. It never bothered my mom, but apparently it bothered this guy.

"He goes 'Lady, I don't know how you put up with this kid.' He says 'I gotta get outta here.'

"I was just a wild little kid. I couldn't help it.

"One night I couldn't sleep. Midge had a bowling ball and our three story house had long flights of wood stairs. So I rolled the ball down the steps. Everybody woke up and was yelling at me."

Which was, of course, the desired effect. He had their attention; now they would exact their revenge.

"We had a laundry chute that went all the way to the basement and I was small enough to fit in the chute. My sisters would put me in at the top and let me drop me all the way down.

"They padded the bottom with pillows and towels so I'd have a better chance of surviving the landing.

"Sometimes they'd lock me in the basement. It was scary, with the old time mangle boards they used to press the bed sheets."

Mangle boards?

"Yeah, like a 6' long steam press." He started to explain. "We had people that would ...."

He didn't want to finish the sentence; he was embarrassed.

Are you trying to say you had maids?

"We had black maids. I had a special black lady who loved me to death. Her name was Carrie. She wasn't there to clean, she was there to watch over me because my mom was always on the go.

"Carrie was a big lady, big and wide. When I played hide and seek with my sisters, I was small enough to hide under her dress.

"If I wanted something that Carrie cooked – like ribs and barbecued chicken – on her day off, my mom would dial the number and hand me the phone.

"I'd ask Carrie to come and she'd say 'OK baby, I'll be there.'

"She'd leave her own children and take three buses to come back and make it for me.

"One time I went with her to take the trash out back. I saw a bunch of rats in the alley, screamed like a little girl and ran back in the house.

"My dad said 'Don't worry about it.' He had a little .25 caliber handgun; goes and gets it and says 'Come on.'

"He takes me outside and starts shooting them – *boom boom* – *boom boom*. That was gross to me, to see them die.

"He picked them up by their tails and threw them in the trash.

"The neighbors heard gunshots and called the police.

"They came and cuffed him up. He got arrested for shooting a .25 within Detroit city limits.

"I was crying 'Don't take my dad!'" Allen laughed. "I don't think he was in jail for 10 fucking minutes."

He worried about his father on that occasion; but his father *never* stopped worrying about him. Alfred hadn't made good on his promise to God and the survival of his 'wild little kid' was *not* assured. The first worst time was proof of that.

"There were three steps from our landing to the storm door. One of the maids had just waxed the floors and covered the landing with a rug.

"I jumped from the top, slipped and flew through the window. Broken shards of glass tore into my arm and a big chunk of v-shaped glass went into my throat. It was just hanging there, it barely missed my jugular. A quarter inch either way and I'm outta there.

"I yanked it out.

"The neighbors came running when they heard the crash. They found me trapped and bleeding in a pile of tangled metal and shattered glass. I didn't know what to do to get out.

"My sisters found me all covered in blood. Somehow they got me untangled, wrapped me in towels and rushed me to Ford Hospital. The doctor told them how lucky I was.

"After that I had so many brushes with death I always thought it was normal."

Was that the first time you felt fear?

"I'm not afraid of dying, what the fuck. It either is or isn't going to happen. It may be that when I was young I used to feel immortal. Not so much now that I hurt all the time."

Allen was on the verge of losing the limitless benefits that go with being the youngest child of doting parents. His mother had one miscarriage before conceiving for the last time.

"My mother was Fertile Myrtle; *nothing* slowed her down. She wanted to go everywhere and she was going to go *no matter what!*

"She was so small she could never move the seat up far enough; when she was pregnant they put wood blocks on the brake and gas pedals so she could reach. Sometimes she sat on phone books.

"Douglas is 3 ½ years younger than me. Douglas Numbnuts. He was a pain in my ass all the time.

"At first we played around together, just hanging out and rough-housing. But he'd always run and tell and I'd get in trouble.

"He enjoyed that.

"Whatever I wanted, he wanted. Wherever I wanted to go, he wanted to go. It was like *Omigod*.

"My dad would always say 'Take your brother with you.'

"I said 'I don't want to take him! He can't go!'

"Suddenly he's my father's favorite, so I was always trying to hurt him.

"My father said 'It's your brother. You don't fight with him!'

"Usually he'd hit me with one of his leather slippers. It hurt; not that much, but a little.

"Then I stabbed Douglas in the eye with a screwdriver. I got my ass beat that time.

"My mom told him to leave me alone. She always protected me."

Except she didn't always know when he needed protecting.

"When I was five my mother was driving with me in the back seat. I opened the door and fell out. She stopped, picked me up and put me back – but I was crying, so she turned around and drove home.

"When we got there David slapped me and said 'Big boys don't cry. You're not hurt now. You're fine!'

"David and Ronnie were around the same age; they were buddies. They wouldn't let me be any kind of a weakling. *A weak kid was not allowed.* They'd put me in football gear and pound the shit out of me.

"I told David 'I'm gonna kick your ass' but I couldn't wet my way out of a paper bag.

"He'd say 'Don't write checks your ass can't cash.'

"My dad used to buy me expensive toys, like airplanes.

"David would say 'Let me show you how to fly that' – and he'd break it.

Despite all that, "I admired David when I was a kid. He was older than me, but we played. It was cool. But then he joined the army and he wasn't around."

Do you think your childhood might have been better if David had been around longer?

"Not really. Him and my brother-in-law were a little rough on me. They knocked me around and beat the shit out of me every day."

He faced similar hardships in Dearborn.

"We visited my widowed grandmother every day.

9

"She was diabetic and couldn't get around very well, so my mother would cook her food and make sure she had everything she needed.

"We lived at Joy Road and Wyoming in Detroit, so it wasn't far – but I never wanted to go. My grandmother would be waiting in the chair when I would come in and she would hold me and kiss on me. It was just so gross.

"My mother was helpful with everybody. We always went to visit someone she knew who had a child with Down's syndrome. It kind of made me feel uncomfortable sometimes; but I learned we're put on earth to do what we can for others. It's not always about us."

While DeeBee was working to instill compassion, her brothers were teaching her son intimidation and violence.

"My grandmother's house was a three-plex, so my mom's two brothers lived there – Freddie and Norman. Uncle Norman was an engineer at Ford.

"At first it was just kid stuff they made me get in trouble for, like throwing eggs at the neighbor's house. But later there was this kid down the street and my uncles hated him.

"Every time I came over they'd send me there to beat him up. He was older and bigger than me and every time I tried I got my ass kicked.

"They just made fun of me after that. They said 'You can't even beat that guy up?'

"It went on for a while. So finally one time I just beat the shit out of him somehow. And they were so happy, 'cuz I was their nephew and they wanted me to be tough. I finally got a pat on the back."

What kind of person do you think you might have been if your brother, brother-in-law and uncles had been a little less brutal?

"Probably I would have been a spoiled brat."

He thought about it a bit longer.

"I would have done all the right things maybe – instead of all the wrong things."

Alfred was wholly committed to raising Allen as a fine young Catholic. He allowed him to go to public school for kindergarten, but sent him to St. Luke Catholic Church in Detroit for first grade.

"I had to wear a little suit. And every morning before school we had to walk to mass two by two to the church.

"I was like *This is retarded.* I'd wake up active and now I have to sit an hour for mass? I didn't want to go at all, ever. I could not stand it.

"After mass, class was the *worst* place to be cooped up all morning.

"I'd just do things because I was bored out of my mind. I'd pick up my lunch box and drop it, make a big ruckus.

"One nun used to hit me on my knuckles with a ruler."

The nuns assigned number of paddle whacks based on the degree of misbehavior. Offenders were sent to a lay male teacher for more severe punishment. It was up to the child to be honest about the number of whacks.

"They'd march us upstairs, there'd be like three or four of us. Then I'm supposed to stand in front of his whole class and tell the teacher the number the nuns gave me?

"I'd always say 'I'm not here to get spanked. Sister just asked me to come up and make sure THEY came.'

"He wasn't buying it, so I'd tell him 'One.'

"And he was like 'C'mon, what's the real number?'"

Allen negotiated. "'Well how about two?'"

"Then he'd take me into a closet and beat me with a wooden paddle with holes in it."

Corporal punishment only reinforced his recidivism.

"I was a constant visitor."

The nuns at St. Andrew's Catholic Church wore long black habits and functional black shoes. Their worn soles barely provided adequate traction for buffed hallways, let alone snow and ice.

"In winter I threw snowballs at them. And I got three or four other kids to go along with me. It was kind of funny; they were slipping around yelling 'You better stop that!'

"Finally Mother Superior came out. She made us write 500 times 'I will not throw snowballs at the nuns.'

"We couldn't do the assignment at school, we had to take it home. It was going to take forever. I wound two pencils together with rubber bands and tried that. My mom helped me. And my sisters.

"Even my dad pitched in. But he complained, he said 'I can't write as sloppy as you!'

He had the most beautiful penmanship, really pretty.

"I'm like 'Who cares about penmanship? What the fuck does that get you? It's the words!'

11

"Anyway, we got it done and I'm *the only one* that handed in the whole thing. My friends didn't get in trouble for not completing the assignment.

"I was so pissed."

Worse still, "The nuns graded based on the way you behaved. In second grade they said I was disruptive.

"They had four spots for each grade. If you got four spots in A, you got to B – four more to C and D. I don't even know how long it took 'til I was stuck in E.

"I told the nun 'What are we going to do now?'

"She says 'You're going to fail. I'll have to call your parents.'

"I said 'Call away.'

"They all thought something could be really wrong with this little fuck. I had to go see a psychologist twice a week for a long time.

"They measured my IQ and realized I was like genius level; school was just too boring for me. They told my parents they could move me up from second to fourth grade.

"My dad said 'Fuck 'em, he's not mature enough.' So I had to stay an extra year in second grade.

"In third grade I finally got a regular teacher and I was kind of teacher's pet. She was really pretty and blonde and if I was bad she made me come sit under her desk.

"I'm down there trying to not look up her skirt. I'm like 'Oh God, what's to do.'

"She opened her legs a little bit and 'I could see.'"

He laughed. "I was interested but I didn't know *why*."

Still in the suits like some Baby Gotti, "When I look at the old pictures, I'm like 'What were they thinking?'

"My parents would dress me up in wool suits and my dad expected me to *take care of them*. I'm a kid, what the fuck do I know?

"We'd have tornado drills where we'd have to go outside and lay down in a ditch.

"We had the atomic bomb blast drills where we had to dive under our desks. Like that's going to save our lives. The explosion's not going to kill you; you'd be lucky if it did.

"So I'm coming home from school in my wool suit and this kid is yelling and screaming at me.

12

"I swing my lunchbox at his head, miss him and bash his sister instead. I felt SO BAD I hit her.

"She's bleeding all over the place and now I have to fight her brother."

Was it a metal lunchbox?

"Yeah. Probably Flintstones or Scooby Doo."

It wasn't a proud moment.

"The girl needed 13 stitches and I ripped my pants in the fight. When I got home my dad said 'What did you do? You ruined 'em!'"

It wouldn't be the last time.

"When David got home from the army, he married a devout Muslim who is now a Haji." [Someone who has done the pilgrimage to Mecca.]

"I remember being little and wearing a tuxedo. I fell down and tore another pair of pants."

He stopped speaking; there was a long silence.

"I hardly saw David again. He became closer with his wife's family than any of us. She's a devout Muslim, her family was praying all the time." He paused; "And she just kind of rules him."

And then he *went off*.

"She's the boss of him. She's a bitch.

"She's got a brother who's about my age and he's a dimwit, half a retard. She used to try to compare him to me and I would just laugh at her. So she doesn't like me at all."

"Between my dad's Catholic relatives and Muslim cousins on my mom's side, my youth was quite interesting. I used to go to the mosque with my cousins when there was youth groups.

"I'd go to all that stuff. It didn't matter to me, I didn't really care. I just thought that what they did was weird sometimes."

Like weird compared to Catholic?

"Catholic is weird too. All religions are weird to me. They're all the same thing.

"My family's not hard practicing Muslims except for David. It was kind of a weird relationship because he really wasn't close to anybody in the family."

His sisters' boyfriends were easier to relate to.

"Nadra is about nine years older than me. She married an Italian guy who was teaching high school in Grosse Pointe.

13

"Midge was short – about 5' – and overweight; but she was pretty in her day. Around 1965 or 66 she married Sam Vicari. We were still living in Detroit, they had their wedding reception at our house.

"I don't know if it's true or not, but they said Sam slept with Diana Ross.

"His brother Dominic Vicari was in dry cleaning business in Grosse Pointe and his son Joe Vicari – who's my age – has Italian restaurants in the Detroit area. He does fabulous.

"Sam was Sicilian, so Midge converted to Catholicism and had four kids back to back. That was like unbelievable. Their oldest son David and I were really close. When they brought him home I was fascinated. I spent a lot of time with them.

"My sister Cindy is six years older. We went at it like cats and dogs sometimes, but we were always really close. *Always*."

While Allen was growing up the spare lots at his house were ideal for hanging out with friends and playing sports.

"All the neighbor kids would come over and play football and baseball on our property.

"There was a protestant church behind our house and it had those basement windows. If you hit a home run, you'd break a window. We broke one at least twice a week, then we'd walk over and see if they went in. We lost some baseballs, but my dad would always buy me more.

"One day the minister comes out with a shoebox. He says 'You live over there?'

"I said 'I don't try to break the windows. If we hit a home run and it breaks the window, I'm sorry.'

"He said 'Don't be scared, stuff happens. Don't worry about it.' He says 'Here' and gives me a shoebox full of the baseballs that I broke all his windows with."

Allen enjoyed reminiscing about this time in his life.

"We played Kick the Can, Smear the Queer ..."

WHAT?

"It's kind of like football except there's no teams. Whoever has the football is queer and has to be chased, attacked and tackled so eventually the other team gets the ball.

"I have no filter. I called my niece Lezbollah – like Hezbollah. She's not even gay. I still catch myself calling gay friends 'homos.'"

There was no harm intended; unless he didn't like you.

"My mom had a sister who was a bitch.

"She worked at Ford as a secretary or something. She drove her brand new Thunderbird convertible to our house, thought she was a big shot. She was parked in the driveway with the top down.

"My dad had the sprinkler on. I moved the sprinkler so every time it fanned, the spray would hit the inside of her car; then I took off.

"When she came out and saw what I did, she waited at the house until I got back and then she came after me.

"I started screaming and running and she's trying to catch me on foot. *That wasn't going to happen.*

"My dad said 'Why did you do that? What's the matter with you?'

"I said 'She's mean!'

"Later she moved to Vegas and became a Blackjack dealer."

"I remember it seemed like suddenly we had all these family members I didn't know in Arizona. Then we were going every year to see 'em and hang out."

"Elaine and her husband got a divorce and she remarried a guy whose sister is my aunt. I can't even tell you how many cousins and relatives I have because I have no idea. I know I've got at least 22 nephews and nieces.

"After a while Elaine's husband decided it was time to move to California; so in the 60s and 70s we'd get in my dad's Cadillac and drive out west every summer.

"When we went to see them, we didn't stay at a hotel; there was none of that. Elaine's husband had opened a liquor store and they were doing OK. They had a nice house, we'd stay for about a month.

"They had a pool and I'd always swim. We had a lot of fun together.

"We had rollout beds everywhere, but nobody was sleeping."

Elaine's family was only one stop on the tour.

"My parents would always go to Vegas and see the bitch aunt. I was too young to gamble, but I wanted to. I tried fixing myself up to look older. I used eye liner to draw a moustache; I used to try everything.

"We'd go here, there, wherever; but we'd always come to Tucson and Phoenix to see my uncles and cousins.

"My one uncle married a Mexican woman. They owned the El Dorado restaurant, one of the best restaurants in the city of Tucson – and that's saying a lot.

"Their son George was born in Mexico, so he had U.S. and Mexican citizenship and spoke English and Spanish without an accent."

One of the most interesting influences in Allen's life, "He was about 8 years older than me."

At the time, 18-year-old George had about zero in common with his 10 year old cousin.

2 Leaving Detroit

"My dad and Uncle Dominic were really good friends, they had a lot in common. This was the second generation of our two families raising their kids together.

"The media called him 'Fats' but we never did. To me he was always Uncle Dominic. He treated us so much like family everyone else did.

"I remember back in those days we had a little door in our house where they delivered milk and orange juice. I guess Peter's dad found out about it because we stopped getting billed."

Dominic Corrado was married to Josephine Vitale, daughter of Paul Vitale. They say Paul controlled all the vice in Greektown – a notorious destination mere blocks from the heart of the city.

"My Aunt Jo only had two kids, Peter and Paul. Their family is really strict on the first son is named after the father's father. The second is named after the mother's father. That's why there's a lot of Peters, Pauls, Ninos and Dominics.

"Uncle Dominic's younger brother Tony married Aunt Jo's sister. Her sister Grace had Peter, Paul, Nino, Dominic and Rosalie. So they're first cousins on both sides too."

While Allen was growing up in Detroit and Dearborn, Peter and Paul were growing up on Middlesex in Grosse Pointe. Allen says "Most of 'the families' lived there; it was the safest street in metro Detroit."

"Uncle Dominic was the biggest property owner in Greektown."

At that time bars and restaurants stayed open later than most and patrons basked in the underworld vibe. They gathered to eat, drink and gamble – everyone from law makers and breakers to sports celebrities and nationally known performers.

Allen grew up hearing all the stories.

"Uncle Dominic owned the Pink Panther for a long time. They named it after the movie with Peter Sellers.

"All the big entertainers used to go to Windsor to entertain and then, after their show, they'd come back across the Ambassador Bridge and go to the Pink Panther.

"After the bars closed they'd go to the Grecian Gardens. Uncle Dominic owned that too.

"They would just go there and drink alcohol out of coffee cups so nobody would know they were drinking cocktails."

Seems like all Detroiters have a Sinatra story – some about his generosity, others about his bad behavior. Allen was not a fan.

"Frank Sinatra was one of the entertainers who'd fly in and hang out at the Pink Panther and Grecian Gardens.

"Sinatra thought he was somebody that everybody loved and cherished. For the most part the masses did, but the people that really knew him knew that he was an ass.

"He was always trying to get girls because he was Frank Sinatra. If you don't have any game or rap or ability to talk to women on your own merit, you're nothing.

"I heard one time Sinatra was hitting on some guy's wife in the Pink Panther. They asked him a few times to stop and he wouldn't.

"Uncle Dominic was a big guy – 6'1" and 280 pounds with hands like paws. Sinatra was tiny. When Uncle Dominic told him to stop, *he stopped.*"

At other times Uncle Dominic sat back and let him suffer the consequences.

"There was this bar in Miami – the Dream Bar. It was owned by Patsy Erra. One night Sinatra was there with his body guards."

According to the book *American Desperado; My Life – from Mafia Soldier to Cocaine Cowboy to Secret Government Asset* by Jon Roberts and Evan Wright, the Dream Bar was a well-known gangster hangout and Erra was "a top boss in the Bonanno family. He was also associated with Sam Giancana, Santo Trafficante, Jr., and Meyer Lansky."

Allen heard "Frank Sinatra pinched Erra's wife's ass, so Erra just started laying into him, beating his ass.

"My Uncle Dominic was there with Mike Terlizzi. When Sinatra's body guards got up to intervene, my Uncle Dominic and Mike told them to 'SIT THE FUCK DOWN!'

"So they sat down and Patsy beat Sinatra's ass."

Very few celebrities were tough enough to mix it up.

"There was an entertainer from Cleveland, Sonny King – a long-time friend of Sinatra. And my Uncle Tony and him were somewhere together and a fight broke out.

"Uncle Tony said 'He's the only entertainer shoved me aside to get in there and beef. *The only one.*'"

If out-of-town celebrities had the time or inclination, they paid homage to mob royalty.

Comedian Norm Crosby built a career on mangling the English language. He appeared on *The Love Boat*, *The Tonight Show Starring Johnny Carson*, *The Dean Martin Show* and more.

"One time Norm Crosby was performing in Windsor. He came to the Detroit House of Corrections after hours to see Uncle Pete, Aunt Jo's brother." (The press said Peter was a capo in the Detroit family.)

"Norm told the warden 'I just came to see Pete Vitale.' He said 'If you let me see him, next week I'll come back and do a show for all the inmates.'

"The warden said 'Sure, if you'll come back and do that, I'll be glad to let you.'

"So Norm got to see Uncle Pete. And true to his word, Crosby came back the next week and did a show for the inmates."

• • •

In 1967 the Ahees were returning from summer vacation when all hell broke.

Late on Sunday, July 23, Detroit police raided an illegal after-hours drinking establishment. Patrons were celebrating the return of two Vietnam War veterans and 82 African Americans were arrested. In the suffocating summer heat, frustration turned to violence.

Allen was 9 years old. I was in high school working part time at Henry Ford Hospital and A.S. was with the National Guard. We didn't know each other then, but we all have personal memories of one of the worst riots in U.S. history.

Allen says "We lived close to Cass High School. I remember driving back going to our house watching everybody breaking windows and taking shit. We could hear gunfire. I remember seeing tanks. And I'm like 'What the heck's going on dad?'

"He said 'I don't know, but it doesn't look good. It's a riot.'

"I had to stay right close to my house. It was just weird. Somehow they didn't come down our street. I don't know why."

I was 16 years old, attending East Detroit High School and working as a co-op student at the hospital. Around noon, after morning classes, four of us would change into white uniforms, grab a sandwich and wait for the bus at Gratiot and 9 Mile.

19

In two bus stops – one hour – we'd arrive at our destination.

If my mother had been paying attention, she would have never let me go. She must have assumed the danger had subsided. It hadn't.

That day only two of us waited for the bus. The ride was somber as a wake.

One of my black coworkers got on at the second stop. A sweet-faced girl with soft gray eyes, she once confided that she'd been raised to believe 'Being black is the cross I have to bear.'

That day she whispered that her family was sleeping under their beds because bullets were coming through the walls.

We arrived to find the National Guard in position on the sixteenth floor of the hospital. It seemed like everything was under control.

A few hours stuck in a dark corner typing death reports will mess with your head. It was a pretty day, so two of us decided to take a break.

We went outside and sat on the front steps. A nurse rushed out and nearly grabbed us by our collars – "GET BACK INSIDE!" There was a sniper at the rear entrance.

The city would never be the same. *Henryford.com* describes it this way. "The events on July 23, 1967 triggered a disaster which would alter Henry Ford Hospital and the city of Detroit forever. A week-long riot ensued – filled with violence, looting and more than 1,600 fires. The injured poured into the emergency rooms of neighborhood hospitals, especially at Henry Ford Hospital, which was in the vicinity of the most serious rioting. The Emergency Room handled 656 cases related to the riot in four days. Of these, almost 400 were serious trauma cases involving gunshot wounds, stabbings or other severe lacerations. The Twelfth Street area was like a combat zone, resulting in at least 44 fatalities. Constant sniper attacks continued, with Henry Ford Hospital as a target since guardsmen and tanks were bivouacked there."

President Johnson sent in U.S. Army troops. Governor Romney deployed 800 state police and 9,000 members of the U.S. National Guard … including A.S. We hadn't met yet.

He says "At first I was at Receiving Hospital, in charge of the shackled prisoners in beds ward. They took away our rifles in the hospital. Fortunately, the guy I was with had a pistol. We made it real clear to the folks in there, 'Don't put us in the position of misinterpreting some of your moves because we *will* shoot you.'

"There are blacks and there are niggers. A nigger approached me and said 'If you didn't have that gun I'd rip it off of you.'

"I hit him in the teeth with it and he took off.

"We were shot at. At one point the two of us were trying to get behind the same light pole, pushing each other out of the way because it was all about survival.

"I witnessed brutality, not that the blacks weren't rioting.

"One guy was just trying to get home from work and he needed to get through a barricade. He was a big guy; he told the white cops 'You have to let me get through.'

"Four of 'em wound up taking him on, beating him up. They put him in the back of the squad car.

"I went up and said 'What the fuck are you doing? The guy's just trying to go home.'

"They said 'Just mind your own business.'

"I remember thinking to myself *You can't have white policemen in black neighborhoods.*"

I asked him how Greektown fared.

He said "It was pretty well known that the people that ran the barbooth games controlled Greektown. No one wanted to have problems with them, so they stayed away.

"The guys at Melrose Linen were heavily armed and ready to defend. When the military was sent in, they basically told them 'You're better armed than we are!'

"A lot went on *around* them, but nothing happened *in* Greektown."

During the riot 7,000 people were arrested and more than 1,000 buildings were burned. Thousands packed it up and moved to the suburbs.

Allen and I thought 'the families' moved to the northern suburbs because of the riot; we were incorrect. There was a family problem.

A.S. explained; "It was kind of like there was a falling out, but not totally. It had to do with money."

The press referred to Jack Tocco as 'suspected Detroit Mafia Boss.'

A.S. says "Jack was very difficult to deal with. He had a degree in finance from U of D. He was maybe the typical business person that took all he could and didn't share with the partners in a fair way.

"His position was that 'We're all in this together' and he wanted to centralize money for a legitimate business. He said 'I have more value; I need to be paid a lot more.'

"They were drawing money out but none of the others could. Shareholders felt they should be getting something, but he said 'No, you're not getting anything.'

"Now we realize that we don't have much to do with the ongoing value. We came through when they needed capital – but now they're saying 'Here's a check and you're out.'

"No negotiations, no phone call, no meeting. 'We want to buy you out.'

"They didn't get to engage with the people who were making the decisions, so they wanted to get as far away as they could … but not too far.

"That's why we left the Grosse Pointe area, to get away from Jack. It was a way to say 'We don't appreciate how we're being treated.'

"If I was Jack I would have interpreted the message as 'We'll still do what we're required to do, but we'll get as far away from you as possible.'

"After that there was a coolness between Jack and Dominic, so he moved his family to Rochester Hills."

The Ahees moved too.

3 Growing Up Mob

"My family moved to one of the new subdivisions that were going up at the time. It was a pretty modest house, about 3,300 square feet – just me, my mother, my father, my brother and two older sisters.

"Uncle Dominic built a big house near 25 Mile and Gunn Road, only 7 or 8 miles away from us. If Peter and Paul weren't at my house, I was at theirs. We saw each other every day.

"My dad and mom were always working – and they had started to fight. I called them the Bickersons. There was never a winner. I'm like 'You guys are so annoying.'

"My dad just wanted to do his thing, which was cook and make bread. He put a pizza oven in their garage and had bricks piled up on the bottom so it would get extra hot – hot enough to bake pita bread. It was unbelievable how good it would come out.

"Every Sunday was massive dinners and there were people like you wouldn't believe. It wasn't unusual to have 20–25 people at our house.

"The dining room was huge, but it wasn't big enough, so my dad finished the basement. They put a big pool table down there and it was nice.

"All my family, my dad's brother, they would come to the house with their kids – my sisters, our friends, whoever. Everybody hugged and kissed and I was always the center of attention.

"Family would make up names for me – 'Hollywood' or 'Ace.' I had one aunt who called me 'Fonzie' like from *Happy Days* and a cousin who called me 'Pacino.'

"One of my dad's friends used to call me 'Beautiful Al.'"

Before you get any ideas, Allen assures "He was married and had kids. Years later, when I'd see his kids, they'd do it too. I'd say 'Oh God, don't say that, please. Your dad can say it but *please* ....'

"I taught all the kids how to play hockey. There was a big pond not far from the house. When it would freeze over we'd skate there. We made nets and we were always playing hockey.

"Gordie Howe used to live right around the corner. I'd go over there and talk to him. One time our junior hockey team got to skate with the old time Red Wings and I started jawing at him. "I said 'You know what? I noticed you're not back checking good enough.'

23

"He took his glove, pushed it at my head and laughed."

"I water skied and snow skied. I could pretty much do anything. I played football and baseball. We had a wooden garage door, so I drew a strike zone on it and we'd play baseball with tennis balls. I'd throw 'em against the door and whoever was at bat had at it. We had fun.

"My mom still went to Dearborn to see family, but not as much. There was too much to do. We didn't have maids any more. She would do everything all day and then get up early in the morning to do everything else.

"My sisters helped her out, they pretty much picked up the slack. I started calling them 'The Buzzards.' They continued to beat me up until I was 11; then I went through a growth spurt and was really strong. It stopped when I could hit back.

"Except Cindy and I started to fight *more* after we moved. She'd do stuff to me and I'd throw stuff at her."

Typical sibling stuff?

"No – I was way, way mean. My dad said I couldn't punch her so I'd throw those big old rotary phones at her. I don't remember what she did to provoke me, but I remember the outcome.

"One time I loogeyed on her. When my dad found out, I got a beating; but I used to terrorize him too. I'd make up names for him. I started calling him 'Otis.'

"The more he didn't like it, the more I used it. Then it stuck; everybody started using it and he couldn't do anything about it."

Douglas was still a problem.

"Whatever happened, it was my fault. When Douglas figured out he could use that to his advantage, he did. I got in trouble for everything, even playing catch.

"We had big bay windows. I don't know who threw the ball – either he missed and I didn't catch it or he threw it and broke the window – but I got blamed.

"When my parents got mad at me I got cussed out in all the languages. Today I'm multi-lingual in profanity.

"My mom was just a little pipsqueak, like a Chihuahua.

"I used to laugh at her because she was tiny, 4'9" and she'd get mad and threaten, 'You think I can't do anything?!'

"She never hit me; well, one time. I'm like 'What are you going to do, HIT me? It would be like a fly!'

"So she hit me with a broom handle and I screamed 'It hurts, it hurts!'

"I was blessed because my family had a little money. There was a golf course in Rochester by our house; it was a good way for her to get rid of me for hours.

"She'd give me money, 'Go have a hamburger there; do whatever you want to do.'

"I started playing golf around sixth grade. As I got older I started taking it serious because I was pretty good."

It was time well spent as the golf course would become one of his favorite – and safest – places to 'discuss business.'

The Outfit had a favorite place too.

A.S. remembers "We played tennis and racquetball at the Warren Tennis Club between 11 and 12 Mile off Hoover. It became a place where people from The Outfit came to play, see their friends and interact. It was a social kind of thing.

"The Outfit was made up of family members, people that were either directly related to or somewhat related to the family. There was a small circle of friends outside, but the decision makers were part of the 'Board of Directors.'

"I met Dominic a few times, but I knew Tony way more. Tony was a friend. He was about 400 lbs., but he was very athletic.

"You'd never expect a guy like that to drive off a springboard. When he was at military school he was a top wrestler and a top diver.

"And you would never think he could play tennis as well as he did.

"On one occasion while playing racquetball I told him 'You're the best racquetball player at this club.'

"He said 'What kind of bullshit is that?'

"I said '*For your size.*'

"You could push any part of his body with your finger and he was hard as a rock."

"The club was owned by Jack and Tony Tocco and Sam Baroni. A lot of people who played there understood what a ferocious competitor Jack was.

"He would call a ball that was in 'out!'

"I'd say 'That was in by a foot and a half!'

"He'd say 'My club, my call.'

"You could see he played tennis like he worked his business.

"When he lost, he'd go to his office for 15 to 20 minutes before he'd come out.

"The Warren Tennis Club was where the inner circle came, along with people who had memberships. Everybody from The Outfit had a locker except there were three of us that weren't part of The Outfit; Gary Vito, a state senator and me.

"Somebody from the FBI wondered how those three people fit in the organization. We knew they would. They weren't names they were familiar with. We used to joke about it.

"Assuming guilt by association, they subpoenaed our phone records every 90 days. They're only allowed to do that four times.

"I was notified by AT&T *after the fact* that it had happened a year earlier. They had to notify me and tell me that."

The Outfit, friends and associates were accustomed to scrutiny and their children were trained to deal with it.

A.S. explained "If you're somebody who can help build their case, they're knocking on your door. It's not guilty by association. If you're not a person of interest and not a target, any surveillance would be because you have the potential to lead them to what they're looking for."

Allen says "I remember my father telling me that 'You never snitch on anybody, never talk about anybody, and you never talk to the police.' *To be a snitch was the worst thing you could be.*

"I said 'I know dad, I know.'

"Even when I was a kid, I knew better. I was raised to never ever tell on anybody, no matter what.

"One day my parents left me and Douglas at home and there was a knock on the storm door.

"I cracked the regular door; the storm door was still shut. I said 'Who are you?'

"They said 'We're the FBI.'

"I said 'So?'

"They said 'Can we come in?'

"I said 'Absolutely no, you cannot come in. My parents don't want me to let any strangers in the house when they're not here.'

"'But we're the FBI.'

"I said 'Well, you're strangers.'

"They go 'We just want to ask you a couple questions about *so and so.*'

"I'm like 'I don't know *so and so*. I don't even know what you're talking about.'

"I said 'I'll see you later' and I just closed the door."

"Midge and Sam's brood got too big for their house in East Detroit so they wound up moving near Utica Road, next to the Zerillis, not far from our house.

"When I was 12 I started working for them. They had a business at 17 Mile & Van Dyke where they sold gas grills and gas fireplaces.

"Midge was the front person and worked the office; Sam did all the installations. He was short and strong and worked like a bulldog.

"When they were building all the subdivisions in Rochester, he worked for the gas company, so he knew how to do everything. He put gas lights in front of houses, installed heat, installed barbecue gas logs and gas fireplaces.

"Sam was really good at it because he was a fanatic about taking care of things; so I used to drive him crazy.

"He bought one of these 3-wheel bicycles that two people can sit in and it had fancy spoke wheels. The Zerillis lived on a hill next to Midge and Sam; their back yards touched.

"The ride up to Mr. Zerilli's circular driveway was really steep. I rode that crazy trike up his driveway, was coming down the other side really fast, turned and the spoked wheel broke and blew.

"Sam got so mad at me he started stuttering. 'You're always f-f-fucking up my s-s-stuff!'

"I just started laughing so hard; he would get so wound up.

"I'd come in and work for them at their store, doing whatever needed to be done.

"At 13 I remember going to Cobo Hall to the Home Improvement Show. I helped load in the equipment and explained everything about the grills. I'd cook Italian sausages and kielbasa and pass out samples.

"I learned how to deal with customers. I learned how to sell. I learned what the quality of everything was – why people should buy certain models as opposed to other models.

"I would give them reasons why they were better – they last longer and stuff.

"I tried to make customers as happy as I could and always did the right thing by them. At the end of the day I'd help load out.

"We sold a lot of barbecue grills. It was simple and it was all common sense.

"I learned a lot working for Midge and Sam. I learned warehousing, where to stack stuff. I learned how to manage inventory. That experience really served me well.

"Sometimes I watched their kids. I'd feed them and make sure they did their homework.

"My nephew Dominic wasn't that smart, so I called him 'Rocketman.' I introduced him like 'You're going to be a rocket scientist. Tell 'em what you're studying.'

"He used to get so mad at me.

"I'd stay with them until Midge came home around 9; then she'd drive me home."

Allen was on his way to becoming 'the cool uncle' – wild and brave and not much older than his nephews and nieces.

"I was starting to push everything right to the edge and I'd recruit everybody to do everything with me."

He was raising his own crew.

"I had an old school train set with whistles on a big table my dad made for me. I'd drive the trains and blow the whistles and there was a town and tunnels and all that kind of stuff.

"It was a very expensive train set. I gave it to The Rocketman and he fucked it all up."

"In the late 60s and early 70s Rochester was still being developed. There wasn't very many people, not like it is now.

"We had hills and creeks and my dad had a motorcycle. I'd steal it and go driving around doing daredevil things that you could get hurt. *It was awesome.*

"When I was 13 my dad bought me a small motorcycle for myself. They were building subdivisions and had just put blacktop on one of the roads. I thought it'd be cool to drive real fast on it.

"I was riding one way at probably 40 mph – turned around and was coming back. The workers got mad and yelled.

"One of 'em jumped in his car and pulled out in front of me. I hit, flew right over the car and landed in wet tar.

"I was hurt, all scraped up and covered with blacktop.

"I messed up their work so I had it coming; *kinda*.

"I pushed the bike back to our house. When my mom got home I was soaking in the bath trying to get the tar off.

"She's like 'What the heck happened to you?'

"My dad knew I might kill myself and he didn't want it on his conscience. He's thinking 'If something happens to this kid, I'm going to blame myself.'"

By that time Alfred was up to three packs of Pall Malls a day. Making good on the promise he made the night Allen was born, he took him to the Anointing of the Sick procession in Indiana and carried his 13-year-old son on his shoulders for a mile.

"It was a line of people with cripples on their backs and some priest out in front.

"I don't know how much I weighed, but I was all muscle, so I wasn't light.

"And it was really hot. I had a burning candle and I was dripping wax on his head. I said 'Can't you go any faster? What's the matter?'

"He's like 'Shut up.'"

Allen made light of the experience, but "Something happened. I got stronger after that."

•   •   •

"Uncle Dominic had 30 acres in Rochester, not far from Stoney Creek and Yates Cider Mill. The plan was – ten acres for Uncle Dominic and ten each for Peter and Paul when they got married and had families.

"He had a meat packing business in Miami, it was one of the biggest. He wanted his sons to work in that business.

"He didn't want them to 'do anything' – and Peter never did. He was always above board, even later, when he knew what I was doing. He was like a voice of conscience.

"Paulie always thought nothing was ever gonna happen, so he would take chances. But mostly we were all straight all the time.

"We made up our own secret language – words we could say in front of someone, so they wouldn't know what we were talking about.

"We had words for like if something was good. We'd say, 'Oh wow, that was so *George*.'

"If it was really good it was 'double' or 'triple George' or 'Chauncey.'

"When you were scared, 'mahartzz' (with a hand gesture) meant 'gonna shit your pants.'

"Ugly girls? There was this girl so ugly I used to call her 'Bowdy.' I started calling my sister Bowdy and she didn't like it."

"Our moms would cook for us every day, so we'd make the rounds just to eat. We're all Mediterranean, so our foods are similar, you know?

"As long as I can remember, my mom always had something going on with the cooking. When she made baklava she'd call me over to hold the ruler so she could cut it. You cut it before you cook it. The phyllo is soft then; otherwise it would be too hard to cut.

"She made her own syrup of sugar and rose water instead of honey.

"Every time we went to Detroit to see family she'd make us stop at Camp Dearborn so she could pick fresh grape leaves. She would use the ones in the jar, but she liked the fresh picked better. We filled up bags and they were so good, the way she made them.

"I can cook except I wish I would have paid more attention to my mother, like what she did with lamb and cabbage. I made her put the rib bones from the lamb underneath and then she stacked them up with seasonings and put a plate on top. And she always made rice pudding with cinnamon."

While Allen's mom was independent and ambitious, "Aunt Josephine was traditional. She kept pretty much to herself. She seemed happy.

"Aunt Jo made awesome, unbelievable Italian food. She would teach my mom Sicilian recipes and my mom would teach her Lebanese recipes.

"To this day me and Peter like to cook. We'd watch our parents cook every day; we usually know what went into it.

"One time me, Peter and Paul were driving back to their house and we hit a pheasant. We threw it in the trunk and pulled into the garage thinking it was dead.

"When we opened the trunk we found out it had just been knocked unconscious. Uncle Dominic broke its neck.

"That night we had pasta with pheasant."

All three boys grew up with the advantages, influence and protection Dominic Corrado's power provided.

"Rochester is a snow belt, so in winter we had snowmobiles. We'd drag our cousins and ourselves around behind the snowmobiles on plastic sleds.

"We made a snowmobile track with a jump over the driveway. We were doing laps, not knowing the maid had parked her car in the driveway.

"Paulie hit it in flight and knocked the muffler off. I was right behind him but I managed to stop. We strung the muffler back up with wire and stuff.

"She was 500 yards down the road before it started falling off.

"We used to ride the snowmobiles on the roads and dare the cops to stop us. We'd just take off at 100 mph. They couldn't catch us on snow in cop cars.

"Before we had our driver's licenses, we had an old Willys Jeep. One day Paul was driving – I was in the passenger seat and his little cousin Nino was in the back.

"He was driving pretty fast, like 60 or 70 mph on a dirt road; he lost control and we hit a tree.

"He got thrown out. I busted the shifter, flew across the whole front of the Jeep and got banged up pretty good. Nino was OK.

"None of us got seriously hurt; but Paul got a beating.

"Uncle Dominic had quite a gun collection because he would hunt big game and stuff like that. We used to steal cardboard human cutouts from in front of the movie theaters, put 'em in the back yard and blow them to shreds with riot pump shotguns.

"We would go to the Warren Tennis Club. All the older people would go and the kids would go too. We'd play tennis and do the sauna.

"In summer we all went on vacation together. Peter and Paul's dad had a cottage on Higgins Lake. Their grandfather had built it, it was a stone cottage with 15 bedrooms.

"We'd be on the boats all day and the ladies would stay inside and cook. Later we'd come in for breaded lobster tails and steaks – omigod, every kind of seafood you could imagine."

A.S. has an old friend who grew up at Higgins Lake.

"Mike McGinnis said when they first came in with the sunglasses everyone thought they were movie producers.

"Then they thought maybe they were gangsters from Detroit; but everyone liked them. They were very generous and nice and owned a lot of property."

Years later James Buccellato and Scott M. Burnstein wrote an article that shared 'the recipe' for The Outfit's prosperity.

"They don't chase the news cameras like in other cities and a lot of them have been very adept of veiling themselves in legitimacy," said former federal prosecutor and organized crime task force member Keith Corbett, of the area's ruling mob powers. "In relative terms, it's been a recipe for success, in that most of them have avoided long, if any, prison sentences and, for the most part, very few people have any idea who they are." (*Organized Crime In Detroit: Forgotten But Not Gone*; CBS Detroit, June 24, 2011)

Unfortunately, the press was *always* watching Uncle Dominic. Allen remembers "One time he accidentally shot himself when he was hunting near the cottage. His gun went off and shot him through his side, down and into his leg. He drove himself all the way back down to Detroit to the hospital.

"We weren't there with him, we found out when we turned on the news. The reporter said 'Fats Corrado shot and in the hospital.' They made it sound like he was in an altercation. They said he got shot; they didn't say if he was stable or if he died.

"Everybody in the family was freaking out. Fortunately Uncle Dominic recovered and the media buzz died down."

Surveillance didn't.

"There came a time when all the older guys' cars were getting stolen. Miraculously the next day they'd find them in perfect shape.

"If somebody steals a car, they don't usually leave it whole. They strip it down for parts in a matter of hours.

"The guys knew something was fishy. They figured the FBI was putting bugs in their cars. As soon as they got the car back, they'd get rid of it."

In 1970 Congress enacted RICO - the Racketeer Influenced and Corrupt Organizations Act.

Allen explained "RICO was specifically designed to go after the mob. They were just assholes. The first guy to get indicted on it was James T. Licavoli.

"I didn't pay much attention at that time; I didn't know what direction my life was going. I just knew I could do what I wanted."

Did your dad ever get into trouble of any kind?

"No. He had enough trouble raising me.

"He used to go to church and tried to get me to go. I said 'I don't want to go.' I had enough church."

Gambling was more fun and The Outfit owned Hazel Park Race Track. A.S. says "It was originally built for hot rod races, but it had lost its capital and was going belly up.

"A member of The Outfit had the foresight to build a race track and get it licensed. It was under the table dealings that got him started, but he ultimately did more above board.

"Men like him were hard to deal with, but he had to have good business skills to make a winning business venture.

"I owned thoroughbred horses and raced at Hazel Park. Because of my relationships, if I had a problem, the problem usually went away."

Case in point ...

"The guy that was training for me somehow got involved with fixing a race and The Outfit wasn't too pleased because it was their track.

"Once it was brought to the trainer's attention, I was threatened. I made a call and the threat went away. In fact, the trainer called the next day and couldn't apologize enough for the 'mistake.'"

A.S. started bookmaking at 15.

"I never considered gambling as illegal. People like us come from cultures that like to gamble and believe it's OK – Greeks, Lebanese, Italians and Sicilians.

"I was a bookmaker in high school in St. Clair Shores. My uncle was an independent bookie, I learned from him. I saw what he did, saw he was making a lot of money, so I thought *Why don't I pick up a few bucks at school?*

"I duplicated his cards and was selling them myself. I had about five guys working for me. I had a nice little business just open to other high school kids.

"One day law enforcement showed up at my school. They were thinking somehow the mafia was trying to penetrate high schools.

"When they busted us, 3 out of 5 were Italians and none of *them* would offer up any information related to what I was doing or me.

"It was the two non-Italians that snitched their guts out, thought they were going to jail.

"One guy's dad was big, he was the president of Local 400 in Dearborn. He came down to the jail where they were holding his son, confronted law enforcement and said 'Either arrest him or let him go; otherwise I'll have a shitload of attorneys in here.'

"They tried to link me to organized crime. I said 'It's not true, I did it on my own. It was organized by me.'

"I got six months verbal probation."

Allen would follow a similar path.

He says "My intuition came from my mother. It was uncanny how she had it. She picked numbers; she'd go to Hazel Park Raceway, bet $2 and win $4,000 or $5,000.

"My aunt used to tell her 'Why don't you step up your bets a little bit? Like to $10?'

"Me, Peter and Paul were gambling with bookies when we were 15 years old.

"Frankie Bags was the ticket puncher at the horse track. I would stand next to Frankie and Paulie would be where they start. In trotters, the horse that breaks first usually wins.

"Paulie's yelling numbers across to me and I'm yelling 'em to Frankie Bags and he's punching 'em in. The 15-20 second lag time was enough for us to get some bets in.

"He'd punch in the numbers and we'd give him the money.

"At the track, you don't get your tickets if you don't pay; and if you lost, you lost.

"But with the bookies – because of who Peter and Paul were – we'd tell 'em we're not paying and there was nothing anyone could do about it.

"People were afraid of their dad.

"Uncle Dominic or Uncle Tony would tell them 'You knew who they were, you guys take their bets? You're not getting paid.'

"That didn't last very long. Soon nobody wanted to take our bets."

"They were still building Rochester Adams when Cindy went to high school; me and Peter got to go to the new school. We were in the same grade, a year ahead of Paulie.

"We cared about being presentable and wearing nice clothes.

"Our families were well-known, we didn't want to dress like bums. We'd get in trouble with our dads if we didn't look right."

Peter wants to set the limo rumor straight.

He explains "We lived in Grosse Pointe and were finishing up a home in Rochester. My father didn't want us to start and then go to another school, so he hired a friend of his who had a limo service to drive us in the morning.

"We were driven in a limo one day and the next day a Dodge Dart; however, everyone remembered the limo and not the Dart. During this time an article came out on front page of Oakland Press, headlines *Mafia Moves to Oakland County.*

"That's how I got to be well known."

Allen and Peter went to school with Madonna. 'The Material Girl' was having trouble adapting to the burbs. Khalil AlHajal of mlive.com wrote about her March, 2015 interview with Howard Stern.

"She spoke about feeling socially isolated after her family moved from Pontiac to Rochester Hills … 'We first grew up in Pontiac, which was a very racially-mixed, mostly black environment and neighborhood, and we went to Catholic schools and we wore uniforms and that was normal life to me.'

"She told Stern: 'When I went to high school, we moved to a suburb that was all white. And we were, a bit, living above of our means... I felt very – because now I didn't have a uniform – so I was aware that my clothes were not as cool as everybody elses or as nice as everybody elses...

"'I just didn't fit in. I just felt like I was with rich people, and I wasn't and I felt out of place. And I felt like they were members of country clubs and they had manicures and they wore nice clothes and I didn't fit in. I felt like a country bumpkin. And I was resentful.'"

Allen was feeling awkward too. "We were half-assed friends, but I was really shy, kind of going through a clumsy phase. I was tall and skinny with braces and glasses.

"We were lab partners in chemistry.

"There are yearbook pictures of us doing a play together. I was Gomez Adams and she was Morticia. She had black hair! She didn't dye it in high school.

"And she was a cheerleader.

"They had the powder puff games where the cheerleaders play football and everybody shows up, even the principal.

"For a while I was the announcer. The only way to get up the scaffold to the announcing stand was a ladder; you climbed and opened the hatch door.

"Me and my friends went up there. I made fun of everybody and we were throwing water balloons.

"The gym teacher tried to come up, but I put my chair on top of the trap door so he couldn't get in. He yelled at me to clean it up and start acting right.

"I got suspended for two weeks for inciting a riot."

"Hobart Jenkins, Superintendent of Schools, was our next door neighbor and a friend of my dad's. My dad was very, very social and they just liked each other. I liked him too.

"When they got home from work he'd come over to our house or my dad would go over there and they'd drink Bloody Marys together.

"If it was snowing, I'd go over to Mr. Jenkins' house at night. He was always a little tipsy by then.

"I'd say 'I think we should cancel school tomorrow.'

"Bart goes 'A little too early for me to call it.'

"I said 'Maybe? Yes? No? C'mon, I can stay up later then.'"

Allen would need the goodwill of an authority figure like Mr. Jenkins.

"My parents and everyone were going to a wedding. I didn't have my driver's license, but Nadra's boyfriend had this car that was kinda cool; and he left the keys at our house.

"I drove it to Peter & Paul's house. They got in and I said 'Let's go do donuts!'

"There was this guy who lived in the middle of nowhere; his front yard didn't have any grass. I thought it would be the perfect surface, but as soon as I drove onto it the car sunk.

"It was like a septic field and we couldn't get out.

"The guy came out and yelled 'If you try to get that car out of there, I'll put a gun ball in your ass!'

"I had to get that car back before my parents came home from the wedding, so we walked back to Peter's house for a Jeep that could pull us out; except the guy was going to shoot us if we tried.

"I had to go to Mr. Jenkins and ask him if he'd call the guy.

"I said 'Tell him I'll work at his house, help repair whatever damage I did or do *whatever* if he'll let me get the car out of there.'

"Mr. Jenkins convinced him to agree and the car was retrieved; but somebody called my parents at the wedding and I got in trouble anyway."

"My dad would beat me when I fucked up, but it didn't work. And my mom would always take my side.

"She took care of me about everything. I knew she had Valium, so I'd go snake some. I'd say 'Mom I'm taking one of your Valium … I love the way they make you feel.'

"I started when I was a kid. I do drugs still. It's my life. I don't feel well.

"My mom never told me no for anything; but my dad did. When I was young, he used to belittle me.

"As I grew up I figured he didn't know any better. He wasn't educated, he didn't really know what to do, how to take advantage of situations – like my mother did.

"I was asking my cousin why I was so much closer to my mom than my dad and he goes, 'I think you really didn't respect your dad like you probably should have.'

"When I was a kid, I didn't really idolize anyone but there were certain people that I respected – like Peter's dad. Uncle Dominic loved me and treated me like one of his own kids.

"You always have the guys that want to try you, see how tough you are. That happened a lot, so Uncle Dominic set us up with boxing lessons.

"Boxing is movement; you know what they're going to try to do and if they're drunk, they're going to flail at you or come up at you. Just give them a couple quick shots and it's all over.

"You try to hit them on the button – on the jaw/cheek.

"Peter, Paulie and I would box in the basement at their house and at my house. That's why we could all fight pretty good.

"If we had a problem at school and they wanted to fight, we'd say 'Let's just put boxing gloves on and fight in the gym.'

"After we'd throw off the gloves and start hitting with our bare hands. It hurt more but we knocked the shit out of 'em.

"Then we'd have a sit-down with Uncle Dominic. He'd have to call their parents and tell them 'Look, you're not going to win.

"You can't fight these guys because they have more power behind them than you can ever imagine. It's best to let it go.'"

"Uncle Dominic owned the milk delivery business and he gave us all employee gas cards – me, Paulie and Peter – so whatever money we had was our money.

"We went to school, got good grades, drove around and did what we wanted. We'd go out at night, fool around and drink beer – usually in Rochester.

"We were still sort of awkward with girls.

"Sometimes we went to this place called the Giraffe on Van Dyke around Utica or Macomb Township. We knew we could get in even though we were underage.

"One night we were there at closing. We were outside while Paul was talking to some Chaldean girl – just talking, nothing really going on. I guess he wanted to go somewhere and do something with her and she didn't want anything to do with it.

"She told him no and he told her to go fuck herself.

"She told her cousins or brothers and all of a sudden ten guys come outside. They were a little older and some of 'em were a lot bigger.

"There's only three of us.

"Uncle Dominic taught us to treat people nice… unless there was a reason that they should be treated another way.

"We didn't not like them; we weren't trying to start a fight. We were taught when we were young: 'You never start a fight, but you never run from a fight; and always stick together and fight together.' That was a code for us.

"So we start talking back and forth and we didn't understand what this one guy was saying – 'I got no ba-time.'

"They started jumping on us and we started fighting one after another. They were hitting Peter and I was hitting them on the head.

"Paulie was one of the best fighters that I knew. In a brawl or street fight, he'd take you out. He happened to have a pair of brass knuckles. He'd hit a guy and it was over with.

"After it was all said and done, we took quite a few shots, but we beat the shit out of 'em – *all of 'em.*

"Then we hear the sirens and the manager says 'Get in here' and he closed the place up.

"Those other guys were left to fend for themselves. They ran or did whatever they could do.

"We went in and got cleaned up as much as we could. When the cops came to the door, the manager says 'Nobody's here. I didn't even know about any fight.'

"After the cops left, we waited a little while and had a couple more drinks.

"When we were driving home we were wondering about 'I got no ba-time.' *I got no bad time?*

"And then we realized what he was really saying was he has *no bedtime*. Like he was ready to go. We accommodated 'em.

"The next day Uncle Dominic sees our faces and says 'What happened?'

"Then he gets a call from some Chaldean guy who tells him 'I guess our kids got into kind of a fight.' He says 'You know, we really don't want any trouble.'

"Uncle Dominic tells us 'OK, then we have to have a sit down with the guy.'

"He told him 'You guys can never win fighting against these guys, there's too much power behind them.'

"So the Chaldean says 'We don't want any problem with you guys anyway.'

"Uncle Dominic said 'OK, very good.'

"Later he grabbed the brass knuckles and threw 'em in the creek in back of the house. He said 'You guys don't need to use things like this.'

"So we used rolled quarters instead."

"When I was growing up The Outfit had all the unions and everything. We used to go to union functions. They were all catered and we got to eat.

"I remember hearing about Hoffa. The older guys were saying 'He's getting a little too cocky; he wants to come take over the union. We like it just the way it's running right now.'

On July 30, 1974 Jimmy Hoffa disappeared from Machus Red Fox on Telegraph in Bloomfield Hills. We all knew Machus.

Allen says "It wasn't far from our house. We used to go by there once in a while."

Most anyone who lived and worked in the Detroit area at that time can tell you where they were when they heard.

The town went wild with rumors. Everyone assumed he'd been hit.

On the 41st anniversary of Hoffa's disappearance *History.com* summed it all up for *This Day in History*.

They wrote: "In 1967, he was convicted of bribery and sentenced to 15 years in prison. While in jail, Hoffa never ceded his office, and when Richard Nixon commuted his sentence in 1971, he was poised to make a comeback. Released on condition of not participating in union activities for 10 years, Hoffa was planning to fight the restriction in court when he disappeared on July 31, 1975, from the parking lot of a restaurant in Detroit …. Several conspiracy theories have been floated about Hoffa's disappearance and the location of his remains, but the truth remains unknown."

For most.

In the 70s I'd be out and about with my floozy friends and they'd make their entrance. Heads swiveled; these were guys who made the papers – real-world mobsters who'd be hanging with Allen in a few years.

You could tell the real thing from the wannabes; they never bragged. They didn't need to.

We saw them at Brownies on Lake St. Clair and in Greektown.

My friend Diana fell in lust with a lesser prince who looked Scarface unstable.

"She grabbed my arm and whispered "How do I get one of those?"

I said "*You don't.*"

When I told Allen about it, he added "You don't *want to*."

Sometimes they'd show up at Archibald's in Birmingham or Excalibur and Oscar's in Southfield.

The most vivid encounter took place at Archibald's at 555 Old Woodward Avenue in Birmingham.

I was working for the Kerbawy Company, an industrial film and live show production company in Troy. Hafe – the Lebanese owner – was like a father to me. His cousin Nick was General Manager of the Detroit Lions and the Pistons.

Our specialty was national new product announcement shows for Cadillac, Audi and Cessna (out of Wichita, Kansas.) It was an exciting job. We hired talent from Broadway and worked with celebrities like Bill Bixby and John Forsythe – the voice of 'Charlie' of *Charlie's Angels*.

Hafe's son and son-in-law worked there, as did Major League Baseball pitcher Hank Aguirre. Hank was a joy. He invited me and my friends to hang out with his buddies from the '67 Tigers – Al Kaline, Jim Northrop, Norm Cash and others.

I hired our secretary. Lisa's resume listed 'bowling and ballet' as hobbies. She remains one of my closest friends.

Dale was on staff as a video producer; she was tough, liberated and fun to hang with. She only lived a few blocks from our destination, so we took separate cars.

Wednesday was always good at Archibald's; the place was packed with the usual upscale professionals.

We had just settled in at the bar when the 'Dark Princes' made their entrance. Everyone turned and looked.

One was especially tall and dark. I was especially fair. The joke was 'blondes have more fun' because they're easier to see in the dark.

Ronnie Morelli – a.k.a. 'Cochise' or 'Hollywood Ronnie' – worked his way through the crowd and introduced himself.

When I mentioned my jazz musician stepfather his whole demeanor changed; like I was real, like I was 'OK.' He nodded approvingly and said "Nick Fiore's little girl."

Further into the conversation Ronnie shrugged backwards towards a conspicuously uncool balding man in a heinous plaid blazer – a big guy sitting alone at a small round table.

Ronnie said he was an FBI agent who'd been tailing him. He seemed more amused than concerned, so I didn't give it another thought.

At 11 or so his entourage started gathering in the doorway to leave for a party on the east side. He invited me to go. I wanted to, but it was a long drive and I had to get up early.

The following morning I was hanging with Lisa at the big white reception desk when Dale burst through the front door; breathless, she slammed a newspaper down on the desk.

"Did you see this? That guy you were talking to last night …."

The front page had Ronnie's picture and a headline that read *'Mafia Hit Man Arrested for Extortion.'*

Tall and strong, Allen was on his way in the world. He didn't know where he was going, but he was going to look great when he got there.

"I was getting so I liked to be cool, coiffed and looking good. They didn't call it metrosexual back in the day. If you got your nails and feet done they thought you were weird; but everyone I grew up with did that, they got manicures.

"I used to get one with clear polish every week; now I just have 'em buff 'em. Polish chips are no good.

Greektown was only a 40 minute drive from Rochester.

"In our teens we had the keys to the Pink Panther. When it was bar time, we'd just lock the door and hang out 'til 4 or 5 in the morning.

"We used to go to the Lions games, me, my dad, Peter, Paul and my little brother. Uncle Dom would have a driver take us to Tiger Stadium. Traffic was bad after the game, so he'd tell us to be ready at the 4th quarter.

"A black limo would pick us up and take us to the Grecian Gardens to eat dinner with him."

The special treatment didn't go to his head. Allen continued to work for Midge and Sam as employee and babysitter.

"I taught The Rocketman how to box in my basement. I'm like 'You're opening up your chin!' And BOOM I'd hit him.

"You gotta remember, I'm 11 years older and a lot taller and he would go DOWN. Me and David were like 'Oh fuck, he's knocked out. Let's wake him up – but he can't go tell we knocked him out.'

"When I was old enough Midge would just give me her station wagon so I could drive the kids home from school. There was this big hunk of railroad that we went up and over. I would go like 100 mph and just fly off the other end.

"There were seat belts in the car, but we just didn't care. The kids would be bouncing off the seats, they loved it.

"Sam couldn't figure out why her car was always out of alignment.

"He was *very, very* particular about his cars, how they looked. He always drove Lincolns, always a Mark.

"I used to say 'Sam, let me drive your car!'

"He says 'NO! *Nobody* drives my car Bussey!'"

Bussey?

"He would just like start sputtering and that was the word that would come out of his mouth. He got upset about things like that. The cars had to be clean. He wouldn't let us touch 'em.

"He was the nicest guy, he'd give you the shirt off his back – but he was a hothead. If something made him mad he would always fight, no matter who it was. He didn't take time to find out if they were connected.

"So this guy – Joe the Monk they called him – he had his own bank for the numbers in Detroit. He was doing good and his son Nick Pitta owned a detail shop.

"Sam took his car to get detailed by Nick.

"Nick did something wrong to the car, forgot to empty the ash tray or vacuum the trunk and Sam went back and beat the shit out of him.

"So now they want to kill Sam. They've got a contract out and everybody's trying to quash it so he doesn't get killed.

"Somebody told me he hid out by sleeping in ['mob underboss'] Vince Meli's basement for two weeks. Nobody could get him to come out.

"Finally my dad went to my uncle Dominic and said 'I hate to ask, but it's my son-in-law. Can you do something?'

"My Uncle Dominic quashed it so Sam got to come home. He saved his life."

Uncle Dominic had the family's back.

"Me and Douglas went to an arcade in Dearborn; he was only 13. A bunch of guys in their 20s tried to take his money and he said 'No!'

"They beat him up pretty badly; kicked him so hard in his nuts he was peeing blood.

"I tried to help him. I got beat up but it didn't do anything to me; at least I could fight back. Douglas was too small.

"Someone called Uncle Dominic. He didn't get obviously upset, he was always stoic. But you don't do that, especially to a 13 year old kid. He told me to find out who they were.

"I went to the owner, found out and told him. He had someone break their knee caps. He made an example of them.

"Up 'til then, nobody in Dearborn knew who we were.

"They did after that."

At 16 Allen had a driver's license, but he didn't have wheels. In the affluent, brand conscious northern suburbs you *were* judged by what you drove and Allen went places where people paid attention.

Pine Knob was a skiing and outdoor entertainment venue in Clarkston, 20 miles north of Detroit.

"Matt Locricchio used to give me free season passes for skiing. We'd take off from school and hit the slopes. We had front row seats to every concert.

"One summer they were raffling off a Pantera. I was 16. I said to my Uncle Dominic 'I want that car.'

"He pulls me aside and says 'If your father says you can have that car, you will win that car.'

"My dad said 'There's no way in hell you're getting that car. You'll kill yourself in a week.'

"I said 'Don't worry about me so much.'

"Later I had a party to go to and my dad had a brand new Cadillac. He let me borrow it.

"So I drank too much and I knew I should stay where I was. I called my dad about 2 a.m., when he was just going to sleep.

"I said 'I'm too drunk to drive; I'm going to stay here for the night.'

"He says 'Get your fucking ass home!'

"I was pretty wasted, having a hard time driving and I sideswiped a tree – took off the whole right side of the car. I could still drive it, but the Cadillac was basically destroyed.

"We had a circular drive so I parked with the damage *away* from the front window; but he was waiting up for me. He knew something was wrong as soon as he saw the lights.

"He rushed out and said 'What happened to the car?'

"I said 'I don't know.'

"He walked around and looked at it and yelled 'What the fuck did you do to it?!'

"I said 'I hit a tree.'"

Alfred *went off.*

"My mother came out and yelled at him – 'It's not his fault, it's *your* fault! He told you he wasn't good to drive!'

"After he calmed down he realized she was right and felt bad about it. He told me 'Don't worry about it.'

"I threw up all over him.

"The next day he came home with a used car for me, a four-door Bonneville, blue with a white vinyl top. That car was a boat."

It sounded like a make-out machine, so I asked how he lost his virginity.

"I was 17 years old, hanging out in a bar in Rochester and some girl in her twenties comes up and says 'Can I go home with you?'

"I told her I still lived with my parents; so we wound up screwing in the back seat."

How was it?

"I really didn't know much."

The Bonneville was destined to log some serious highway miles.

"I'd drive with Midge and the kids to California or Arizona to visit our sisters. We'd take our time. We had a big station wagon, we were all in there. When my mom came she'd bring coolers full of food. We ate pretty good – breaded steak filet sandwiches in pita bread. We'd stop at places and hang out.

"Sam would be home working. Sometimes he'd come later and meet us.

"One time I was supposed to drive my car and Midge was going to drive her car. David and Dominic were going to ride with me, but I had stayed out all night the day we were leaving.

"So I'm sleeping at my other sister's house and Midge calls. 'Alright, we're leaving. Get up, we gotta go. We're going to drive all night.'

"I drove all day knowing we weren't stopping at night. I'm thinking *Omigod, I can't make it.*

"We had CB radios and we're driving and I start falling asleep and swerving; she starts yelling at me, 'Wake up wake up!!!'

"So I woke up. I told David 'Here's what we're going to do. I can't slow down and I can't pull off. You gotta drive, I can't do it anymore.' I said 'Uncle Al has to have a nap.'

"He was only 14 years old. I made him switch on the fly and he did a great job.

"I showed him exactly everything he had to do to keep it between the lines. David drove a few hours and we finally stopped for the night. We stayed on the top floor of a hotel in this big fancy room.

"When I was refreshed, we started throwing melons off the balcony."

He remembers his teens as mostly good times.

"I was close to family and we had everything that we wanted. We had good friends – Peter and Paul. We were together all the time.

"We weren't into drugs or anything like that. Our dads used to tell us we'd get a beating if we did drugs; but it was OK to drink, which was weird."

Allen graduated from Rochester Adams High School in 1976. Looking back, he has one favorite memory.

"Mr. Berube taught Humanities. Everyone liked him, I heard he became Vice Principal.

"Me, Peter, Paul and another friend of ours had an assignment for his class. We could pick what we wanted to do, so we made a movie about a book we were supposed to read – *The Iliad and the Odyssey*.

"It was us pretending to be figures from Greek mythology. Paul's grandfather lived in Clarkston and he had a horse, so we filmed it there.

"I didn't go to our 20 year anniversary, but Peter went. He said Mr. Berube told him 'Al was so funny - and that movie you guys made? It was just hilarious. It was my favorite class of all time.'"

Lottery for the draft ran from 1972 to 1975 and young men born between 1953 and 1956 were inducted. Allen – born in '57 – missed it by a year.

"I was lucky I was born in a window. A few years earlier, I coulda went to Vietnam; a few years later I coulda been in Iraq or something."

Unlike many others, it didn't really matter. *He knew people.*

"There was no way I was going to go."

4 Moving to Tucson

"In 1976 one of my elderly uncles asked my parents to come to Arizona and take care of him. Uncle Willie had a lot of property that he said he'd leave to my parents and my brother and myself. He didn't have a family of his own and he didn't trust anybody."

As is often the case with people who can't be trusted.

The timing was probably as good as it was going to get. Allen was ready for college, Douglas would be starting high school and his sisters were married with families.

"I didn't care about moving, I always liked California and Arizona. I had to go to college, so I might as well go there.

"But first I told them 'I'm staying in Michigan for the summer. I took a semester at Oakland Community College and stayed with my cousin Michael and his parents."

Allen's parents and brother drove the 2,000 miles from Rochester to Tucson; extended family was waiting at the other end.

"My father's cousin Sol had served as a state senator in the 60s. I called him 'Uncle' Sol because he was older. He got me out of beefs before I started getting into real trouble."

Sol would be a bad influence on Allen, but he had a positive effect on his father.

"My dad had emphysema. He'd had it a long time – he was smoking Pall Malls with no filters for a lot of years. It's going to take its toll.

"So Sol and my dad both decided to quit smoking. They couldn't quit on their own, so they went to this thing together.

"After that first semester at Oakland I transferred to University of Arizona. When I first went there I had to take a math test so they could see where they're going to start me off.

"I graded so high I had to take all these stupid hard, really retarded math classes and I really hated them. I'm like *Oh fuck, why didn't I just pretend I couldn't do it.*

"I never knew what I wanted to do, but the business law teacher thought I was great for some reason. Not that I remember anything from the class."

Rumors had preceded his family prior to their relocation.

"Before I came back I remember somebody telling me there was something in the papers that made the Lebanese community think we had a mob connection.

"I never saw the article, but that was the rumor. Either that or somebody said something.

"It didn't stop anyone from wanting to be with us.

"I wasn't in Arizona very long before this woman came over to welcome my parents and introduce herself. She was from a wealthy Lebanese family that was in the produce business. It was one of the biggest in the state, they'd been in it forever.

"So she sees me – I'm dark, I'm Lebanese, but I look more Italian than anything.

"I had a really thick beard, but I always was clean shaven with really dark eyes and a whole lot of wavy hair. Everybody that cut it said 'You've got the most beautiful head of hair *ever*.'

"And when you move to a place where you wear flip flops every day, you gotta get mani-pedis. I have nice feet. You don't want your toes to look like talons.

"This woman thought I was handsome, 'dashing.' She said 'Oh, I have a niece for you! You are so gorgeous!'"

"Habibi was my first serious girlfriend. That wasn't her real name, that's what I called her. She was really pretty, looked like Kim Kardashian – so we dated.

"She was a few years older than me and we had a good thing. Habibi was already in school, in a sorority, so I could go there and hang out. She was studying to become a schoolteacher and I helped her with her assignments.

"The head basketball coach and his assistant used to see me out with her and they'd say 'You have the finest filly in the yard. I don't know how you do it.'

"I'm like 'I don't know dude.'

"Her dad had just bought her a Pontiac Trans Am like in Smokey and the Bandit. I'd drive it and pick her up whenever, wherever.

"Some days I needed to pick her up from school because I was out fucking around all day, I didn't always go to class.

"Habibi was Lebanese, I was Lebanese; it worked out for a while.

"I tried to teach her to drive a '67 'Vette that belonged to my cousin Roxy. It was the fastback with the split window.

"She wanted to drive it bad, but it had the four-speed manual transmission.

"I said 'OK, get behind the wheel.' I tried to teach her but she kept stalling it out. I told her 'Here, after we get around the corner I'll show you how and we'll try again.'

"I put it in first and I'm trying to go around the corner and the tires are spinning. I tried to slow down so I could go straight, but I drifted into the curb and broke the axle.

"This was before cell phones, so I had to walk to a pay phone. I said 'Hey Roxy, we got a problem.'

"He says 'What the fuck did you do?'

"I'm like 'I hit a curb and broke the axle. I don't know. It won't go.'

"So I had it towed to the dealership. Needless to say, the parts weren't readily available. It took a while to pay for the repairs."

Money was no longer flowing like wine; his parents had experienced a disheartening setback.

"When Uncle Willie died we found out he had a cousin in Brazil who was kind of a shady character. And the cousin got a woman pregnant. She talked Uncle Willie into leaving everything he promised us to her and her son.

"My parents were both hard working people, so they managed to do OK on their own. They opened an auto detail shop and worked a deal with dealerships to pick up 3 to 15 cars a day. They'd get them looking like new and send them back.

"Cars weren't expensive like they are now. My parents bought me a new car, a 1976 Cutlass Supreme – metallic brown with the 350 Rocket V-8. It cost about $5,500 with all the options on it.

"I think payments were about $150 a month. It wasn't like they went out on a limb and got me a Cadillac."

Not getting a new Cadillac was as close to *deprived* as he got in those days.

"Don't get me wrong, it was nice. At that time I didn't care. My dad just didn't want me to have fast cars because I was always speeding and there were a lot of mountain roads. He didn't want me to kill myself.

"In '76 there were only 250,000 people out here. It was like the wild, wild, west.

"We could do whatever we wanted and Uncle Sol was awesome – he took care of everything I needed. He had a successful carpet store on Broadway between Swan and Craycroft.

"When I'd walk in he'd say 'What do you want now?!'

"I'd say 'I dunno, I can't help it!'

"At 18 I didn't need money; I just needed to get out of traffic tickets. Uncle Sol fixed ticket after ticket.

"Finally the cops stopped writing me tickets. One told me 'I'm not even wasting the paper.'"

Uncle Sol was *resolving* the moving violations, but his father was *paying* the parking tickets.

"You couldn't park on campus in certain places, so I just parked anywhere I wanted. I got a ticket every day. Finally my dad got mad because my tickets were like $800 – $900.

"He'd yell 'What's the matter with you?!'

"So I found the guy that was writing the tickets and started talking to him, started bringing him food from my mom; and you know, we kind of became buddies.

"He said 'Alright, I'm gonna make a deal. You can park wherever you want and when I see your car, I'll put a ticket on it; but it won't be a *real* ticket. Don't worry about it.'

"Allen tried to get the same consideration for his friends, but the guy said "No, I can't take care of all these people.""

Suddenly Alfred and DeeBee were having problems with *both* sons.

"Douglas started doing drugs and stealing from my parents. They'd give him credit cards and he would go buy stuff and return it so he could get cash for drugs.

"He'd come home paranoid. He'd say 'The house is bugged' and this and that.

"My parents knew he was on something and they'd want him to go to rehab.

"He'd agree to go to rehab, but then he'd steal all the credit information out of their computers, charge stuff and return it to get more drugs.

"One thing I know about recovering addicts is it always starts with alcohol usually. That's why the best is AA. From what I know.

"Douglas stole their jewelry and pawned it; but my parents were friends with the people that owned the pawn shop.

"So the guy would buy the jewelry from Douglas, give him some money and call my parents. They had to buy their jewelry back. It went on like that."

Something had to give.

"My dad told me 'Your car is paid for, college is paid for, and you have a place to live. You take it from here.'

"I said 'Well I need money.'

"He goes 'Money doesn't grow on trees. You're going to have to get a job champ.'

"I didn't want to go to work so I came up with the idea of doing parlay cards as a freshman in college. My cousin Paul – Sol's son – used to help me.

"I pretty much knew what was going on with sports betting, who's good, who's bad, who's injured. And there were certain tendencies – they all loved the Dallas Cowboys back then. Arizona didn't have the Cardinals yet.

"At that time they didn't make the lines right away, so if I waited, I'd lose a day. I always did mine first thing Monday morning, whether the lines were out or not. I'd number them and put in all the college games and pro games – print point totals and everything.

"Every Monday we'd have to type it up on an old fashioned typewriter and take it to the printing place. The guy that printed and cut the cards called me Mr. Big because he knew I could get things done. I paid a group of guys to pass them out.

"You pick three teams minimum and bet whatever it is you want to bet; and if your three football teams hit, it paid 8 for 1. If you bet $100 you'd win $800.

"You could pick up to ten games; that paid 1,000 for 1. Nobody ever won that." In fact, "Nobody ever won anyway. Some guys would hit a few hundred and I'd be happy to pay them.

"The police would play, everyone was playing. I was taking them to the car dealerships. Nobody ever said anything about it.

"Every night after I got my money I'd call Dave Quant. We were good friends at the time. We went to this nice place for dinner and one night he goes 'You're a rookie bookie.'

"I was taking in $3,000 – $4,000 a week. I'm like *this is awesome*. I could buy things.

"I've been driving the Cutlass for a while so I said 'Dad I want to get a new car.'

"I wanted an Eldorado. I could make a $300 or $400 car payment but my dad said 'You're not getting that.' He said 'You don't need an Eldorado when you're in college.' He wanted us to be low profile.

"An Oldsmobile was OK with him, so I got a brand new 1978 Toronado with the Rocket V8. It was maroon. It was pretty much the same thing.

"I had money and a new car. I could go and do what I wanted, go here and go there."

Tucson was an alien planet compared to Rochester Hills.

"At first I was like 'It's brown! There's no grass!' But you learn to appreciate the subtle things of the high desert. It's gorgeous, absolutely gorgeous, especially the sunsets. I became hooked.

"A lot of Westerns and John Wayne movies like Eldorado were filmed in Tucson – some of the Ponderosa and Bonanza series.

"Tucson and Phoenix are 100 miles apart and the speed limit's 75. With radar detectors you can make it in an hour or less.

"I'd have friends come here and party. Or I'd go up on the weekend. I have some good friends up there.

"I missed the lakes, but then I found out there's all kinds of lakes in Arizona. Lake Powell is absolutely gorgeous; and Lake Havasu.

"I bought boats. I learned to barefoot water ski. Slalom skiing was great.

"When I found out there's snow skiing, I'm like 'Let's go!' I did everything I liked to do in Michigan.

"Randolph Golf Course was a public course in Tucson. It's right across from the Doubletree. There was a guy named Homero Blancas who was the head pro. He played on the tour, before the senior tour even came out. He gave me lessons on the short game every day. He was a really nice guy.

"The assistant pro was Ron Castillo. We'd go out and play in golf tournaments. We had fun. I learned Spanish by living here."

"In the summer after my freshman year there was no football, I wasn't making money and I didn't want to stay in Arizona. It gets so hot it's like a ghost town.

"The heat depends on the elevation. Phoenix is the worst, it doesn't even cool off at night.

"It's all paved; when the sun goes down the heat comes right back up from the asphalt. You sweat like Mike Tyson taking the S.A.T.

"Me and Habibi were only seeing each other off and on, so it wasn't any big deal if I went away for a few months.

"I drove back to Michigan and stayed in Grosse Pointe with my sister Nadra. From her house it's only 8 miles to Greektown.

"While I was there Paulie and I opened an arcade around the corner from the Grecian Gardens. It was commercial property and there was nothing there. Uncle Dominic owned it, so we didn't have to pay rent.

"We put in a bunch of arcade machines and all the little black kids came and played the games.

"We had an oven, we'd make pizza and this and that and we did pretty good.

"There was this long alley outside the back door at the Grecian Gardens; that's where they'd put the trash. It was a feast for the rats."

In downtown Detroit, Norway rats can measure 18" from the nose to the tip of the tail.

"When I was little I was always afraid of 'em, so me and Paulie would dare each other to run down that alley at night. Paulie used to set traps for them.

"And he had this German shepherd that was so mean he'd charge the sliding door and jump at it. His paws would go *clack, clack, clack* and you could hear his teeth on the glass. If he got you, he would tear you apart.

"I'd say 'Put that thing in a cage so we can go outside.'

"He'd put him in the cage and I'm thinking *He's ok, he's calmed down*. I went down by the cage and he's still trying to kill ya.

"This dog. If he got ahold of you he probably *would* kill you. So that's just Paulie. That's how he was.

"We were doing alright. We would go out to all the bars and stuff.

"One night Paulie was pitching quarters and he won $32,000 – some obscene number. He'd go for $1,000, double or nothing. So we just split the money and spent it all.

"Paulie said the guy we won the money from took him to his house and he followed him downstairs where he got the money out of the safe.

"Paulie goes 'There's probably a lot of money in the safe. We should rob this guy.'"

Their plan included walkie talkies and 'two white guys' who would set the victim up with a date so he'd be out of the house.

They knew he had an alarm.

"We had people walking the corners in case he came back. These guys cut the alarm wires and we went in; but nobody could find the safe.

"Then these white kids I didn't even know started stealing everything like liquor and this and that; and they got caught. We knew those guys were going to probably tell so we went to Paulie's grandparents in Clarkston and hid out.

"The white kids didn't know me, but I think they told on Paulie. My Uncle Tony told me to get in my car and go home.

"I always travel with my pillows and blankets. I threw all my stuff in the Toronado. I had pillows on both sides of me and I drove home to Arizona. It was alright; I was getting out of trouble."

He thought it all through as he drove.

"I'm thinking *Why the fuck did you bring these fucking morons? They had a Milwaukee saw that could open the safe but we couldn't even find the safe.*

"I decided that was not my gig. Burglary was not for me. You don't want to go in someone's house. I would never do that. And I would never deal with strangers again.

"Aunt Josephine called shortly after I left Michigan; Uncle Dominic had a really bad stroke. I knew he wasn't going to last.

"His death took everyone by surprise. My dad went to the funeral but I couldn't go.

"Like The Sopranos, we feel it but don't show it. Everybody grieves in their own way."

Peter added 'Sicilians are stoic, not emotional like Italians.'

His father's original vision for the family land fell through. Allen says "When Mr. Corrado died they sold the house. Peter got married and Paulie was out in Las Vegas doing his thing."

Allen was back in the action with Uncle Sol in no time.

"There were two dog racing tracks in South Tucson, the Mexican part of town. In the summer they switched to Amado Dog Track because it was higher in elevation, a little cooler at night for the dogs.

"Habibi's real name was Denise but my Uncle Sol called her 'Danoose.' We'd go to Amado because nobody would know us down there except the degenerate gamblers in our families.

"It was kind of a long drive, but Uncle Sol used to be there every night. He was a very good bettor of dogs.

"He knew the trainers, knew what was going on.

"So we'd go down there and I'd say 'I need some money, give me a winner.'

"He'd go 'OK, relax. Just be ready when I tell you and then you go bet what and how I tell you to bet.'

"I said 'OK.'

"He'd say 'Take this dog and bet him in a wheel with every dog in the race.' So if the dog won I'd win the trifecta. And you gotta hope that the dog runs first or even second.

"That way, if it runs second with a bunch of long shots, you're going to make a bunch of money. I'd make $300 or 400 on the bet.

"Habibi and I would leave and we wouldn't even get halfway back to Tucson, we'd pull over to the side of the road and have sex.

"Everything was going great until her parents caught us naked on the couch. They didn't like that at all. They're like 'What did you do to our daughter?!' They thought I defiled her.

"We had to sneak around after that. We used to go to school together in the morning and hang out. We'd go in the library and I'd bang her on the piano. I banged her everywhere.

"We'd go to the bar sometimes or just take a drive. There's all kinds of places in Tucson in the mountains. It was just a couple hundred thousand people there. We used to make love in the car all the time.

"We'd drive all the way to the east side of town where I eventually built my house. There was nothing there at the time. I told my parents 'This property is going to be worth a fortune one day' but they didn't listen. I was just a college kid."

But now he *was* old enough to hang with his cousin George.

"By this time George is bald, 5'10", stocky and very strong – a real cowboy. He could do rodeo riding and roping and shit."

Was he shaved or naturally bald?

"Naturally bald with a little hair on the sides. He said it came from 'doing too many U-turns under the sheets.'

"His parents still had the El Dorado restaurant. His father was partners and best friends with my Uncle Willie who was supposed to leave us all the stuff.

"The Mexicans called George's father 'Nacho' out of respect. He could always be trusted to help people who crossed the border. He let them stay in apartments in back of the restaurant.

"His parents bought the property right across the street and George opened a disco.

"In South Tucson it's all Mexican people, so his disco was cowboyish with Mexican music mostly. I remember concrete floors; maybe tile."

Why did he call it a disco?

"Because he had a disco ball."

I laughed; he didn't.

"The place was nice but it wasn't my thing.

"That's why I didn't want to go there at night.

"Sometimes I'd have plans with Habibi, but he'd call and tell me 'Come over, I gotta stock the bar.'

"We'd be stocking and all these girls would be coming in and we'd just get shitfaced.

"He'd say 'C'mon, you gotta drink another beer.'

"I'd say 'I gotta go meet Habibi.'

"He'd say 'Fuck her. Drink more.'

"I started calling him 'Zib'; it means little dick in Arabic."

"George was a real deal rodeo riding cowboy with the hat, rodeo buckles and boots. He was president of 'El Charros' – Mexican cowboys – and he had an arena.

"On rodeo week they have a parade and they'd wear their traditional clothes. Women rode side saddle in costume.

"I rode horses in Michigan and then, when we went to Arizona, George saw how good I was, that I could ride any horse. He'd throw me on the wildest horse and I'd just hang on and they'd all calm down. He'd be amazed. I just had a way with the animals.

"They had this one horse they called 'The Widow Maker' because he threw everybody off. I just got on him. They know when you're not having it and they kind of calm down. You pet them and get to know them.

"I'd train the horses for the girls to ride and work with them if they were acting up. Then I rode every day."

How did George decide you were man enough to hang with him?

"He had a baby bull we were trying to load in a trailer. I had a 2 x 4. He had the lead line around the center pole and I'm hitting it in the ass with a 2 x 4. It wasn't moving.

"George said 'Turn the board around and hit it with the nails.'

"So I turned it around and he kind of moved."

Once he'd been accepted as an equal, Allen became George's student. George took pilot lessons and became a cocaine cowboy, dealing with a cartel and flying drugs like Mickey Munday who flew for Pablo Escobar and the Medellin Cartel.

"George would fly through washes so they couldn't get him on radar. Or he'd fly right over the freeway and just drop it somewhere."

Sounds like you might have learned things from him?

"Yeah, a lot."

Legal or illegal?

"Mostly illegal."

George's first arrest was for transporting cocaine.

"They caught him and took a bunch of property away from him – something like $10 million worth.

"Bob Hirsh was his attorney. Hirsh knew my Uncle Sol. He used to get so many people off of every charge. He defended Bonanno, Pete Licavoli and Charley 'Bats' Battaglia.

"One guy found his wife screwing another guy and killed her with three blasts from a shotgun. Hirsh got him off – 'Not guilty by reason of insanity.'

"Another guy stabbed his wife 26 times 'while sleepwalking.' Hirsh got him acquitted. They changed laws because of him.

"George had to go to jail, but not for long."

"George was a sharpshooter, a national champion. In the National Guard, he won their shooting competitions almost every year. In Arizona 200 meters was the size of a chicken, 300 meters was a turkey, 400 was a javelina.

"He could take somebody out from a long way if need be.

"One night I saw him unloading his shooting rifle before we walked out the side door of the bar. He pointed it at me.

"I said 'Why are you pointing that at me? I know it's not loaded.'

"He says 'Oh, you think so?'

"The muzzle blast crossed the top of my head and blew my hair back."

That was supposed to be funny?

"Yeah. He was fun; that was a joke. I was goading him into it. I didn't know it was loaded. I was *for sure* it wasn't loaded.

"I was wrong."

"Eventually Uncle Sol went to Las Vegas and lost a quarter million. He didn't want to burden his family with it, so he ended up committing suicide. He drove up to Mt. Lemmon, pulled off and shot himself in the head.

"His wife is still alive. She loved him; he was a great guy. She travels a lot, was going all over the world with one of her cousins.

"In the 50s – when he was an Intelligence Officer in the Air Force – Uncle Sol bought a Rolex. My cousin was into watches, so his mom told him 'Here, I'm going to give you your dad's Rolex.'

"There was no band, it was just the face.

"My cousin said 'Well it's really not fair to my sister and brother. Let me do some research and see what it's worth.'

"He didn't want to go through the jewelers in the family; he likes to do things on his own. He went online and found some experts.

"Turned out it was a very rare watch worth $80,000.

"He sold it and split the money with his siblings. His dad would have liked that."

Things began to cool with Da-noose.

"We had fun for a while, but then I got bored with the shenanigans with the parents and all that shit. I was lucky enough to be able to corral a few other fillies."

Monogamy made no sense; it was mathematically unsound.

"You go out with one girl for what – 2 or 3 months? In that time period I could be banging 50 girls. It's *much* better coverage."

5 Expanding the Circle

"Tucson had the first Canyon Ranch; now they put 'em in the cities. It's beautiful, a health place. You go in, they make you eat right and exercise.

"Now Tucson is *full* of spas and resorts – Miraval, Loews Ventana, Westin LaPaloma. It's a circle; you go out and see people you know.

"The Licavolis moved from Detroit to Tucson. It has one of the best climates in the country. You could do business by phone and it's a hop, skip and a jump away from the west coast.

"I played cards one night with Peter Licavoli, took him for a lot of money and he wanted it back. I said 'Go fuck yourself.'

"I used to go out with Carl Meli, the Monacos – Billy Monaco and his brothers. They're really nice people.

"Paulie was living here in Tucson with me for a while. He never was much of a gambler. People that gamble gamble.

"Frankie Bags married one of the Licavoli daughters and they would always fight. Every morning we'd get up, we'd go get Frankie Bags and it'd be the three of us – we'd go around town doing this and that until happy hour; then we'd go drink."

When Paulie went back to Vegas, he and Allen stayed in touch.

U of A was the first time Allen ventured out from his circle. Making new friends was easy.

"People just naturally always liked to be around me; I'm hilarious."

I asked how he knew someone was worthy of his attention and he gave it serious consideration.

"They had to be smart and fun, from good families. And they all had money. That way we were all equal."

Three of Allen's friends – Charlie, Karl and Dale – had just graduated from the elite Cate Prep in Santa Barbara.

"I met them when I was a freshman. Charlie's grandfather was a banker; he wound up following in his footsteps.

"Karl's father had started Burger King. He opened up a whole bunch of Burger Kings in Scottsdale.

"This was back in the day and they didn't catch on. He went broke and they moved to Tucson. Karl became an architect.

"Dale's father and brother were cardiologists. Dale got a degree in Information Management Systems. Within a few years he would be 'like a comptroller' for Allen's drug operation.

"I met Ray at U of A too. We became really good friends. He was a big time Calvin Klein model. He went on to open his own studio in Manhattan. He knows a lot of people and is very, very successful."

"One day at college Ray says 'You're getting high today.'
"I said 'OK.'
"We were out in the desert. It was duskish. We don't have street lights in a lot of places. We have special lights so you can see the stars. When they came out it was electric, just amazing.

"We had a good time.
"I said 'This shit's great! No wonder they wanted to keep it away from me!'

"After a while I was getting high all the time. I didn't party 'til I came out west and then it was all hands on deck. I drink, but I'm not an alcoholic. If I drank it was vodka tonic or vodka soda with a piece of fruit, lemon or lime.

"I'm a rare breed in that I can do drugs. I did cocaine; I did pills. I never did crack and I never did heroin. I wouldn't do things like that.

"But then I started doing Quaaludes, those were my favorites – like lemons. The Mexicans made some. You just kind of get a really good buzz. I used to take 'em and carry them and give them to people.

"I always had 30 or 40 Quaaludes on me – not for profit or anything – just for fun. I'd pass 'em out to people I knew … mostly."

What do you think of the way Cosby used them?

"I think he's a sick fuck. I never used 'em for that. There's a big difference if girls took them willingly or he dosed them by putting them in their drinks. He should have to pay the consequences, whatever they are.

"Guys like that, to me he's demented. You don't take advantage of people for any reason, especially you don't drug a woman so you can have sex with her.

"She doesn't even know what's going on. It's the most idiotic thing. It woulda been better for him to go pay for it.

"He's a freak, he's weird.

"I'm a freak … but girls want to be with me. I don't have to do stupid shit. I party because I like to party. You want to join in, you're more than welcome.

"I don't expect anything ever in return."

Partying was easy; making it home in one piece wasn't.

"Most of these people at the bars were in college and they had to drive home. The roads were in the mountains, in the foothills. The kids lived below that, they had to drive down winding roads that were dangerous. There were a lot of accidents.

"We always used to race on those roads because it was cool as fuck, just awesome. I always had radar detectors, but I still got so many tickets. I would always be going 110 or 120.

"After a while there were so many accidents on Hacienda Del Sol that they closed it. People were getting hurt and there were a few deaths.

"My mother, no matter what time I came home at night, if I came home at 3 or 4 in the morning, she would want to make me something to eat before I went to bed. Whatever I wanted.

"I'd say 'What do you have left over? Heat it up.'

"My mom could make everything. She could taste something and know what was in it and how to make it.

"If she wasn't cooking for us she was cooking for somebody else. They'd ask her how to make certain Lebanese dishes that were labor intensive; they've got to be done right to taste good.

"She was always helping and teaching and eventually she made a business out of it.

"There wasn't any Lebanese restaurants in Tucson at the time; despite the fact that there were a lot of Arab students in Tucson for some reason.

"In the early eighties they opened The Sheik on the east side of town – Wilmot and Broadway in Tucson. It was nice. They had a liquor license and a belly dancer.

"My mother had a better sense for business than my dad did, but he could bake like you couldn't believe. People used to wait outside in line just to get in on Friday and Saturday nights; sometimes Thursday nights too.

"When Douglas worked in their restaurant, he would yell and scream. I don't know if it was because he was high or what, but he was bad.

"I was already kind of doing my thing, but I did some restaurant work. I had to have a good work ethic, they instilled that in me.

"They said 'No matter what you do at night, come time when you're supposed to be here, you're going to be here! That's it!'

"You get to the point where there's a rush and everybody's running around and working quickly. You have to be able to take it and be calm – make sure everything comes out and people are satisfied.

"At the restaurant everything had to be perfectly spotless all the time. My dad was a clean freak, had like 98 on their health department assessments.

"I'd come through with a bunch of friends after the bars closed and mess up everything. I'd cook burgers, drink beers and hang out 'til all hours.

"The only thing my dad cared about was 'Couldn't you just put the dishes in the sink?'"

Sundays the restaurant was closed and the family tradition continued.

"My mom would just say she was making *whatever* and I'd show up at their house with all my friends. They always liked her food, even the rice. She might add pine nuts, or butter and vermicelli; fry that and put it in the rice – then add water and seasonings. There was a little cinnamon too; just a hint.

"My parents had a nice house and all my nieces and nephews would come around. They were small, they'd come hang out. Sometimes I'd jump off the roof into the pool.

"My dad's like 'What is that pounding on the roof?'

"I'd get a running start and BOOM."

Allen was swimming hard, full of phlegm and spit.

"Douglas was laughing hard with his head thrown back. I took aim and hocked a loogie that hit him right in the mouth.

"He started wailing to my dad."

"Midge and Sam wound up getting divorced, but he would still come to Arizona and see my folks and hang out. It was nice.

"Midge went out with George the Animal Steel for a while. He coached high school football. He acted like a total retard in the ring, dyeing his tongue green and biting that thing in the corner of the ring – but in real life he was just a pretty normal guy."

• • •

"In the early 80s my sisters opened an electronics and appliance store in Huntington Beach.

"Elaine's husband Kelly taught me about running a business. I was still in college, so I'd drive out, stay at their house and work for them in the summertime.

"In the beginning I was doing a lot of manual labor. I drove the delivery truck and delivered appliances. Then, during business hours, you'd run into a lot of different things. People buy merchandise and they use it and don't like it and bring it back.

"We were working on small margin, so you couldn't just take everything back.

"If there was valid reason for the return, if something was wrong – definitely, we'll fix and replace it to make the customer happy.

"After a while they had me handling all the returns, all the complaints, because they knew I could deal with people. I wouldn't offend them."

"We were the largest Cannon and Nikon dealers in the United States. And living in southern California, we were a little more ostentatious with the cars, with going out to dinner every night. We'd spend a couple thousand dollars.

"I'd get up real early and play 9 holes with the pro. I took golf lessons from the guy that gave Tiger Woods lessons when he was young; I was starting to take it more seriously. The golf course is a great place to have conversations and make a few bucks.

"Around this time there was fighting near my mom's property in the Middle East. She sold some strategic piece and made pretty good money. The store was already doing good, but she gave them more money to help 'em out.

"She wanted to do something nice for all her children.

"She bought me gold bracelets. I said 'Just buy me a Rolex.' But no, she bought me a bunch of gold shit instead.

"They have Rolexes in Lebanon, but maybe she couldn't get 'em as cheap as we can get them here. Or maybe my dad thought it would draw attention.

"After a while I moved from Elaine and Kelly's house to Newport Beach. Our store was still growing; my uncles had two stores in San Diego and another guy had a store in LA.

"The guys in San Diego were all from Dix Avenue in Dearborn. They grew up together and they'd all help each other. If we needed something or they needed something, we moved money back and forth.

"If there was a train load of something coming in that had to be paid for and we were short of cash, I'd just drive down to San Diego, pick up the money and take it back.

"Atari video games were hot and – compared to gaming today – that stuff was more expensive back then. If I could buy a truckload, we'd get money from somebody for a few days and sell out that fast.

"We charged customers what we paid for them, just so we could bring business in and sell other merchandise.

"Most of the big ticket items were 'floor planned' so we didn't have to tie up our money.

"We'd be moving money around all over the place, so I learned all about banking. I learned how to tell fake bills from real bills and went to the bank every day to make deposits.

"We were doing 60 to 65 million a year in sales at the one store. Around the holidays we hired armored cars to come take our money and make our deposits."

There was no conscious plan to engage in illegal enterprise, but "I learned if it looked like business, business was business. I learned if you didn't stand out, if you didn't look like you were doing anything wrong, nobody would even take a second look.

"If something happened that they needed more help, I'd take off a couple of weeks of school. I was still doing my parlay cards and stuff."

When Allen needed to blow off steam, he could always count on his party uncle. While Uncle Sol had worked to get him *out* of trouble, Uncle George paved the way.

"My Uncle George was Lebanese – not really a relative, but he loved me like a son. His wife had passed away.

"He lived in Laguna but he also had a 5,000 square foot party house in Palm Springs – 5 bedrooms, 5 baths – right across from William Holden's house.

"Uncle George only cared about collecting Lladro and making sure I had fun. He owned George Chevrolet in LA, but he didn't care about the dealership, he gave it to his son-in-law to run. I was really good friends with his daughter and son-in-law.

"He kept his own personal space way in the back of the dealership, in the Parts Department. He had his Lladro there and people would come and shop. It was quite funny.

"In 1984 I told him I wanted a new Corvette.

"He said 'They're in high demand.' Then he turns to his son-in-law and says 'Tim, get him a car.'

"I said 'I want a red one.'

"So I got a red one, a four speed."

Allen was staying with his sister in Palm Springs when a pedestrian made an unfortunate remark about his new car.

"I said 'Your mom gave it to me because I fucked her really good.'

"He threw a bottle at me.

"I sped up to hit him and missed.

"We were near a hotel driveway that was at an angle where he could take a short cut and get to the street before me.

"When I got there, there was water in the gutter; I did a 180 while I was going against the traffic, sped up, did another 180 and he was right in the middle of the road.

"I knocked him up in the air and took off.

"After a night of partying I came back the same way. It was probably 3:30 a.m. and there was yellow tape all around the back of the hotel where it happened.

"My nephew said 'They're looking everywhere for you.'

"I'm like 'Aw shit.'

"I told my sister 'I'm going back to the beach.'

"She says 'What are you talking about?'

"I said 'I just can't sleep. I want to go back to the beach.'

"I took the back streets and got out of there.

"My nephew sort of followed the story; the guy lived. I got in trouble in Palm Springs a lot; but I had great lawyers so I would always would get out."

"This girl started working at the electronics store. She was beautiful with a smoking body – and she was nice. Her family owned a Chevrolet dealership and her boyfriend went to Cate.

"She was friends with my cousin Patty – Uncle George's daughter. We became friendly.

"She says 'Come over to my house, I'm going to fix you up with my sister.'

"Lo and behold, I end up banging *her*. But her boyfriend is coming in the front door while I'm running out the back trying to get my pants on.

"I took off so fast I spun out. Karl and Charlie laughed so hard, those guys could not contain themselves.

"Turns out her boyfriend was a douchebag. He broke up with her and we started dating for a little while … but I never got serious with girls too much. I would date 'em for a little while and then we'd just go our separate ways.

"I was kind of a hound; whereas Peter got married right after college. He always knew who he was going to marry, it was no secret. She's a great lady. I like her a lot.

"They came out to Newport Beach for their honeymoon.

"I saw him and we stayed in nice hotels. I'd tell him where to go during the day while I was working.

"We went somewhere later and we're looking around and *what the fuck* – there was all kinds of feds in the lobby. We're like 'Wonder what they're here for?'

"Turns out they were there for us, to see what we were up to. We weren't up to anything! What a pain in the ass, it's like we can't even hang out."

Life wasn't nearly so complicated with his U of A crew.

"Karl was an architect in the '84 Olympics. That spring he was working on setting up all the venues, so on Saturday nights we'd drive my Corvette to Palm Springs.

"Uncle George had a Screen Actor's Guild card. He knew people, he could get models and actresses hooked up with jobs.

"He would invite girls he knew to the house on Saturday. It was a routine that he set up. We'd go out to dinner, come home, spend time by the pool and hang out.

"Karl was like 'These girls are fucking beautiful.'

"I said 'Well what'd you expect, some dogs here?'"

Then came the Olympics.

"President Reagan opened the games for his home state. David L. Wolper produced the opening and closing ceremonies.

"We went to all the big events, but having tickets to the closing ceremony was a huge deal. We had great seats, but somehow we got separated in the crowd heading into the Coliseum.

"Karl had both of our tickets on him so I couldn't get in. I'm running around looking for him and he's running around looking for me. Finally I talked my way in.

"After about 30 minutes Karl shows up – sweating hard. I'm sitting there talking to girls and having a beer."

Music from *2001 a Space Odyssey* blared as a 52-foot diameter UFO descended in a blaze of sound and light. Some people thought it was real.

"Karl says 'This is unbelievable. You're the only guy on earth who could talk his way into this event.'

"A while later Karl goes 'You know how we can make some money at school? Selling coke.'

"I said 'Well, we could try it.'

"So he gave me a kilo.

"I said 'How are we going to get this back to Tucson Karl?'

"He said 'We're just going to put it in our pants and fly in an airplane. You take half and I'll take half.'

"And away we went.

"It ended up not being a real money making proposition because our friends came over and everyone partied. We really didn't sell much.

"I realized I'm not cut out to make money from my friends. Not then; not ever."

Back in Tucson "Dale went out and bought a new Corvette because I had one."

Same color?

"No, he got bronze/brown – it was weird looking. So now he and Augie Busch both had Corvettes.

"Augie was great grandson or grandson of the Anheuser Busch people. He went to U of A for a little while. I just knew him to say 'Hi.' He was a horse's ass.

"Not overly arrogant, but he wasn't the nicest guy. I met him a few times and it just never changed. But Dale liked him and they hung out.

"They used to race through the desert on River Road before they straightened it out. It was very windey, very dangerous – especially at high speeds.

"One time Augie was with some girl, drinking and driving his Corvette really fast. He flew off the road and crashed his car. He ran away because he was drunk. He left the girl in the car to bleed to death.

"Obviously people like him don't get consequences. Someone called his family and told them what happened. The jet was there right after the crash to get him. They flew him out of town that night.

"If he would have saved her life, what's going to happen? He might get a DUI, maybe? But because he's Augie Busch and he's got 250 lawyers behind him, Pima County doesn't want to deal with it.

"Later Dale was driving really fast – probably racing somebody – and the road went from two lanes to one on a curve; no warning signs, nothing.

"You're not supposed to be going that fast.

"He broke the front end and he knows the car is never going to be the same. He comes over at 4 a.m. and begs me to call my friend at the junkyard and have it crushed.

"I used to do that for friends once in a while. I'd say 'Here, crush this – I don't want anything left.' I'd tell the friend to say it was stolen."

How did you get into crushing cars?

"I knew people and I did things out of necessity. I knew the guy that owned the junkyard, so BOOM. I got stuff handled.

"In Dale's case, I wasn't going to wake the guy up and make him crush the car that late at night."

"I'm still going back and forth from California and Tucson for work. I learned more working the electronics store than I learned at school.

"College wasn't a college, I was just having fun. I paid people to do my assignments. I studied business and finance but I knew it already. And the teachers always knew I knew. They weren't teaching me anything.

"I kept going to school until finally I didn't sign up for a semester and I'm like 'fuck it.' I was only a few credits short of graduating. I knew I didn't need to learn any more.

"I didn't graduate; I worked full-time for the electronics store. They made me VP.

"I did some commercials for the store, just winged it. I was popping out of refrigerators saying 'We've got the coolest deals!'

"It wasn't that hard, not at all; and the business was 60 million a year. Back in those days that was a lot of money. I was *making* a lot of money, but I was too busy working to spend it. We were busy from morning to night.

"One of my uncles knew Muhammed Ali. He used to come to our store and do book signings. He would stay until everybody got an autograph or got to talk to him – no matter how late it was. He denied no one.

"He liked to do magic tricks, although he was no good at 'em.

"After the book signings we'd go to dinner at Antonello in South Coast Plaza, on the corner of Newport Beach and Costa Mesa – a premier shopping place in the country. Antonio Gagnolo has been there forever, we're really good friends with him.

"Ali used to hang out with me and we talked. He liked me because I used to see him all the time in Vegas. Whoever was with me couldn't believe it.

"Like one time I'm walking on the street with three or four guy friends and they said 'That's Muhammed Ali!'

"I say 'I know him!'

"They go 'Yeah, sure.'

"His memory wasn't so good, but the guy who took care of him sees me and goes 'Allen!'

"Then Ali recognizes me and we go over there. He says 'You got some friends? You guys want to have breakfast with the champ?'

"They're all like freaking out now. I said 'Sure!'

"And he goes 'You want to walk into the fight with me?'

"I said 'Yeah, of course!'

"So we're walking into the Spinks vs. Holmes fight. I had my hand on his shoulder and they're yelling 'Ali! Ali!' – everybody in the whole place. It was amazing.

"I leaned over and said in his ear 'They're saying Ahee, not Ali!' And he started laughing.

"I used to have pictures with him and I boxing around, sparring around, stuff like that."

"When business at the store started to go down we hired a big firm to find out why. They analyzed who was valuable, who's doing the work that needs to be done and who's not.

"We were paying a lot of money for it. They came in and stayed for month. They evaluated and found out people were stealing.

"We started taking the trash out ourselves. I wouldn't let anyone take it out. The back doors remained locked while we checked it.

"We had a security guard up front, but I caught people just taking off, taking things, expensive items and walking out the front door like nothing happened.

"Sometimes they'd get caught – sometimes I would chase 'em down.

"You can't imagine how many young kids are in jail because they steal to support their habit. They just run out with a TV – or as many as they can put in a cart. When the alarm goes off, there's someone outside waiting and they take off. They sell 'em and get high.

"After we'd close we had dinner at Antonello's in Newport Beach. We had a big table every night.

"By the time we got done eating, we didn't get home 'til 11; and we'd get up in the morning and do it all over again – six days a week.

"I left there because I didn't want to work like that. I decided *I'm coming back to Tucson.*

"When I came back I got my real estate license. I had a friend who was building homes and subdivisions at R.A., so I got a job with him. It was just him and me and it was good money – *easy* money for me right then.

"I like real estate because you're selling somebody's dream. They're going to build their home and make things that are really, really nice.

"R.A. had three different models and we ran the office. People would come in and we'd show them through. Usually they picked one. I did the paperwork, got 'em financed and they bought a house. It was that simple.

"I was still living with my parents when Dale introduced me to Phil; the two of us became really good friends. *Later I'd find out Phil never liked Dale, never trusted him. Hates him to this day.*

"Phil's brother Mike was doing construction and owned his own house, but he was thinking about moving back to Phoenix to work in real estate.

"When he finally made his decision, he said 'You guys should just take over my place.'

"His house was in my parents' subdivision – a nice place in a really nice area. It was on a curve with nearly 3,000 square feet on one level. We didn't have a pool, but we had a big back yard with a garage around the side and a two car garage in the front.

"Me, Phil and Dale lived there for a long time. We just went out and partied; then we'd go back, have fun and stay up all night."

"So I'm in Tucson driving my red Corvette and she just obviously stood out. She was blonde and beautiful with big breasts.

"I pulled over and started talking to her.

"She said she was in nursing school, so I asked her to take my pulse on my dick.

"I used to call her Lurch because she was so tall.

"I don't know how she got her house, but it was really nice; maybe somebody was letting her use it.

"She told me her father was really wealthy, but that didn't matter to me. I only liked her for quick booty calls and such.

"One time on my way to pick her up I stopped at Jack in the Box to get burgers and onion rings. When I got to her place, I put the rings on my dick and made her eat them off. I said 'Don't miss any spots.'

"Then when she was giving me head, she said 'Your dick tastes like onion rings.'

"I said 'It could be worse. I'll stick it in you and it'll taste like pussy.'

"Lurch liked me a lot, more than I liked her. A lot of guys wanted to sleep with her but she wouldn't do it.

"A friend of Dale's was trying to get at her and she shut him down. I told her 'Do me a favor. Just have sex with him.'

"She got mad at me for that. She said 'I thought we were exclusive!'

"I said 'We're exclusive *right now.*'"

"I was completely wild all the time. If there was a reason to party, I'm all in. If there's no reason, there's no reason.

"I'd stay up for two days in a row. Sometimes I'd sleep in the day, hang out by a pool and relax. When I couldn't sleep in the day, I'd get up and away we went.

"I remember one time I backed out and forgot to open the garage door. It looked like a bat cave. That was in the middle of the day, not late at night when I was fucked up or anything.

"Years later, in his testimony, Dale would say he liked to be with me because I was fun and I had money; and he had money and we could do whatever we wanted.

"Dale didn't have a hard time getting girls when he'd hang out with me and Phil. There was always plenty of girls and he could talk.

"He was OK; not hideous looking. Lurch hung out with this girl who hooked up with him for a while.

"Lurch was sad when she had to move away, but I was OK about it. I wasn't exactly monogamous.

"She ran into Madonna somewhere in Florida. Lurch said 'I think we have a mutual friend.'

"Madonna says 'I don't talk about my past.'"

"They used to call Phil the Italian Stallion. He's a very, very good looking guy and some girl said he had the perfect dick.

"We used to compare dicks. We'd pull 'em out and measure."
Sometimes they compared them in action.

"There were these two gorgeous girls and Phil says 'Why don't we take 'em to Palm Springs?'

"It was private; it was perfect. It was over 5,000 sq. feet, 5 bedrooms, each with its own bath.

"We would have everything there – pool table, ping pong table, darts, bar room games, the pool ... all fenced in. We could stay in and have food catered.

"Nobody was ever there unless they were going for the weekend. I asked my parents; they weren't going. I called my sister, who would have been the only one that might go. We were in the clear.

"So Phil and I took the girls separately. I drove my Porsche and Phil had a two door gray market Mercedes."

Gray market cars were considered the forbidden fruit of the automotive world; they weren't legal in the U.S. without expensive modifications and American cars didn't come close.

"We drove in tandem to Palm Springs.

"We got there, hung out and then it was off to the bedroom. The master bedroom had two king sized beds.

"A few years later, I don't know where Phil was or where I was at the time, but he calls and says 'Turn on the TV; you're never going to believe who's on!'

"Heidi Fleiss was on Oprah and her top escort was the girl that I was with. The papers said she was a $1,500-an-hour prostitute. Someone said Charlie Sheen was her best customer."

Allen's real estate career continued to thrive.

"Before long we sold out the whole development for R.A. – more than 100 homes. So that was pretty cool, except I didn't want to just sit there.

"Phil tells me 'You can make more money working with us at JNC.' They were a big time developer.

"Dale was already working there, so Phil told me to come down.

"Before long I was selling investments and making $10,000 a week – a lot of money for back then.

"I got jobs for most of my friends. John Catanzaro was a pretty nice guy. I sold him some investments and got him to come in and be a salesman.

"Most of my friends worked for JNC except Ray. He was a model, so he'd go off on shoots. He was in GQ almost every month for years."

DEALING WEED

6 Dealing Dope

"I was only working a couple hours a day and Ray didn't have a schedule to keep, so we were hanging out all the time. We'd go places and spend money. We spent like $15,000 on a competition ski boat and went water skiing.

"So I asked Ray, 'How are you getting your cash? I know how I'm getting it – how are *you* getting it?'

"He says 'I'm sending about 7 or 8 pounds of marijuana to my sister in New Jersey every week.'

"I said 'REALLY! Of marijuana!'

"Ray said he'd send her 7 pounds, so he was making good money; 7 pounds was about $400/lb. and he was probably selling it for $1,200 to $1,300/lb. That's seven grand a week. That ain't hay.

"So I said 'Where do you get it?'

"He says 'Wherever I can; here and there.'

"I'm thinking *I know enough people.* I said 'Would you mind – if I get it – would you buy it from me?'

"He said 'If you can get it, I'll buy it from you; it just has to be good quality.'

"So I said 'OK.'

"I called Ernie, a big land developer who made a lot of his money in dope. I knew him from real estate. I figure he'll know someone.

"I call Ernie and he says 'What do you need?'

"I say '7 pounds?'

"He says 'Yeah, just come over to the house and pick it up.'

"I drove up there and he said 'Here, just take it.' I didn't even pay. People were always kind of nice with me.

"I threw it in the back of my Corvette – where anyone could see it – and drove all the way across town to Ray's place. I pulled into the garage and we opened it. 'Oh yeah, this is good!'

"So that's how I started. Except now I had a source but I didn't really know anything about selling.

"My nephew David had stayed in Detroit to go to Wayne State and play football. I called him and said 'Find out who you know that sells weed.'

"He goes 'Well, let me check.'

"Calls me back the next day.

"He knew a guy – Joe something or other – a white kid. He was the first guy in Detroit I started dealing with. He was pretty trustworthy actually.

"David says 'Can you get him 80 pounds? Joe will pay you $1,200 a pound if you can bring it to him.'

"I said 'I can bring it to him.'"

"Mike recommended flying product in special Zero Halliburton steel suitcases because they're lightweight, airtight and waterproof. They were at least 40" wide and real deep.

"I could fit 40 pounds in each Halliburton bag. You had to sit on them to close 'em sometimes. They had locks and a release valve to let all the air out.

"They come in stainless steel and black. When average people saw a big stainless steel suitcase coming through the airport, they're like 'What's that?' I chose black because they attracted less attention. Nobody notices black.

"I started taking 80 pounds to this guy every week or 10 days. It was always Tucson to Detroit, but I'd fly out of Phoenix because it was a busier airport.

"In the old days you had to walk up the stairs to get to the plane, then down the stairs onto the runway. You don't want to fly with drugs in suitcases out of Tucson. Big suitcases look suspicious in a small airport.

"Detroit was my main hub, in and out of Detroit. I had access to warehouses and people I could trust. Back then there were no dogs at the airport, they didn't check your luggage or x-ray anything.

"When I landed my nephew would always be waiting outside. He'd heave the bags into his trunk, take them to the guy and wait to get paid.

"Once I landed at Detroit Metro I'd just tear it up. I'd go to Windsor to the strip clubs and bring girls back to the hotel.

"I always took everything for granted, the people that I knew. 'Hollywood Ronnie' Morelli and Billie Bagnasco. 'Billie Bags' and Billie's brother Frank all had a place together. And they always had girls over there because Billie got all the looks.

"I had money, so we went out. I used to love Lelli's downtown, especially the zip sauce on the steaks."

Bobby 'the Animal' LaPuma was part of the crew.

The press said he was top enforcer for Tony Jack and Billy Giacalone.

"Him and Paulie used to do everything. No guys would ever bother us.

"I had family in Detroit, so everyone was happy to see me.

"At first Cindy's kids never really knew what I did or anything, but over the years they'd always ask me for stuff. Like I would get sports memorabilia, signed jerseys from hotshot NFL players.

"My niece wanted a signed jersey from Yzerman when he was young and playing for Detroit. I think she still has it.

"Her brother wanted a signed jersey from Chad Johnson – Chad Ochocinco of the Bengals. My friend Ricky was the linebacker coach for the Bengals. I asked him if he could get me a jersey.

"He said 'You only have to pay for the Jersey, I won't charge for the signature.'

"I told him 'I'll beat his ass!' So I got my nephew a Jersey.

"My cousin Raymond knew Tom Ilitch. He got a signed jersey and had it framed.

"I was visiting everybody. I stopped to see Nadra in Grosse Pointe – who's married to the brother-in-law that doesn't like me now.

"The side of their driveway was kind of narrow with a spigot sticking out from the brick. I was on my way to play golf, backed out and it started spurting all over.

"I told my brother-in-law 'Oh wow – I'd like to stay and help but I got a tee time.'

"He goes 'You're such an ass.'

"I stopped to play golf with Frankie Fish. He was a nice guy. He was older – older than us – and we'd always hang out with those guys.

"Frankie had a fish market downtown and he wanted to expand his product line. He had a lot of black people coming in and he'd sell product to them."

Golf was a little different in the city; more imaginative.

"Everybody would come at night to hang out at the arcade, Frankie Fish, Joe Dana, just a bunch of people would come.

"There was a little patch of grass on the sidewalk in Greektown – the alley where the Grecian Gardens was.

"You could see the Blue Cross building from there. They told us the FBI had offices on one of the floors and they pointed 'em out.

"I used a 7 iron and blasted golf balls at that window. They don't break-break; they leave big round marks where the glass cracks.

"I played golf at the Hillcrest Country Club in Macomb County. We're related to all of the Thomases.

"Raymond Thomas had the Crystal Gardens and they used to book all kinds of people. Midge sang with Paul Anka when he was performing.

"I saw Whitney Houston when she was just coming up. She was beautiful. I wanted to meet her, but her mother wouldn't let me.

"I met Buddy Hackett and Joey Bishop. After performances I was allowed to go back in their dressing rooms to have cocktails and just talk. I really didn't say much. They knew anyone who came back was blessed.

"They all respected and feared the mob; more fear than anything else. Like 'If I can lift you up, I can bring you down.'"

"I don't remember how my parents found out what I was doing, but they did and it really wasn't a big deal. They were with me.

"The dope would come in nice and moist. It was really fresh, so I bought a trash compactor and took it to their house. I told them 'I gotta compact it here.' It was a safe place.

"I'd fly every week or 10 days, but then they kept wanting more and more, so I had to *get* more and *make* more to *bring* more.

"I went from two suitcases to four suitcases. Soon I was taking 160 pounds almost every time I flew."

Weight and bulk weren't a problem.

"You just drive up, drop them off and the skycaps take them in. Give them $20 and they loved it. Throw 'em in the car and take 'em to the guy.

"I'd have some money they'd give me right away, so I'd just hang out for a couple days. I'd party, see family and get paid.

"Sometimes I stayed with one of my sisters. Other times I stayed at a hotel in the Ren Cen or one of the older places in Detroit.

"On the return trip I'd carry from $250,000 to $300,000 in my Louis Vuitton bag.

"Karl used to say 'I see you brought your wallet.'"

What did you do with the Halliburton cases?

"Usually you just leave what you transport in – but those cases are expensive. I brought them home empty."

Most flights were uneventful.

"Except one time I was coming back from Detroit in bad weather. We had to circle Chicago for three or four hours.

"Just as we got the green light to land and are making our descent, a woman comes running down the aisle with her hand over her mouth.

"The vomit hit my cashmere sweater and soaked down the layers to my skin; it was the grossest, most disgusting thing ever.

"When we landed I didn't have time to do much of anything but run from one terminal to the other carrying my bag.

"When I boarded the next plane, I asked the stewardess, 'Could I possibly get a drink?'

"She says 'I think you've had enough.'

"I told her what happened and she started laughing. She said 'If you'll tell everyone that story I'll give you free drinks.'

"So I had to stand and tell the story to the whole plane."

"I was in Tucson just working and doing the marijuana when Dale said he wanted to help. He looked right. He's a white boy – 5'8" with glasses. He was very, very smart with a devious mind. He had his master's in management information systems by then.

"Dale was in charge of bringing the money back. He'd tell me the money that was owed, but I always knew already. He helped with logistics too.

"Mike was doing real estate and construction; when he needed extra money he offered to fly loads. He was in Phoenix with his wife and kids, so I'd have the stuff taken up to Phoenix. He'd fly it, wait a couple days, take the money and come back.

"He used to pay my American Express Platinum Card every month. In those days you could pay in cash and nobody really cared.

"If Mike couldn't stay and wait for the money, I would have Dale pick it up.

"He knew my family, he knew everybody.

"When Dale flew he'd wear pantyhose and pack the money in there. He'd get on the plane, go in the bathroom, take the pantyhose off and put the money in his carry-on. Or just sit with it in his pantyhose."

"When my parents wanted to remodel the restaurant, I said 'How much money do you need? Take what you want!'

"I helped them whenever I could.

"There was this Mexican Congressman that was friends with my parents, he used to come to their restaurant. He'd bring them fresh fish and this and that.

"We just started talking one day and he said 'You need anything?'

"I said 'Yeah, I could use some weed.'

"He goes 'How much?'

"I say 'Like 400 to 500 lbs.'

"He said 'OK, I see you next week.'

"He used to put 500 to 600 pounds in his van and tell me 'Whatever you want to give me for it.'

"After that I told him what I needed and I got it.

"He always drove it in his van and they never checked him. That's how I was operating back then."

Business was good.

"Nobody else was doing what we were doing, nobody could. They didn't have the cities, the connections and the places to off it.

"My sister Cindy says 'You were an asshole then.' When I had all my money.

"There's no denying it. I enjoy the finer things in life.

"By then I was a member of the Ventana Canyon Country Club and I lived in a townhome on the golf course. 'Ventana' means window; you can see the whole city, it's really pretty.

"They built homes on the golf course and there were big 3-bedroom condominiums. We were the first people to move there. We had a private Jacuzzi and a community pool.

"The coaches for U of A lived there. Phil dated Lute Olson's daughter. They'd come over and we'd party.

"Jerry Kindall the baseball coach lived there. I knew him through my Uncle Sol's brother; he was a general in the Army Reserve."

"There was a spot on the golf course that was way up high, the third tee; golf carts can hardly get up there, you have to walk.

"At night I'd take a blanket and bottles of wine and tell the guards I'm going to the third tee to watch the stars. I took girls up there all the time. It was the total place.

"A lot of pretty girls lost their virginity there.

"I don't know why they picked me to be the first, I don't understand it.

"One stripper used to come over to my house after her gig and we'd … it wasn't making love, but we had sex. I'd be really hard again really fast and she'd say 'Oh my God, you're going to make somebody a great husband!'

"One of my cousins called me 'Al the Tank' because it just didn't go down.

"I usually made rounds at college during the day. I knew girls' class schedules so I'd go to their house and have sex and then I'd go to another one. I had to keep myself occupied.

"So I'm out at a bar and there's this little blonde girl from ASU. I didn't know her. She says 'Why don't you take me back to my apartment?'

"I was drinking a big glass of wine. I took it and drove her.

"This guy Matthew came with us. He was kind of a big guy; you'd think he could take care of himself.

"Turns out the girl was at the bar with her boyfriend. She was trying to make him jealous and it worked. He and his buddies followed us back to her place and they're like 'We're going to kick your fucking ass.'

"I'm thinking *Oh man, not this again.*

"I came at her boyfriend with the glass, punched him in the face and he started bleeding. Punched the second guy until the glass was just a stem. The third guy, I beat him up.

"The fourth guy didn't want anything to do with it. He said 'Please don't hit me!'

"Everybody else was running away.

"Four guys against one and this Matthew didn't even try to help; fucking pussy.

"I said 'You're a piece of shit' and I left him there. I said 'Get your punk ass out of here, I'm not giving you a ride. Get your own ride home.'

"My fist was all bloody but I couldn't go to the hospital because I knew these guys would be going. I went to Karl's house and he says 'What happened to you?'

"I said 'I kinda got in a fight.'

"He goes 'Looks like you bipped and slashed somebody with a wine glass.'

81

"Karl was in architectural school with this Matthew. He taped me up but he was laughing so hard.

"I've got scars on my wrist and thumb from hitting those guys. The stem did the most damage."

Allen made friends and his parents made friends; sometimes theirs became his.

"There was this guy Ron who started off as a personal injury lawyer. I knew him through my family. He would always go out with us and everybody knew he hated his wife.

"I figured his marriage wouldn't last because he never spent any time at home. Turns out he was with his secretary the whole time.

"When his wife threw him out he came and lived with me. He had tons of money, he just didn't want to give half his practice to her.

"I had a room with a futon, I said 'You can sleep here.'

"Futon Ron switched his practice to become not just a personal injury lawyer, but also medical malpractice. He stayed with me until he bought a house.

"If I brought him a client he'd always give me a percentage of what he made. We became really good friends."

Futon Ron shared Allen's love of cars.

"I *always* had really fast cars. What good is it to have a fast car if you've got to drive it slow? I can't drive 55. I'm going to go as fast as I can go.

"I got tickets for doing 145 mph. Policeman looks at my car, he says 'If I had this car I'd probably be doing the same thing.'

"There's a place called Dead Man's Curve in Tucson; it had a warning sign with an arrow pointing the other way.

"I took us airborne around that curve at 110 mph, chopped off the top of the sign and landed in a wash in the desert.

"I looked at Ron and said 'You OK?'

"He said 'Yeah, you?'

"I said 'We better get outta here before the cops come.'

"The Porsche had a little damage underneath, but no big deal. They used to give me brand new cars off the showroom while taking care of mine."

Damage was no big deal unless someone else caused it.

"I went out with my nephew Rodney one night and I brought a girl back home. It's like 2 or 3 in the morning.

"We were going to bed and I told him to go to bed.

"I wake up and my car's not there. He's not there. I'm like 'What the fuck, this fucking guy!' I had my Bronco, so I took the girl home and then I went to his fraternity house.

"He was in bed sleeping. I grabbed him and started smacking him around yelling 'WHERE'S MY FUCKING CAR!'

"The other students thought it was hilarious.

"Rodney says 'We gotta talk about it.'

"I say 'We got nothing to talk about – I told you to go to sleep last night.' I started slapping him again, I said 'You better take me to where the fucking car is.'

"Turns out he wrapped my Porsche around a fucking fire hydrant and got a DUI. I see it and I say 'I'm not driving this car.'

"I went to the Porsche dealership, told them 'Give me what it's worth and get me a new one; a Carrera convertible.'

"I had a special paint job on it, like silver pearl.

"I had CDs before CDs were even anything. People were still playing cassettes. A stereo store offered to put a CD changer in my car if they could use it for photo shoots.

"I said 'OK, but I want it to sound crystal clear at 130 mph with the top down.'

"They said 'No problem' and they hooked it up. They took out my back seat and put subwoofers in there. It was pretty badass.

"This was in the 80s. I was one of the first people that had that kind of stereo system in my car; the rappers weren't even hip to that yet.

"It was so loud, had so much bass you could hear me for miles. I like every kind of music, but hip hop is my favorite. I used to play *Fuck tha Police* by N.W.A."

"I bought a truck, Porsches, Beemers and all kinds of stuff because I was making so much money.

"I had money in the bank. I'd pay for some in cash – sometimes I'd put it on my Amex platinum card and pay it off at the end of the month. I don't like making payments, it seems to not be the right thing to do. Just buy it, just pay; and if you can't pay, you don't need.

"I'd go into all the dealerships dressed in t-shirt, shorts and flip flops; and they didn't notice that I had a $20,000 watch on.

"They'd ask 'What do you want?'

"I said 'I'd like a car. I'm here for a fucking car.'

"They'd say 'How do you plan to pay for it?'

"I'd say 'Cash fucking money.'

"I'd have my Louis Vuitton bag with a couple hundred grand in there. 'How about this? Is this going to be enough for you jackass?'

"Then they'd change their tune and apologize.

"I'd say 'Save your sorry for your ass; you won't be getting a commission.'

"I dressed how I wanted to dress. I had so many clothes you wouldn't believe it. I was dressing for Tucson and Telluride – desert climate and mountain. I traveled all over for stuff.

"Me and Charlie Ganz used to get a big suite at the Waldorf in New York for two weeks every year. We'd get deals on summer stuff for Arizona and I could buy winter stuff cheap. Everything was top of the line.

"When I went out I'd wear $100,000 worth of clothes counting jewelry. The shoes were $2,500, pants were $7,800, jacket $4,000 to $5,000 – shirt $300 to 400 bucks. A $25,000 watch.

"I had full length furs and shearlings – I must have had 50 coats. I had ostrich skin cowboy boots.

"My dry cleaning bill was $400/week.

"I'd walk back into the dealership and say 'Get away from me. Aren't you the asshole that wouldn't talk to me last time?'

"After a while, when they saw me coming, they knew I was coming to buy a car. I got good discounts because I got so many. Vito – manager of the BMW place – gave me exactly their cost and added $1,500. I said 'OK, can't beat that.'"

"My friend Danny would let me do anything in his restaurants. His father owned Scordato's in Tucson, then he passed. Danny had brothers and sisters, but he was the only one that had the desire to keep the restaurant going.

"I used to go and – if it was nice outside – I'd sit outside and smoke weed between courses.

"I'd stay there after they'd close and drink whatever he wanted. A lot of times he wanted to drink 75 or 150 year old Grand Marnier.

"I'd buy really good wines. I'd tell him 'Get me two cases of this, two cases of that.' I'd pay cash, carry it to my truck and take it home to my wine cellar."

His friends in New York were living similarly lavish lifestyles.

"Slavik's family was rich – really rich. They have houses everywhere. They believe in buying all their properties in prime spots. His father won't let him buy apartment buildings outside of Manhattan.

"Sometimes I stayed at Slavik's; he has a carriage house right across the George Washington Bridge in Alpine, New Jersey. JZ lives in there, P. Diddy lives in there.

"Ray's got a studio and office where he does all the ads for Hugo Boss, Victoria's Secret, all the top brands. He picks the models, does the photo work, does everything.

"When the models came into his office he'd point at me and tell 'em 'This is the guy that's going to make the final decision whether you get the job or not.'

"And we'd go to this cool place with a club atmosphere. They've got a pool room in the back, a dance floor and a bar area. In the front is the seating – they've got booths and stuff. It's called Pop Burgers, it was on all the food channels. Roy owns it, I know him through Ray.

"Ray would say 'Let's go there.'

"We'd hang out, get a booth, play pool, drink and smoke and nobody cared.

"I'd tell my friend Slavik where I was. I love him dearly. I'd be in a booth with the models, but when Slavik came, I'd start ignoring them. They'd get mad and say 'We're hardly getting to know each other! I want to go home!'

"Ray goes 'You know, those girls are weird because they're insecure. You wouldn't think so, being as beautiful as they are.'

"Sometimes Ray hooked me up with a friend's penthouse in Manhattan. The guy said 'Leave me some beer in the fridge when you go.' That's all he wanted for it."

• • •

"Three Finger Bubba only had a forefinger and a thumb on his right hand. I think it was just a birth defect. And he always wanted to shake your hand. It kinda grossed me out.

"His dad was in the porn business. Bubba used to drive a Corvette. He was always flashy, was always going to the strip clubs.

"He had a partner named Dana. We started doing business together. When I started getting product through them, the business just *took off*.

"Soon we're selling so much weed we had to drive it."

There was a seasonal nature to the business.

"Dope is harvested in the fall, so the big players don't work in the summer. We didn't do anything either. There's less people working and the same number of police, so they catch people. They could smell the dope.

"Dale's family had a bunch of places on Coronado Island in San Diego. Every summer I'd get a place and stay there for at least a month.

"Once we acquired product, we were working hard and fast to get it out. You're not going to sit on it; you want it gone and away from you.

"When dope is harvested you don't need to rewrap it. The bails come half-assed wrapped; you just take it from there and make sure it's wrapped correctly.

"I'd get stuff that would smell so strong you could not cover the smell; but we had a system on how to pack it. We'd use brake grease, baby powder, Bounce sheets, all different smells so you couldn't detect the weed through the paper.

"When we first started out I used to do it. And then my dad would help me. He was a stickler, he enjoyed the work. Then we had people doing it and I'd tell him 'Here, make sure they do it right.'

"We'd wrap it in those big rolls of Saran Wrap, like the ones at Costco. Somebody would hold the roll and the other person would start wrapping and twisting lengthwise, all over. It would be a couple inches thick before you'd stop.

"My mom wanted to help, but it's hard work; not an easy thing – especially at her size.

"Everybody that was wrapping had to wear plastic gloves because if you touch the weed and then you're wrapping, the smell will be on the outside too.

"Then you'd put a layer of grease and wrap and keep wrapping and wrapping – baby powder – wrap and wrap – another layer of grease.

"Finally we'd put contact paper on the outside, like what you put on the bottom of your drawers.

"When we were done a 15 to 20 lb. bail would be like 2' tall and 3' long, maybe more. Some are bigger, some are smaller.

"When we were finished you couldn't smell anything. So that way if a cop said 'Oh, I smell something,' we knew they couldn't."

"In the wintertime, temps are about 60 in Tucson – cool but not cold. You don't want product to freeze, so we'd load everybody up before Christmas.

"There was no shortage of drivers. Depending on how much product they had, they could make $6,000 to $7,000 a trip; plus expenses.

"Some of my drivers kept receipts. Like Dale would keep receipts for gas and hotel, but I didn't really care. I never kept ledgers or anything like that because I knew paperwork's the best way to get caught. I kept all the figures in my head, I knew how much they were supposed to get to the penny.

"The type of vehicles we used depended on the time of year. We started buying Suburbans; we had a couple that worked out of those.

"In warmer weather we'd add bikes and put big duffle bags on the roof. You could fit 150 to 200 lbs. in those giant hockey bags and keep 'em in plain sight.

"Bikes on the roof or snow skis, it's all part of telling the story if you did happen to get pulled over, which – thank God – didn't happen all that much; but it happened enough.

"In the wintertime, we'd pack the Suburbans with 600 or 700 pounds in duffle bags in the back and skis on top. Everything had to look right."

Police dogs were an ongoing concern.

"The dogs always alert and it is total bullshit. I've had stuff in my car because I smoke marijuana. They'll bring the dogs even if I don't have anything. If the cops want it to alert, they say it alerted and that's totally bullshit.

"They're pushing back on that; it's highly illegal. I had guys that would take dogs.

"If you get pulled over with a dog in your car – like a Shih Tzu – they can't use a dog to give them probable cause because a police dog will come to the car and alert because he smells the other dog. It's just the way it is.

"I knew a guy who had a small dachshund.

"He used to go with him on every trip."

"When some of my family found out what was going on, they wanted to help.

"Midge was always ready to go. She wanted to drive as often as she could.

"I said 'Hey you want to take a trip to Detroit? I'll pay you $6,000.'

"She said 'ABSOLUTELY!' She was making money. She'd buy books on tape and just go.

"Midge had a Grand Marquis; I had to have the shocks done so it didn't sag from the weight. It all went to Detroit and some would come back to Chicago. I had a guy in Chicago.

"My mom used to beg, she wanted to go all the time. She hated the government; she thought they were as corrupt as everyone else. She said 'They take advantage. It's their world and we're nothing.'

"She wanted to go with my sister. I'd say 'Mom, do whatever you want.' It made them happy, they got to hang out. I didn't worry about them, they were two old ladies.

"They got stopped one time. My mom kept running her mouth, so the cop waved 'em off. He said 'OK, you guys can go.'

"My friend Shewy would go all the time. We became friends when he was at ASU and I was at U of A. We met at a bar in Tucson and became really good friends. So he would say 'If you need a driver ...'

"I'm like 'You're in buddy.'

"I never asked anybody to do anything I wouldn't do myself. I always thought that was the fair way to be. If you don't treat people right they're going to snitch on you."

"I had 20 to 30 drivers over the years. Some were family, some were friends and some were friends of friends. They'd say 'My dad's retired; he'd drive as many times as you want.' Same as a mule. They just take it where it has to go."

Allen trained his drivers so they'd be safe.

"I told them 'You can never speed. You have to blend in. Set the cruise control and when you get there, you get there.'

"I told them not to drive through the night. I said 'Stop and get a good night's sleep and drive in the morning when the sun's up. There's a lot of activity during the day; nothing's going on at night.'

"I believed you avoid suspicion by doing the obvious. If you do things everybody's doing and act normal, it draws no suspicion to you. It's when you start acting like you're trying to hide something that things get weird and they start paying attention.

"I picked specific routes and had them avoid certain states so they wouldn't get pulled over. You have to go west to go east. If they went the way I told them and did what I told them everybody got through.

"There are other routes you can go, but I didn't want my drivers to cut across Four Corners – which connects Arizona, Colorado, New Mexico, and Utah. Some people did because it's a shorter route.

"The problem with New Mexico is they have checkpoints. They have the right to search your car and if they suspect anything, they're pulling you over; so you don't go there.

"And you don't go through Texas, it's hot as a firecracker. There's a lot of police. I-55 goes all the way from Chihuahua to Chicago and every illegal immigrant is on that road.

"I told them 'If you get pulled over, tell the cops THEY CAN'T SEARCH YOUR CAR!'

"We took off pretty quick and there are things that can happen. A friend's brother was living in Vegas and he wants to come and drive a load.

"I said 'No problem, come on.'

"He came and I told him the way to go. He drove an Olds '98, something of that nature.

"He didn't do what I said – he tried to take a short cut; they call it Cocaine Alley. Lo and behold he gets pulled over with 280 pounds of marijuana in the car.

"He took the trunk key off the key ring and stuffed it under a pile of cigarette butts in the ash tray.

"So the cop asked if he could search his car.

"He said 'No, you can't search my car.'

"The cop ended up popping the trunk with a screwdriver and hammer.

"My guy calls me and I called the lawyer I used to take care of all my problems like this.

"I said 'Give me the best lawyer where he's at and bond him out. Tell me how much money you need and I'll get it to you tomorrow.'

"I bonded him out the day before Christmas Eve.

"He got out in time to have Christmas with his wife.

"I got every case like this dropped. BOOM – illegal search and seizure. Whatever they find, they can't use it against you. You're going to lose the load and your money, but that's the risk of doing business.

"If I lost a load when I was first starting out, I had to pay for it and keep working. I'd tell my supplier, 'Alright, I have a brand new Ford Bronco. You guys can have it for what I owe you.'"

Sometimes getting paid was a problem.

"I was getting product for a bunch of Jewish kids that were sending it to LA and all over. One of the kids, Howie Z, decided he wanted to stiff me for $40,000.

"I'm a very personable guy, but they think they can take advantage? Mistake kindness for weakness? Fuck no. I never took any shit from anyone.

"So I called Ray and asked 'Where's Howie working at right now?'

"He says 'He's working in this office somewhere in LA.'

"I sent my cousin – 6'4", 270 pounds – and a coupla friends as big as he was. I paid their fare and told them where to go.

"They walked into his office and told him they were going to fucking kill him if he didn't give them the money.

"In about a half hour my cousin got the money from them and they came home.

"And then I told Howie, I said 'Don't ever try to fuck with me again because there won't be no next time. Next time I'll just take you out.'"

"I always knew things could go wrong. You had to fight through setbacks. You just get so high and BOOM, something would happen and you'd get a huge setback.

"My cousin in Macomb County [Michigan] knew a guy that owned a party store. And in the back of the parking lot there was a tractor trailer.

"We rented the trailer from him and used to keep the dope in there. Nobody really knew what was in it; nobody knew what was going on. My cousin would go in and get it and deliver it where it had to go."

The bust is still a mystery to Allen.

"I don't know who told or how they told, but somebody told.

"Macomb County cops cut the lock, found the dope, took the dope and asked the guy working the party store 'Whose was that?'

"He said 'I don't know. I have no idea. Could be anybody, I don't use it. I haven't been back there in a long time.'"

A.S. is friends with the guy who owned the store. He explained "We all kind of were a nucleus of people who had things in common. That trailer was behind Tommy F.'s meat market and grocery store. It was his trailer. He's known Raymond forever.

"Tommy was struggling with his market. At some point they said 'Hey, what are you doing with that trailer back there? You want to rent it out?'

"He said there was no written agreement, they just asked and gave him whatever money they wanted to give him. Tommy told me 'I have no idea what they did with the stuff in the trailer, but it was full of what they were selling.'

"I believe that when the cops opened the trailer they saw it was filled with a million dollars' worth of marijuana. It was the biggest bust in Macomb County up to that point.

"Tommy says he told the cops 'It's none of my business. I didn't give a fuck. I just knew they were going to give me money to rent it from me. If you think I'm part of it, check my bank account.'

"They took Tommy's trailer and he never got it back. He said 'Not that it was important to me, but they could have asked me.'"

The bust was a blow to Allen's business. He says "This was when we were just starting to get our legs under us. We lost 800 pounds of marijuana – about a million dollars at the time."

The timing could have been much worse.

"We'd been using that trailer for a long time, there was always a lot of stuff in there. They happened to catch it in February when we were getting ready to send more.

"If they hit us when it was full, they probably could have got a couple tons – worth as much as $4.8 million.

"The way it went down, nothing came of it, nobody got in trouble. We just picked up our bootstraps, pulled them up tight and went back to work."

Did you ever have second thoughts?

"No, if I'm doing it, I know the risks. I was in it from the early days. It wasn't as illegal as it is today. It was like kinda demoralizing, but you fought through it and did it again. You just go on instinct.

"When my parents found out how much money I was making with the drug thing, they didn't care. They said 'Just be careful.'

"I said 'I try.'

"And I was. We were good for a long time, but things happen."

7 Expanding the Business

"I started selling drugs with just Mike and Dale and then the need for weed kept growing. Everybody knew we'd be off for 30 days at Christmastime so they'd load up for the holidays. We'd sell tons and then take off from mid-December to mid-January and go skiing.

"George was just running the disco. He wasn't really doing anything.

"I said 'George, I'm selling a lot of fucking dope.'

"He goes 'How much?'

"I said 'As much as I can get.'

"George goes 'Alright, let me talk to somebody.'

"He had friends in Hermosillo. They said 'Yeah' – they would bring it by the semi and we'd unload it at his mom's house in a subdivision. He'd put it in the attic, in the rafters.

"So George and I became partners."

How did you know the quality was good?

"By the look, the smell. Sometimes if it's moist, it's fresh and that can mold when we wrap it. You've got to tell your people 'Open it right away so it can breathe.'

"When it molds it smells like ammonia. When it's got that smell, it's worthless, but there's tricks you can try. If it went bad you could throw it in the tub, separate it, throw a bunch of lemons in there and spray it with Ozium and some kind of soda pop, like 7-up. If that didn't work, you're out whatever it is.

"And people want a nice looking bud. If it's shake, they really don't want it. Shake ends up at the bottom; it's dope, just particles. You can smoke it, but you don't sell it.

"If there's shake, you take off some of the weight. If I sent 2,000 pounds and a guy told me there's 50 pounds in shake, I'd say 'OK, no problem, you don't have to pay for it.'

"A lot depends on where in the country it comes from, how it is when it gets here. In Juarez and El Paso there's so much traffic they compact it so they can put it underneath the floor boards.

"When it's fresh and moist they put it in a press and it comes out a block. Sometimes it comes out like bricks, thinner than a concrete brick. You can put it in the microwave and it'll puff up – but not much.

"I told 'em 'We call those nigger brick. The niggers buy that. And I don't deal with too many niggers.'

"They got the hint. Things were just going along; they knew what to bring.

"We took product to the ranch and made the Mexicans wrap it. The ranch was in Marana, which is right next to Tucson. It was 16 sections of Bureau of Land Management land we'd leased 'to put cattle on.' A section is approximately 618 acres; times 16, that's a lot of land.

"It had a locked gate and a fence. You couldn't get in, you had to drive through a wash for probably 6 or 7 miles to get out to the trailer where the Mexicans lived. They took care of things.

"It was so far into the property the only way you could see it was from the air; and there was no reason for anyone to be flying a helicopter around there.

"There was only one way in and the gate was locked. We'd stage the vehicles there. It was close to the freeway, nobody could get in or out. We did that for probably a couple years."

When shit went down, George was ready for it.

"He'd been into guns and hunting his whole life.

"We were in Mexico and some guy was trying to screw us on a deal. George had an automatic; he fired off about 10 or 12 shots in the air – got the barrel really hot and branded the guy on the face.

"That got his attention.

"George told the guy 'You ever try anything again, the bullets will go in your head.'

"Things settled into place. By then George and I were moving tons and tons and tons of marijuana."

Allen's success drew attention within certain circles.

"During the time I got into the business, Joe Bonanno had moved out of New York and was living in Tucson. He was old and people wanted to get rid of him."

According to *Joe Bonanno – The Youngest American Mafia Boss Ever* on *JoeBrunoontheMob.com* "While Bonanno was in Tuscon, where he was supposedly allowed to keep whatever rackets he had assembled there, there were several bomb attempts at the homes of Joe and Bill Bonanno, and also at the homes of some of their Tuscon crime associates. However, no one was killed, and soon the other New

York bosses came to believe Bonanno when he said he would stay out of the East Coast rackets completely, and concentrate only on Arizona."

So now Allen was making big bucks on Bonanno's turf. 'Tribute' – ongoing financial proof of respect – was expected.

"My Uncle Dominic had stood up in Bonanno's wedding, but he didn't know me from Adam. All they knew was I was from Detroit and I was making big money. So he sent one of his guys to shake me down.

"The guy says 'You know, you gotta pay tribute to Mr. Bonnano.'

"I got a piece of paper and wrote a number down. I said 'Call this number. If you still want me to pay, we'll figure something out.'

"Joe called me in for a sit-down.

"Vince Meli was running things back then. Vince goes 'You know, because of who you are and everything, you don't have to pay anybody. You don't have to worry about anything; we'll take care of everything here. I only have one request. Do not let my son get involved.'

"So I kept his son out of it. He wanted to get involved in the worst way, but he stayed clean.

"A couple days later Bonanno's supposed muscleman gets in touch with me. He says 'Why didn't you just tell me who you were connected with?' He was so embarrassed.

"I said 'I'm not that way; I don't do things like that. You got to *find out* the way it is.'

"He goes 'I'm so sorry and Mr. Bonanno is sorry, so you know.'

"Him and I became pretty good friends.

"Bonanno's dead now. Part of the Godfather was based on him. He was one of the guys they tried to portray, but he wasn't the Godfather.

"In the early days, when the drugs were just coming in, there was heroin and cocaine and stuff like that. So the mob didn't want to get involved because it was a bad thing."

I told him the *Tucson Citizen* quoted Bonanno as saying "Our tradition was to protect your wife, your daughter, the poor and the innocent. That's what the Mafia means."

Allen laughed. "Yeah. It was the first two."

There was another organization that was going to be very interested in Allen's income.

"The IRS likes to know where the money comes from. You don't want to raise suspicion, so me and Phil got money from Bubba and Dana and opened a workout place.

"We named it 'Gym's.' It had aerobics, weight equipment, stuff like that. It was in an old grocery store in a really good area. There was plenty of parking, everything you could want.

"All the kids from U of A signed up and beautiful girls worked out there. You don't know how many times I heard guys say 'I met my wife there!'

"Brooke Burke from *Dancing with the Stars* worked out there. One guy goes 'I should have married Brooke, she's so fine!'

"I never even knew who she was really. I didn't pay attention. I'd come in all hung over and sometimes they'd talk me into doing an aerobics class. I wasn't really into that kind of working out.

"I used to train with LaMonte and Ricky the way they trained for football. LaMonte had me on a regimen; we'd run and do cross training.

"I met one of their brothers first. He says 'You and LaMonte would probably really get along.'

"There was a bunch of bars and I used to go out almost every night – the Flying V, the Cactus Club, Bobby McGee's. Everybody knew me.

"We were at one of my favorite bars and I kept saying 'Hey motherfucker!'

"LaMonte was getting mad; he hated me at first but we became friends. Now we're like brothers.

"They had no idea what I did. They played in the NFL, they couldn't take chances like that. I said I was in the family business; they didn't question it any further than that."

"Gym's was going good. Phil was working mostly doing that.

"We were signing people up, doing alright and then Michael came to work for me. He'd make some trips, he took care of those kinds of things for me; or I'd go.

"I was always going somewhere on a plane, doing this, doing that. We did good together.

"Michael had two young kids and a wife. Michael's wife came down and decorated my place. They lived in Phoenix. Sometimes I'd go up there and hang out with them. I enjoyed it.

"That's what makes the world is family. You have to have your family and you have to have people involved that you can trust more than anything.

"If you can't trust them you know you've got to get rid of them. You can still be family or friends, but you can't do business with people that aren't trustworthy, people that only think about short term.

"My older brother had nothing to do with my business.

"My nephew David – something happened and he fucked up and lost $100,000. I said 'Don't worry about it, we'll work it off.'

"He says 'No, I don't want to work anymore.' It was kind of like he got married and I guess maybe his wife didn't want him involved; for whatever reason, he didn't want to do it.

"My cousin George from Detroit said he could do it, but one thing after another kept going wrong with him. They were small things, like sometimes we'd mail stuff and it would get caught. It was a cluster fuck.

"So I went to his brother Raymond, who was older. I said 'Raymond, you gotta do this. We're going to make *so much money*.'

"He jumped in and everything started running smooth. We still had ups and downs because of how things go, but that's just the way it went."

"Midge was working for me, so she and Rocketman had money. When she moved to Arizona, The Rocketman got a professional boxer to help him get in good shape; but when he got in arguments and stuff he just wouldn't pull the trigger. I always had to come and save him. Whereas his brother David, him and I would fight back to back.

"I told The Rocketman 'If you know you're going to get in a fight, you throw the first punch no matter what. You have to be aggressive, that's *it*.'

"Rocketman could fight but it's like not in him. He wants to have fun and when he gets drunk he's nonfunctional.

"I'd fight for him. He'd be there in a bar just jawing. When there's a situation, you don't talk – you just hit.

"I'd come up, 'What's going on?' 'Before the guy could get a few words out, I just smacked him right in the jaw.

"He dropped dead on the ground. You don't talk, you just fight.

"Don't talk about it, BE about it. I never tell anybody I'm going to do something. I'll be saying 'No, we don't need to fight' and then BOOM, I smash 'em.

"It's just common sense. Never let someone else hit you first. NEVER. Uncle Dominic taught us that."

"When my nephews and nieces were young they'd ask me 'What should I do when I grow up?'

"I'd say – 'Unless you're going to be a professional – doctor or lawyer – just go to school and get your degree. Things will happen to you along the way and you'll figure out what you want to do.

"I said 'Do whatever makes you happy.'

"Everybody listened.

"The Rocketman had residency, so he went to U of A. And then my nephews and everyone started going to U of A and they all wanted to be around me.

"By then everybody in my family knew I was dealing drugs. One of the nephews probably told 'em.

"Elaine, Nadra and Cindy all told me 'You're just taking the easy road.' They wanted me to be a lawyer. They just thought I wasn't applying myself.

"In California, a partner at this big law firm said 'Come intern here for me.' At Newport Beach, another guy said 'Go to law school; I'll make you a partner the day you graduate.'

"Futon Ron, the ex-friend piece of shit attorney that's living in my house now, he told me 'You go to law school, you can come and work in my firm.' He goes 'You will kill 'em. You would absolutely kill 'em.'

"Because of the way I could talk to people. He just thought I would never lose.

"And I didn't do it. I knew I could do it but I didn't want to do it.

"For some of my family to say I was taking the easy road is just degrading because they had no idea of the amount of work that went into it. There's nothing easy about it.

"They didn't understand that you have to apply yourself 10 times more to do what I was doing than anything else; especially at my level. It had to be run as a business. It could be no other way or you're a ship lost at sea.

"You don't keep records when you're dealing drugs.

"Everything was in my mind right down to the dollar. I knew what was owed to me and what was on the street.

"A lot of others tried and failed because they didn't have the self-control to do what was right. When they made money it came right out of the box, spending like there was no tomorrow. A lot of 'em got caught that way.

"I was never like that. I spent money, believe me; but I was also making legit money.

"Fat Bob and his partners at the law firm used to come to my parents' restaurant. They were from the same firm as *my* lawyers.

"We became friends; he's a little older than me. We'd do ludes and coke, whatever.

"He knew I was working with JNC and he says 'Why don't we do our own property investments?'

"I was still at JNC when I did my first real estate deal with him. We used to hang out and go places.

"In 1985 JNC took us all to the Super Bowl in New Orleans; it was the Bears against the Patriots. They paid for everything, so I brought Fat Bob; I got him a ticket and we sat together.

"I was skinny as a rail, 6'1" and weighed 160 pounds. We'd go out to eat. I could eat anything I wanted, but him - he couldn't. He was kind of a closet eater and he had a dog. He'd order prime rib and supposedly he'd have leftovers for the dog. And so he'd eat some and take the rest home.

"I knew the dog never got it.

"One time we went to a fight and made a bet with a guy in the seats next to us. He was there with his wife.

"The guy lost and said he didn't have the money; so we started roughing him up. Come to find out his wife had the money in her purse. I grabbed it and said 'Fuck you!'

"They pushed Fat Bob down between some seats and he was so fat he got stuck. I said 'How am I gonna get you outta there? Do I have to go get some butter?'"

"I used to say JNC stood for 'just no clue.' Everything was going smooth with them until I found out they were shystey. They'd do a partnership for the purchase of the land and another for the development; but they'd pay too much for the land.

"By that time there was so much debt on the land, you'd be lucky to break even. I knew we could never collect the debt.

"They got me to do some things. We'd get an investor to sign a note for $100,000 and give them a kickback of $10,000. I'd make $10,000 to $15,000 and they would take the notes to a big time insurance company back east that had agreed to lend on the note.

"I had everybody signing notes. People were signing and they didn't have that kind of capital. I knew if everything went to shit they couldn't collect because the people didn't have enough money.

"JNC built a huge state of the art building and spent all the money on themselves instead of doing the right thing.

"He put us in other deals and nothing ever worked out with him; and then we find out that he's committing fraud all over the place.

"He got kickbacks and really fucked his partners over. He got money from friends and everybody lost their money; everybody lost everything.

"It was just a matter of time before he goes to jail or somebody knocks him off, so I left there; but they kept calling me to come back. 'We have a project, we need you.'

"I said 'OK, I'll come back for a little bit.' I'd sell a few and then quit again; I kept going back and forth.

"I finally quit and turned over litigation to Fat Bob. He protected the investors so they couldn't collect on the notes.

"JNC couldn't touch the people because they should have been screened better. You can't have one guy sign a note for 6 or 7 million when he's only worth a couple hundred grand.

"Eventually everyone at JNC went to jail.

"Turns out Fat Bob was just a greedy pig fuck. He screwed me out of most everything we worked on together. I don't know how much money he made on litigation, but he didn't give me any. I got him the case and he should have; but he's just a greedy pig fuck.

"After JNC collapsed, Phil went to work somewhere else.

"Catanzaro went off and opened his own store in Tucson. He would buy baseball cards; he was always into memorabilia and things like that. He was really straight, but he could get me unregistered guns if I needed them."

"Cowboy George had a roping arena in South Tucson. I went partners on it with him. We hardly ever used it for business.

"It was for our pleasure. It was a place where we'd go, hang out and have fun on the weekends.

"We had horses and grandstands. We used to do roping events and give out prize money. We had a place to cook. We'd get tortillas, make carne asada and grill stuff. We'd just eat, drink and do coke.

"We boarded horses, so some of our friends kept their horses there. Back then you could ride in the arena or go out of the arena and there's places to ride.

"When they filmed the movies in Tucson and the actors didn't know how to ride, we'd teach 'em. They asked me if I wanted to be an extra. I said 'No, that's alright. I don't need to do that.'

"We had a lot of stuff at the arena besides the horses; we used the property to store equipment. We had back hoes, bore machines, Forerunner ATVs, all kinds of stuff. We always had illegals staying in the trailer guarding the place.

"The arena was a way of life. It's how we grew up. We kept it tight. If you're around people you trust, there's less things to go wrong.

"We originally had 6 acres but we sold 3 to a guy who was just kind of a scumbag dealer. He did things I'd never do.

"I wouldn't sell heroin, I wouldn't sell acid and I wouldn't sell cocaine; I would *do* cocaine, but I wouldn't sell it.

"He got his drugs from Mexico. He'd send his wife, have her stuff heroin inside of her vagina and come across that way.

"It never occurred to us that the DEA might be watching them."

"Our main guy in Hermosillo was a friend, he was always cool with us. He was making tons but he didn't care about the money so much. He liked us. We had fun.

"He'd call us and say 'I'm coming with a semi full of dope – be ready.'

"So we'd be ready. We'd have his cash and he'd be happy.

"I had given him my Jeep; it was all lifted up and the main guy down there wanted to use it. They were bringing the dope to drop off when they somehow got made. Somebody told or something happened – the DEA came screeching into the arena.

"The police were chasing him, but he leaped out of the Jeep, jumped a barbed wire fence and spent the night in a dumpster.

"The barbed wire sliced him up pretty good.

"In the morning he found a way to call us. We went and got him and took him to my place. I had a vet come stitch him up."

A vet?

"A regular doctor's going to ask questions.

"We figured the DEA had to be paying attention to the scumbags because we weren't doing anything. Well *not much*, because there were always people around. It's in a neighborhood. Nobody would say anything, but it was better not to push it – unless we had no choice.

"The police confiscated my Jeep, but they couldn't keep it because I wasn't driving.

"After that, our friend in Hermosillo couldn't come back; or maybe he didn't really want to.

"Suddenly me and George weren't getting enough dope.

"So I'm out playing golf with Fat Bob and he says 'There's somebody you should meet.'"

Fat Bob had no idea Allen was dealing drugs. He figured he was helping two friends establish a real estate connection. Maybe there'd be a buck or two in it for him somewhere along the way.

"Ozzie was around 6' tall and weighed 260 or 270; he liked junk food. We're playing golf and riding in the carts together and somehow we started talking about marijuana.

"I told him 'Our source in Hermosillo is gone now; I can still get it, but it's getting to be more of a hassle.'

"Ozzie said he wasn't moving as much product as I was able to move. He didn't have the buyers that I had; but he said he had cartel connections.

"We hooked up and fortuitously we became like brothers. Ozzie and I and George got together and started getting weed from Ozzie's connections."

"Ozzie and me were always afraid of being listened to, so usually we went to parks in Tucson. Agua Caliente was one, it had a natural spring. We'd go to the park and throw the ball around, sit down in the middle and talk for a while.

"As our business grew, we worked out of Denver and West Virginia, which was deep in the Bible belt; close to the east coast, close to Detroit.

"We had a sheriff in Clarksburg; his daughter had a place to store it. We only went there once.

"They treated us like kings and made us steaks, but we didn't like the town. We stuck out like *My Cousin Vinny*.

"We didn't want to draw attention to them or what we were doing. We wanted out so bad we chartered a plane and flew to Pittsburgh."

"After that whole high speed chase at the arena, the DEA started following me and George. Eventually they put a camera on the light pole to watch the lot and see what was going on with us at all times.

"The DEA watched and waited and finally they decided to raid George's house. He's a sharpshooter, so they don't find just one gun – he had like 16 or 17.

"That was the beginning of the end for him. Felon in possession of a firearm is a big deal.

"Usually if you have a really good lawyer you might be able to get off, explain it being in your house because you own a bar – which he did.

"So I went to see Michael Piccarreta. Me and Pic used to be pretty close. He used to come to my parents' restaurant all the time.

"Pic was a partner with Fat Bob until he found out Bob was cheating on a land deal that we did. Fat Bob screwed his partners in the law firm. He screwed everybody he could screw.

"I go to see Pic about George and ask him 'What can you do?'

"If he had one gun it might have been ok, but then he lied to Pic and that pissed him off.

"George got five years in the federal pen. But he never said anything about me, which is what they were probably after.

"George's wife lived with his mother while he was in jail. They had a big house on the west side and I lived all the way on the east side of town.

"He had a lot of money at the time and she kept coming to me, saying 'George says to give me this much money.'

"I said to him 'You know, you're going broke giving her this money.'

"She kept taking his stuff little by little. Eventually she took everything and then divorced him. When he got out she was with another guy."

"Me and Ozzie started doing some real estate deals.

"There was this property on Sabino Road right off Catalina Highway that goes up to Mount Lemmon. That was 65 acres.

"It was zoned suburban ranch, which is 3.3 acres per home site. We put the roads and utilities in and got 18 lots out of it.

"We named it Elin Ranch, after Ozzie's mom; that made him happy.

"We wrote the deed restrictions. You could have horses, but not a lot of horses, it's just not enough property; but there's plenty of places to ride around there.

"We put a trailer out there and started selling for $65,000. A lot of people were buying two lots. I said 'We gotta slow down, raise the price.'

"We started selling for $125,000 and sold out.

"I sold a lot to Ricky Byrdsong and his wife. He was an assistant coach at Arizona and we became really good friends. He wound up getting the head coaching job at Northwestern.

"I was honest with them. I told them they could build a great house there and they wouldn't lose money on it.

"I kept the two end lots. Ozzie and I did a spec home on one and I gave the other as a down payment for the house that I built. It was a like for like trade, we didn't have to pay tax.

"And then on Sunrise there was 115 acres, something like that. It went from Sunrise down Kolb to Snyder. It was owned by Pulte homes and that market tanked. It was appraised at 2.7 million dollars.

"We bought it from the bank for 500 grand and gave the banker 50 grand. We did a double closing, sold it for 1.8 million and we got another piece of property – 65 acres – that was legitimately worth a million bucks.

"The first thing we did was the engineering for that property. We figured out where the homes would go. We were going to have to shave off the hilltop to make it flat for ingress and egress.

"That meant going before the city council. We sent Freddy Krueger in to do that because he was a good weasel.

"That wasn't his real name, but we called him Freddy Krueger because he'd get paranoid, say weird things and act funny. He didn't take offense at the nickname; if he did, we wouldn't stop anyway.

"Freddy was a shyster, the shystiest of them all - but he never took advantage of me.

"I think he was a little bit scared. I didn't threaten him in any way. I just went about my business.

"Nobody knew who I was.

"It wound up being a big argument with city council, but eventually we got our way. It's called Bonita Ridge now, there's probably 60 homes on 30 acres. They're like condos, you go through the guard gate to get to higher priced homes up in the mountains.

"We cut Freddy in, we all took a third. He was happy about it.

"And right across the street there was another piece of property we tried to get, but we were short on cash right then. We could have bought it for a million.

"A grocery store chain – a Bashas' – went in three weeks later and bought it for 5 million. That made me sick."

One real estate deal bothered Allen's conscience.

"Ozzie knew this German family that invested in real estate in Tucson. They had a big brewery in Germany and they pretty much relied on our partner Freddy Krueger to do their deals.

"One of the brothers lives in Scottsdale – queer as a football bat – so Freddy just thought it would be easier to do business if Ozzie and I pretended we were gay.

"I told Ozzie 'I don't think we should do that. I don't want to do that.'

"I had friends who were gay, it never bothered me. You're gay, you're gay; I'm not. It's cool. Gay guys used to always want to hang out and be my friend. I don't know what they wanted to do, but they liked me for some reason.

"In the end I went along with it. I don't even know how I did it.

"We did the deal, made a lot of money and he never knew we weren't gay … until Ozzie eventually told him.

"I said 'Oh man, why'd you do that?'

"Ozzie told me he found out he had AIDS. He said 'I just wanted to tell him the truth.' He felt guilty; like we took advantage.

"In the end it didn't matter because he made money and we made money. We bought 130 acres on Kolb and Sunrise, paid $500,000 for the property, sold it for 1.8 million and they threw in another piece of property that had a real cash value of a million at that time.

"So essentially we walked away with 2.3 million between the three of us."

"Another time I was scheduled to close a couple million dollar real estate deal at 9 in the morning; but my cousins were in L.A.

"So I flew out, partied all night, flew back to Tucson and went straight to the closing. All I had to do was sign.

"I got my money, we celebrated and I said 'See you guys later.'

"Went home and went to bed."

8 Connecting with the Cartel

"In the 80s I met with the top people and they loved me. Nobody called them cartels back then. My guys were older gentlemen, well respected and established. They had all their own stuff.

"They were relatives of one family that had the power; they were in the Mexican congress. That government has always been corrupt.

"Just the two main guys would meet with me and Ozzie. They'd say 'We're coming up' and they'd come across the border.

"Nobody really cared. There were no guns back then. I was in the business before they started bringing tons and tons of cocaine through.

"We'd meet at Burger King, where nobody would suspect anything. They didn't want to take chances with people, so you don't know their real name half the time. Sometimes you do, but most of the time you don't.

"That was the day of those bright colored shorts. I'd wear pink ones and a t-shirt and my nickname became 'The Pink Panther.' They knew my real name but they never told anybody.

"They had a nickname for Ozzie too – 'Cacheton' – *fat cheeks*.

"Nobody called us 'gringo' or 'whetto' – the disrespectful nicknames they use for white boys. They liked us because whatever we told 'em, we always did. If we had a problem we'd go straight to them and they'd help."

They were impressed by Allen's mob connection.

"I don't know if somebody had told them or what, but I didn't. It's not something you do. People that are *don't*, you just *don't*. Maybe Dale said something.

"At any rate, the cartel guys respected me because they knew *American Mafioso*. Sometimes they called me 'Mafioso.' It gave them a sense of relief that I could handle things across the border and I didn't really need them to do things. Then they were like 'Whatever you want, you got.'

"They would ask us what we needed, hook us up and we would just do our thing and get rid of it.

"After a while, they'd say 'Come over here' and they'd have a house full of dope from floor to ceiling."

Were you ever blindfolded?

"If they don't want you to see where you're going, they'll put you in the trunk. They never did that with me.

"Me and Ozzie would spend hours inspecting product. We'd cut the blocks open and grade 'em. Nowadays it goes from 1 to 10; in those days we went a, b, c, d ... we would only take b+ or better. And then there was some that was nice and fluffy.

"When we were starting out the cartel would see us every couple weeks because we had issues with the quality. It was a problem because my guys wanted the best we could get and a lot of times we'd look at something – but when it arrived, it was something different, so I'd say 'We're not taking it.'

"They'd say 'Can you get rid of it?'

"And I'd have to say 'At what price?' To get rid of it we had to sell it to outlaws and black people who didn't have much money.

"And then we had to go back and forth before we came to an agreement. The guy that worked for them didn't know that we were supposed to get *the best of the best.*

"We spent a couple months telling 'em what it had to be like. Finally they put their foot down and told their guys 'This is what they get; nothing less!'

"After a while they just brought what they knew I wanted so I didn't have to go there. They said 'OK, we'll get this over there for you.' They tried to bring it across without people knowing; otherwise, everybody's got their hand out.

"They were good to work with because they knew they were going to make a fortune with us.

"As soon as we started getting all their best stuff, BOOM – it took off. They'd come across at the ranches. We used to pay the ranchers to let 'em cross.

"They'd take advantage of the monsoons we get. They're really harsh, like 60 and 70 mph winds with lightning, intense rain and flash floods. It's a good time to cross because most won't risk it. The current's so strong it will carry cars away."

"I kind of justified what I was doing in my own mind, for my own sake – whether it's true or not – that I was *only* selling marijuana. It kind of made me feel like I wasn't doing something terribly wrong.

"I'm not hurting anyone. It's much less destructive than alcohol, they can't prove permanent brain damage.

"It helps with some conditions and it wasn't getting to the kids. That's what the difference is. Like now there's some kids that have certain illnesses that medical marijuana helps them.

"I justified it that way.

"The cartel always wanted to give me coke. They said 'Just take 50 kilo – 100 pounds of cocaine.'

"I was making good money selling marijuana. I wasn't going to screw that up.

"Cocaine is a much more dangerous business. That's what turned the drug business on its ear. The Mexicans grow the marijuana, but the cocaine that they get comes from Colombia.

"It started to get increasingly difficult to get marijuana across because the Colombians were bringing cocaine through Mexico and everybody knew.

"It made everything more difficult and more dangerous. There's so much money involved they'll kill anyone for any reason.

"The cartel always knew if something happened, I'd tell them and show them the proof and we'd take the hit together. There was no fighting at that time.

"I do not like violence too much. It's a necessary evil, but if it can be avoided, it should be avoided. When there were problems, I could usually handle them on my own. But if I needed the cartel's help, I'd tell them. They dealt with it by any means necessary.

"If somebody needed to be killed, they got killed; but it wasn't like it is now. They'd help, they didn't care. We were moving so much product they didn't give a shit.

"I could handle things across the border and I didn't really need them to do most things; but I usually made the Mexicans do the dirty work. I could make a phone call.

"They'd send up guys that were really small – tiny and dressed like kids. Nobody is looking at kids size-wise, clothing-wise.

"They'd just walk up to somebody and BANG-BANG – off they'd go, back to Mexico like nothing happened.

"It's no joke. If 20% of the people in this country didn't want to do drugs, there would be no market.

"When you're dealing in something that's that kind of money, you do not play around. *Nobody plays around*. The cartels were going to do whatever I needed.

"Sounds harsh, but that's the way life is sometimes."

How did it feel to make those calls?

"I didn't really want to, but you gotta do what you gotta do. You can't let it slide; it sends the wrong message and a lot of people who work for you are affected. Once your business starts growing, more and more people are depending on the income.

"I always felt I could end peoples' lives or make them better. Most of the time I made them better.

"There was a few times that it worked out that people got the wrong end of the stick because they didn't do the right thing. Like this guy had his own stuff and thought he can circumvent some people and me.

"He made a deal with us and tried to change the deal and that's how things got out of hand.

"The cartel was going to take care of it. They wanted me to come down and see.

"I told 'em 'I really don't want to.'

"They said 'No, we really want you to come down here.'

"That happened a lot. When you steal, you steal; there's repercussions that are going to happen.

"There was a motorcycle gang up in the Bay area that used to get dope from us. It wasn't the Outlaws, maybe a faction of the Angels.

"A friend of mine told 'em their bill was a few hundred thousand dollars.

"They told us 'Go fuck yourselves.'

"It was like *What are we gonna do?*

"So we told our Mexican friends; they said 'Give us a place where they are.'

"We found out, told the Mexicans and asked them to 'Just let us know.'

"They went in and chopped 'em all down with shotguns. The next call we get is 'We have your money.'

"My friend went and picked it up. There was nothing left to be said.

"It made news in the Bay area that motorcycle gang guys got shot up. Wherever it happened, I didn't know; I didn't want to know. The less I knew the better.

"Some people that do bad things deserve bad things to happen. They get tossed in the trunk and they go to Mexico. It's a big desert; bury 'em deep and they're never heard from again."

"When we first started out they may have been using the tunnels to get product to me. They'd just say BOOM and it's here at this house or that house."

The first drug-smuggling tunnel was found in Nogales in 1990; maybe earlier. Allen's attorney told him about it; he had a photo of it on his wall.

Allen explained "It was below a pool table that had hydraulics. If you went into the person's house you would never know."

According to *The Narco Tunnels of Nogales* by Adam Higginbotham (8/2/12 for *Bloomberg.com*), the tunnel was "270 feet long, with its southern entrance concealed beneath a pool table at a house in Agua Prieta, Mexico, the favored cross-border drug transfer point for 'Shorty' Guzman, infamous head of the Sinaloa cartel. When the spigot of a tap outside the house was turned, the table rose eight feet into the air on hydraulic rams, revealing a vaulted, concrete-lined tunnel strung with electric lights and equipped with a wheeled cart. The passageway emerged beneath the drainage grate of a truck-washing station in Douglas, built on land sold to Guzman's lawyer by a local judge. Customs agents who examined the tunnel said that it looked like something out of a James Bond movie."

Allen says "Before there were engineers and architects, people died building 'em. Some of the people they didn't really trust, they'd have 'em work on the tunnels; they'd kill 'em and just keep building.

"They're all over now. When one gets found, they fill it with concrete so they can't use it. Then they dig more."

"The business just ballooned, it kept getting bigger and bigger and bigger."

Working with the cartel added to the security of Allen's operation.

"We had cartel connections in the DEA – somebody's cousin. He would know when our names came up, who was hot and who was not. He'd tell them and they'd tell us 'Chill out – we'll take care of it.'

"That helped a lot. We'd close down, go on vacation, not do anything wrong and let 'em follow us.

"I used to bust their chops so bad, they absolutely hated me.

"They try to do a lot of things to blend in but they stick out. They have a look about them – like their shoes. They can't afford nice shoes. I'm wearing Gucci and they're wearing garbage shoes. And their clothes – they don't make enough money to buy nice clothes.

"You could tell; you could pick 'em out.

"They'll confiscate cars and drive around in the same cars to try to set up other people. Everybody in the business *knows* the guy's car just got confiscated and sees the car. It was like 'Oh, hi guys. You're fooling everybody.'

"After a month or two we'd come back and everything was kosher again."

"Dale could see we'd be needing more help. He said, 'You know, The Rocketman's going to be good for us.'

"By then he was 5'6", stocky, a good looking kid. When he was younger he was funny and fun to hang out with; but he was changing.

"Nobody in our family was an alcoholic. My mom never drank, and not because of religious reasons. She just said she was allergic to alcohol.

"Nobody in our family was an alcoholic except The Rocketman. He was a bed wetter. He'd get so drunk he couldn't wake up.

"His father had died of a brain aneurysm, so Dale told me 'We just need to get him some discipline' – because he had none.

"I sent him to Outward Bound in Arizona, out in the desert. He didn't want to go, but when he went he kind of liked it alright. After that he would hustle and he would do what I told him.

"I'd use Rodney too, but for different things. He didn't understand how to hustle. Rodney lived in California, he grew up there and I saw him all the time; but Dominic grew up in Detroit and I raised him."

Did Rocketman remind you of his father?

"Yeah. In fact I used to call him 'Sam' all the time."

While Allen was trying to keep a lid on The Rocketman, his guys were doing the same with *him*.

"Everybody tried to keep me low profile. My partners and business associates; they didn't want me drawing attention to the operation.

"Dale was one of my best friends. He pretty much kept me in the background.

"Only a few buyers knew who I was. I don't want the buyer of what I'm selling to inadvertently get in trouble and tell on me. Why should he know who the hell I am?

"The further I was from what happened, the better.

"A lot of times dealers do things to show off and it's not about that. It's about business. You have to use your head.

"They're mostly just street guys. Instead of using their heads, they use intimidation and fear. We never did things like that; we were way more professional.

"You try to stay away from those guys. They know who you are and you know who they are. You don't usually interact except with people that you mesh with.

"I had a friend Lance who had everything going for him. He was doing OK, making good money, but he was a cocaine addict.

"I'd go out with him and his girlfriend. Sometimes it was fun, sometimes it was draining – a pain in the ass. So I just stopped hanging out with him.

"I heard he's just all fucked up, still a drug addict. So he lost everything."

Allen spent some years off the leash too.

"The things I used to do in those days – I was a monster. I don't know if it was drug fueled, alcohol fueled or what.

"I didn't have to do much to make money and I was out in the bars every night with all my friends and we just partied. I wasn't flashing cash, I just used my credit card and opened a tab.

"One time we were in L.A. partying and Ricky had an exhibition game. He got us all nosebleed tickets and we took a limo.

"I brought the girl Uncle George set me up with in Palm Springs. She was drop dead gorgeous.

"I told her to bring some of her friends and she did.

"I would go into everyone's room, make sure they were screwing around and ask if I could join in.

"I'd go back to her and she'd say 'Now you want to come to me?'

"Later I said 'Let's get outta here. Let's go to my friend's restaurant.'

"I'm half undressed stumbling out of the limo as Antonio is walking out the front door. He's upset, like 'Omigod Allen, what are you doing? Get your clothes on!'

"I said 'OK, relax!'

"He says 'This is my business! You're killing me over here!'"

"At the NBA finals me and Oz got a limo so we wouldn't have to park; and we just happened to be next to Charlie Sheen.

"Soon him, me and Oz were getting all fucked up, doing cocaine, getting hookers and it was just like a day in the life.

"You go outside after the game and there's a zillion limos. Like 'Omigod, they're all the same!' Just try to figure out which one's yours when you're that fucked up; it's not an easy thing.

"So then after the game we hung out. We went out and had drinks. I think we went to his house and partied and had some girls over.

"Sheen was a decent guy. He wasn't smoking crack or anything like that at the time. Crack is garbage, a terrible thing to put in your body. Like compare me to my little brother; we're night and day."

"I've been to the NBA finals, World Series, everything.

"The Kentucky Derby is tops, it really is. The girls are trying to look nice, wearing the hats; they're easy pickings.

"But the Derby's only good if you're in an owner's box with someone who has a horse in the race; then it's *cool*.

"I was in there with Fred Willis. He owned the Porsche dealership in Tucson and I bought so many cars he said I could go anytime I wanted to go.

"I said 'Hey, why not?' I drank the Julep, I drank everything. I don't say 'No,' I say 'Mo!'

"LaMonte and me always went on vacations and did everything together. We'd travel to go see Ricky's games. We'd get on a plane and go to Vegas all the time.

"I would go for a day or two and gamble all night and all day. I didn't want to go to shows, didn't want to do any of that shit. The only interest I had was in eating and gambling.

"They don't care whether you win or lose, they care how much you play. If you play Blackjack eight hours a day and your average bet is $500, they'll give you whatever you want.

"They give you your own casino host. You call him (or her) and say 'I'm coming in' and he says 'OK, I'll take care of everything.'

"He asks 'What time does your flight land?'

"They send a limo. They stock the room. We'd have ours stocked with every alcohol and shrimp, lobster, crab and filets.

"It was pretty good. After you go a couple times they know what your likes and dislikes are.

"Paulie was in Vegas, I'd go there to see him all the time.

"One time I'm there and this guy comes up to me and says 'Hi, how are you?'

"I said 'Good, how are you?' I didn't know him. I said 'Have we ever met?'

"He says 'You probably don't remember, but you had the top suite at the Las Vegas Hilton.' He goes 'I think there were about 80 hookers there. Everybody was having fun, just partying away. It was the most amazing thing I ever saw.'"

Sometimes – when you're having too much fun – you can get sloppy with the details.

"I had gotten a check for $75,000. I cashed it and went to Vegas. I don't know what I did with it, I could give a fuck less. I don't know if I won, lost, whatever.

"But I do know that I never paid taxes on the check. I completely forgot."

9 Calling the Shots

"I used to tell people 'Life is not checkers; it's chess. You have to think far, far ahead.' The only ones that could make business decisions would be me, Ozzie and my cousin Raymond in Detroit. Nobody else. Only people we could trust.

"I was a long way away from Detroit and communication was key. If I had to meet a cousin, we'd pick a city, someplace where nobody knew anybody.

"We would meet face to face and talk to figure some things out. I'd fly out of Tucson to wherever. We did it a few times, we'd just get up in the morning and fly to Kansas City or some other city and meet, go eat, and talk.

"I tried to avoid talking on the phone. Telephones were the only way they could catch you without a snitch.

"In the beginning we started using pay phones, so I would carry change. You learned to say 'Call me at my cousin Raymond's' and he'd call me there. Or 'Tell me the number' and I'd write it down and find a pay phone.

"I'd always use a little pad; I'd write and throw away a couple pages so they couldn't read the impressions under the pages. It was just a part of the way you had to run things. Today they have apps that only last so long and they dissolve.

"Later I had cell phones. They were just coming out and they were big. They charged you a lot of money back in the 80s. A Nokia cost $2,500 a month.

"An attorney told me 'Don't say anything on a cell phone that you wouldn't say to judge in an open court.'

"That sunk in. He knew what I was doing so that kind of advice really was helpful. I never talked on them, NEVER. It had to be that way.

"You can't take a chance of somebody eavesdropping on that conversation.

"If they hear that there's 2,000 pounds being shipped cross country or somewhere, they can make up any story. They don't have to tell how they heard it.

"We used scramblers too; they were a pain in the ass. They were really big and really expensive and I couldn't use them with everyone.

"I'd hook one up to my phone and whoever I was talking to had to have one. We set the settings the same. We could talk perfectly clearly and anybody trying to listen couldn't hear anything.

"I stopped using those because I didn't want to supply them for everyone and I figured they'd find a way to descramble 'em."

"Sometimes me and Ozzie didn't let our own people know what we were doing.

"We'd have our meetings in the middle of the park, any park. We'd drive around and find the right place because even at that time they had super sensitive microphones where they could hear you from a long ways off; they can pick up your conversation.

"So we'd sit in the park and talk softly, quietly and nobody was really around us. That way we didn't have to really worry about anything.

"There's people reading lips. There's all kinds of ways that people get caught that didn't even know they did something wrong. You don't know how you got caught 'til you got caught.

"Any time there was a problem, Ozzie'd say 'Oh, the stress, we're under so much stress.'

"I'd say 'Would you stop it!'

"Ozzie was a stress eater. He liked to eat junk food – a whole big bag of Spicy Doritos.

"Stress doesn't bother me much really. I've been under stress pretty much my whole adult life. Some people eat, some do drugs and some drink. I do everything. The difference is I'm not fat, I'm not a drug addict and I'm not an alcoholic.

"On weekends we'd be doing coke and drinking and gambling. We were pretty good at this betting thing. We made money.

"We'd wait 'til the last possible second to see where the line's going, what the money's coming in on; usually the late money is the smart money. We'd wait until right by kickoff and get our bets in.

"We'd bet every sporting event there was, probably $25,000 a game and five to seven games during the course of the day.

"By the weekend we'd be either up or down a quarter mil. And sometimes, if we liked a game on Monday night, we'd bet it all to try to get our money back.

"The bookie was a friend of ours, 'Big Dumb Jack.' I think it was legal for him because he had a place offshore.

"Ozzie and I had a $250,000 line of credit with him. He'd take our bets and he always paid with a smile.

"One time I think I owed him a couple hundred grand and we didn't have it right then.

"He talked like a cartoon character. He said 'Oh fuck you guys, I always pay you right on time and now I gotta wait.'

"It was pretty funny.

"If we owed him a bunch of money, he'd take a trip down to Tucson and we'd pony up to pay."

• • •

"We had excellent product and things were going great.

"When the cars became too small, we started renting motorhomes. We would do two or three motor homes a month, filled with 3 or 4,000 pounds – as much as we could stuff in there.

"It used to take us over an hour to drive them to the staging area, fill 'em with dope, make sure everything was wrapped nice and then bring 'em back to the gate.

"It would take us probably another hour to get back to the road. We'd meet the driver somewhere and they'd take off right from there. It was really close to I-10.

"If it was like my sister and mom or dad, they'd just get on the freeway and go. We'd make sure we timed it so they could get past Phoenix and up towards Las Vegas that first day.

"My parents were still the Bickersons, but she'd go on her little trips and that would give my dad a break.

"My mom used to love to go on trips with my sister in the motor home. They were both short – people would think they were sisters. They got in and had the time of their lives driving.

"Ozzie's friend Turk drove with horses. You have to know what you're doing when you do that. He put the dope in the horse trailer.

"There's a spot up on the top, in the very front and you can probably put 600 to 700 pounds in there. Then we'd add hay and stuff like that – and put the horses in.

"Turk didn't go east, he'd pick his own routes to the west coast. You've got to stop and walk the horses, get them water and feed. He drove roads where the horses wouldn't have to stand in the van the whole time.

"We did things with loading U-Hauls. We'd pack the dope all the way in the front – 2,000 to 3,000 pounds – and go out and buy furniture.

"I'd usually have a couple drive so it looked like they were coming back from school or whatever. Maybe add a refrigerator and a couch so it would look like they're moving. I'd have 'em tow a car behind.

"And they all had their stories. I'd tell them what they were supposed to say if they got pulled over.

"I had everything covered for people. I made it easy for them to *not* get in trouble.

"When we started shipping in semis, the weights had to be correct. We'd make sure the bill of ladings were right so that when they went through the weigh stations there were no issues.

"We had people in New York; it was some Italians guys in Brooklyn that we knew. They had connections, so it was all taken care of. I used to send it to them and they were good.

"We were sending three tons a month to Detroit. I was with my cousin and we took on another partner because we were getting semi-trucks full of dope brought to the neighborhoods. We'd store it at my aunt's house.

"Chicago would get what Detroit didn't use. The Rocketman always said he wanted to move to Chicago after he graduated, so I set him up. He could make money selling drugs – which is what he did.

"I'd bring 500 to 700 pounds of weed up to him and it'd already be packed. Or I'd send someone else and pay the guy $1,500 to $2,000 to drive, it didn't matter to me.

"One guy – a Greek guy in Chicago – ripped us off for $160,000. His family is loaded.

"He went to the Four Seasons in Chicago with his girlfriend. They got a big suite and they were smoking crack cocaine for I don't know how long.

"He didn't know me by sight, but The Rocketman knew who he was. We ran into him with one of his buddies one night. We started partying and I'm being nice and this and that and I say 'Hey, let's go over to my nephew's after the bars close. We'll party some more.'

"It was nearly 6 in the morning when I got him there.

"I said 'You don't know who I am but I'm going to tell you who I am. And you're going to go get my fucking money or I'm going to take your friend here and throw him off the fucking roof.'

"His jaw dropped. He said 'Omigod, I'm so sorry.'

"It's early, so I said 'You go and you get your ass back here as soon as possible with as much money as you can possibly dig up *right now*.'

"He owed $160,000; he came back with $65,000, so I let him and his friend go for the time being. *Ozzie didn't want him hurt.*

"Every time I'd see him somewhere he'd try to avoid me.

"In Chicago they've got the East Bank Club, it's a really expensive athletic club with food and a bar. They call it 'the West Bank Club' because there's a lot of Jews there.

"So he was in there with his girlfriend getting primped. They were getting haircuts and manicures and that kind of stuff.

"He spots me and he knows he's in trouble.

"I see he's got a nice watch. I take that and all the money in his pockets. I don't remember what kind of car he was driving, but I took that too; it was convenient.

"I said 'The only reason you're alive is because of Ozzie. And don't think you can take advantage of the situation.'

"He ended up paying off his debt. That was it. It worked out."

"Me and The Rocketman were still really, really close at that time. He helped. Him and I used to talk on the phone with the scramblers.

"You always have people that want better stuff than the Mexican stuff. The best weed we could get was Canadian, from British Columbia. It's really expensive – $4,000 to $5,000 a pound.

"We used to bring 1,000 pounds to Chicago every month. They'd sell out in a day, day and a half.

"I used to have a connection in B.C., but The Rocketman fucked it up.

"Detroit was my main hub and now I had The Rocketman in Chicago making money; *but he always shorted it*. I knew it and I made up the difference for him."

The Mexicans weren't nearly so accommodating.

"They will kill anyone, even family members, for anything having to do with money.

"Only one of their people would come to my house and only for one reason – to pick up money.

"I remember one time one of their nephews came to my house. He came to talk to us and I didn't think anything of it.

"I had like $2,000 to $3,000 on my dresser and he stole it.

"I didn't want to tell them because it was no big deal. My mom used to tell me if people stole from me, don't worry about it. 'They need it worse than you.'

"But I told Ozzie and he insisted; 'No, we have to tell 'em.'

"So we told them and they dealt with him their own special way. *You don't steal.* That's not how they are. If you steal, you're going to pay.

"The nephew was never seen again. More than likely they murdered him.

"I told Oz it made me feel bad, but you have to get used to it. It's business. Somebody was trying to do things that they shouldn't do.

"I shoulda done it to Rocketman is what I shoulda done. But I would never do that. He's family.

"I had a niece that worked for me for a while. She did a trip with my dad. When the money came up $10,000 short, she tried to blame him.

"I said 'No, don't try to blame my dad. That's not going to work.'

"Some relatives did whatever they could because I'm easy going. They knew I wasn't going to do anything to my family.

"I just cut them out. That hurt them worse."

Allen's illegal enterprise was exploding around the time the Partnership for a Drug-Free America was dropping eggs into a hot pan for the *This is your brain on drugs* campaign.

I asked how he felt about it.

"It was just stupid. Fry your brains? You can't. You can fuck up your brains with the *wrong* drugs, but marijuana?

"If you do cocaine you can have a heart attack any time because it's a jolt. The first time I got out of prison I did some and waited for a second ... a minute; *here ya go* – I didn't die.

"Reagan and the war on drugs was such a farce. We all knew the borders were pretty much open at that time.

"The generals were making millions and millions and millions of dollars every month. In fact, the Mexican government moved the generals around so they couldn't take over in one place. That was back when Mexico *had* a government.

"Who do you think was bringing in the most cocaine?

"The government.

"I knew one of the guys that was big time in Washington, in the CIA. In the 70s they had George Bush as head of the CIA and in the 80s they had Howdy Doody [Ronald Reagan] as president.

"Bush served as Raegan's vice president for two terms – then he was president.

"They were getting cocaine *from* Noriega, putting it on the streets and spending the money on arms for Iran and Iraq so they could kill each other.

"Noriega's still in prison; he's never getting out. It was the U.S. government that did it to him. This is the Iran-Contra stuff.

"Reagan had his wife saying 'Just Say No' while they're bringing in the drugs. Do you think they were trying to stop it? Oliver North, all those guys?

"Did they get in trouble? Not really.

"I knew a guy that was working with him. I can't use his name, but that's exactly how it went down. They needed a fall guy, so they got the guy from Panama.

"They did it to fund their own agenda. It was all about oil. Who do you think controls the Saudi oil? The Bushes.

"Saddam Hussein – after the first time, he didn't do anything. He was a dictator, he kept things in line over there.

"In earlier years in this country, there was integrity. But in the 80s that's what they were doing. That's what it was about – money. Now look at it. Just for greed."

"In the early days there wasn't crack cocaine. The blacks figured out how to make that later. The laws hurt poor blacks more than any other group."

According to drugpolicy.org, "The number of people behind bars for nonviolent drug law offenses increased from 50,000 in 1980 to over 400,000 by 1997."

Allen says "You think they're here to protect us? They're listening to our phone calls. They want their finger on the pulse of everything. It's not a good situation – and now they blame terrorism.

"Even right now, the U.S. is giving weapons that are ending up in the terrorists' hands.

"It's the real deal. I knew what they were doing. That's why I never got involved in cocaine. I didn't want the headaches that go with policing the situation.

"Smuggling cocaine is like that movie *Sicario* with Emily Blunt, Josh Brolin and Benicio del Toro. You don't know who's who or who's what.

"Me, I know everybody. Everybody at a certain level knew me. Even the people that didn't know me knew I was somebody because of where I was – in the mountains and fields."

We talked about an article I read on the making of the movie - *How the 'Sicario' Team Took a Road Trip Through One of the World's Deadliest Cities'* by Austin Siegemund-Broka. (December 02, 2015 for *Hollywoodreporter.com*).

It said "During their research trip in Juarez, the filmmakers came across hundreds of posters for missing women; images of them and of the shoes they found in the city's 'killing field' haunted them throughout the shoot."

It's not news to Allen.

"There's people buried everywhere in the desert. They used to just bury 'em in shallow graves and throw 'em by the river. Or just shove all the bodies together, use a big bulldozer and push 'em into a wash.

"But if they really want to send a message they'll hang em. More recently than back then. I have seen it. It's new. You turn a blind eye. You don't look at it. I don't.

"The way the cartels run their business is cruel. They're Mexicans – it's amazing, you know –- how they're willing to do anything. They always take care of people, but when it comes to business – who's paying, who didn't pay – there's no conscience.

"They had families but they were just dangerous people who wouldn't go anywhere without people with guns.

"They're all Catholics, they support the churches – but if the church leaders speak out against them, they don't care who you are. They'll come and do the shootouts and bomb the cars. Blow up the whole car; they don't care who's in it.

"The U.S. doesn't want that violent aspect of it getting into our country. And the reason it started like it did is because of cocaine.

"After the DEA choked off Florida, the cartels had to bring it through Mexico, up through Texas, Arizona, New Mexico and California. It's all here. So that brought more heat.

"Before that happened, getting the pot was easy. When I got into the business, it was a piece of cake. Nobody cared, nobody paid any attention.

"Now we have fucking tunnels. We have everything for the cocaine because it's such a high dollar product. It's just not anything I wanted any part of.

"Say you give somebody 10 kilos of cocaine at $35,000. That's $350,000 and it's not that low key. You don't know what's going on with the FBI and the cartels. It's cowboy shit.

"When you go to a meeting to do a deal, you've got to carry guns. It's more aggravation because the cartels *will not play* when it comes to the cocaine. They're very very strict on that.

"Whereas marijuana is a mellow drug. To fuck up a good marijuana deal, you have to be really stupid. Not that people don't try to take advantage of any situation when they can."

"I was doing very, very well.

"I used to keep $10,000 in the secret compartment in my Porsche – $2,000 each in rubber bands. When one stack was spent, I'd put the rubber band on my wrist.

"I'd come home and count the rubber bands and know how much money I spent. It kind of caught on with the rappers.

"I was taking my nephews and nieces to bars when they were 15 or 16. They liked that I could get them in.

"I'd give the doormen money, they didn't care. When you're spending $5,000 a week in a bar, they don't mind. You can get away with a *lot* of shit.

"When my nephews went home drunk, my mom would say 'Omigod, what are you doing to these kids?'"

The Flying V was on home turf at Lowes Ventana.

"I went there two nights a week – sometimes three. I was spending at least $2,400 a night. They appreciated my business so much they built a patio just for me.

"Everybody knew I'd be there on Friday and Saturday.

"There was a long line to get in but I never had to wait in line for anything. I pulled up, left my car and walked in with like 15 guys.

"That bar was rocking. Girls walked around and sold shots and we just partied all night.

"I used to do cocaine in there, nobody would say anything. I'd carry a big bag full of powder in my pocket – sometimes in little bottles, sometimes in a one-hitter like an inhaler.

"Turn the thing and tap it.

"The coke goes where the inhaler is and nobody knows what you're doing.

"Sometimes we'd carry a big baggie full of cocaine. Not just like a little bit, not a sandwich bag – it was a freezer bag. And we'd just pull it out."

"I was like 6'1", 170 pounds – but I knew how to fight.

"All the time, all my life I would get in more bar fights than anyone. *I was all violent all the time.* I never start fights; but I can end 'em.

"And you didn't want to piss me off because I was always with football player friends. We'd go out and nobody's going to be foolish enough to mess with them.

"LaMonte and Ricky were always with me. These guys are black. Race doesn't really mean anything to me, it's the person. They made something of themselves, they're smart.

"I helped 'em in some real estate deals. JNC tried to wine and dine and take 'em on a helicopter tour around Tucson, showing 'em properties to buy. They wanted them involved because they knew they had money.

"I told 'em point blank 'If you put a dollar in there I'll kill you myself.'

"They were like guardian angels.

"Ricky is 6'3" and 300 pounds – but he always says he's 6' 2 ¾". He got drafted out of high school to play professional baseball and wanted to play football. But to me, you know, you have to do whatever it is you got to do.

"He played for the Broncos, Raiders and Cardinals. He was coaching the defensive line at Memphis. He used to coach the Redskins, Bengals and Raiders.

"LaMonte is 6'2" and about 250 pounds. Who's gonna mess with me? LaMonte was my black conscience. Whenever I wanted to do something bad, he'd kind of like calm things down."

If he could catch it in time.

"One night he was between me and the bouncer at this strip club; and the bouncer's just being loud and obnoxious, throwing me out and being a jerk about it.

"So I whispered in LaMonte's ear, 'Just turn your shoulder a little bit.' I cold cocked the bouncer, knocked him out and kept going.

"We were like *Ballers* on HBO. We were balling before anyone knew what balling was. We'd go out at happy hour and stay out all night.

"We'd do dollar bets. Ricky or LaMonte would pick a girl and bet me a dollar that I couldn't go home with her. And if she got lippy I'd say 'You know what honey? You were just a dollar bet.'

"I used to stir girls' drinks with my dick. I had a large unit and my friend Karl used to beg me, 'Get it angry, get it hard – not all the way, just angry and amazing.'

"I'd do it. I'd bring it out and squeeze it and people would either laugh in amazement or run. You never knew what kind of reaction you were going to get.

"Management would say 'Please don't do that. Don't put your dick in girls' drinks.'

"But they never threw me out.

"I had Julius who's 6'3" 330 pounds; he was a defensive lineman at U of A. If somebody did something, he'd rip through the kitchen grabbing pots and pans. They'd have to close the bar sometimes.

"And then I'd always go home the same way and sometimes there was this one cop who would stop me.

"He was first on scene when my cousin got in an ATV accident in the wash. He broke his neck and got paralyzed from the neck down. This cop got him the help he needed to save his life.

"So he'd see me driving 110 mph and pull me over EVERY TIME – like five times. And he'd say 'Do you know what happened to your cousin?! I'm not giving you a ticket but SLOW DOWN! I know you've been drinking!'

"Not once did he give me a ticket because he knew me, knew my family name and liked my family.

"Sometimes – high and drunk after a night of partying – I'd be driving home, take my gun out and shoot up in the air.

"That's dangerous. If you shoot straight up the bullet will come down just as fast. I could have shot myself. Or there might be people behind me. They coulda got killed.

"Then I'd have to take downers to sleep. I'd have good dreams, vivid dreams. I was a mess, a blessed mess.

"I had couches all over, but I'd wake up and strangers would be sleeping it off on my floor. I'm like 'What the fuck! Who the fuck are you?'

"One afternoon I woke up and those freaks had painted my walls with whatever they could find."

"Brian Williams and me hung out all the time at U of A. He was one of my best friends. I met him through another basketball player.

"I had season tickets for 25 years so I knew all of the basketball players because I sat in the front row – even some of the opposing players from UCLA because I'd yell at 'em.

"When Brian got his first contract, I helped him pick out his car. He played in Detroit; then he played in Chicago and won championships with Michael Jordan."

Brian's father Tony was one of the original Platters. The group started in L.A. in 1953 and went on to become one of the most popular black groups of the fifties.

In 1960 Tony left the group to sign with Frank Sinatra's Reprise label. Three years later Tony married Helen – a model he met in Las Vegas; Brian was born in 1969.

The Platters were inducted into the Rock and Roll Hall of Fame in 1990. Allen says "Brian used to try to play the trumpet, but he was terrible at it.

"He was 6'11" – a good looking black guy with light skin. Some people thought he was gay because he was metrosexual.

"We would go out and do things together. He never drank, never did drugs. He would do anything for me and I'd do anything for him.

"He'd call after the bars closed and say he's coming home with a girl, so I'd leave the front door open. Then he'd knock on my bedroom door and say 'Where's the olive oil?'

"I said 'I don't want to know what you're going to do but DON'T FUCK UP MY SHEETS!'

"He's like 'No, I won't, I promise.'

"He'd walk around in the morning in a tiny leopard banana hammock.

"I'd say 'For the love of God, put some fucking clothes on!'"

"That happened a lot with my friends, always bringing girls to my place for the night.

"One night my cousin George from Detroit was visiting. I don't know how he locked himself out, but I wake up to see him climbing in the window.

"I'm like 'What the fuck! Go back, I'll let you in the door!'

"So he goes back and this girl comes in. George had met her at the bar. She was drunk and obnoxious and she said something mouthy so I said 'You know what? Get the fuck outta here!'

"I threw her out.

"My townhouse was in a private gated community. She had nowhere to go, she had to walk to the guard gate and call for a cab.

"I did that a lot of times with girls at my house. I told them 'You've got to go.'

"I thought *I'm never going to get married.*

"Then I met this girl Marnie and she said 'My roommate would be perfect for you.'

"I'm like 'Yeah, yeah, I've heard that a bazillion times.'"

10 Romancing Missy

"I was supposed to meet them at the Flying V. Marnie dragged her out and I was already drunk and sweaty and she hated me. HATED me.

"She was 20 with blonde hair, blue eyes and a nice body.

"I'm about 31 and I'm looking at her and for whatever reason I knew I was going to marry her.

"It wasn't because she was a challenge; she didn't tell me she hated me. It was just something about the way I felt. I didn't think of anything other than that.

"I'd go and hang out with her and we'd talk and eventually she began to like me.

"She was at U of A, struggling with Economics. She goes 'If I don't do good on the final, I'm going to fail.'

"I picked her up from school and said 'How'd it go?'

"She says 'I think it went real well. I cheated off this guy next to me.'

"I say 'What did he look like?'

"She described The Rocketman.

"I said 'Oh fuck; you failed.'

"She says 'What do you mean I failed?'

"I said 'That was my nephew and he doesn't know shit!'

"We became friends. I found out her parents are both very, very smart people, they both graduated from Michigan. Her father's a lawyer, he's in the Michigan Law School Hall of Fame.

"When she asked me what I did – point blank – I told her the honest to God truth; 'I'm a drug dealer.'

"It was no big deal. I found out Missy had been doing drugs since tenth grade. She was an Olympic-level swimmer – didn't make the team, missed by a fraction of seconds; but swimming didn't stop her from partying. She still did that."

She had other issues as well.

"She told me she was anorexic in high school. She'd put rolls of quarters in her pockets because her dad used to make her weigh in. With the quarters, he wouldn't know she was losing weight.

"Once she was with me I said 'You're not doing that. I don't give a fuck, I don't want you skinnier than you are.'

131

"I don't know if she was bulimic as well, but I have my suspicions.

"She'd come over and we'd go out. I wanted everything to be nice for her, so I hired Ella – a Mexican lady – to clean my house.

"We started going together right around the holidays, so she asked her parents if she could bring me skiing.

"They said 'Yeah, he definitely can come to Vail and stay with us.' So I had to get her a Christmas present because we're dating now.

"My cousin Greg the jeweler just happened to call me. He had this custom diamond necklace they made for some person and the transaction fell through. It was really expensive, worth about 40 Gs.

"He said 'I don't even care, I don't want the rest of the family to know. I'll let you have it for $5,000.'

"He had already had it made, probably couldn't sell it to anyone else. He was going to take a loss on it, so he might as well take a loss and get a deduction.

"I said 'OK.'

"It had a 2 carat diamond in the middle and diamonds that got smaller all the way around.

"Her parents were impressed.

"And it just so happens that Dale and his brother were there, they came to ski. *Everyone* was impressed."

"You come out here you gotta know how to ski. I was already going on ski trips two or three times a year. Vail, Aspen, Beaver Creek – so many places. The cold dry states had the best snow. On dry snow you can just BOMB.

"Then I'd go somewhere in Mexico and hang out where the water's really warm. You have no idea how much influence I had down there.

"I didn't drink the water in Mexico, I only drank beer and special tequilas that I liked. When I brushed my teeth, I rinsed my mouth out with beer.

"I would be drunk driving in Mexico and have a police escort. The Chief of Police was a friend.

"One time I made a wrong turn and the whole police department, the whole town was trying to find me. They said 'We've been looking everywhere for you!'

"He knew I was going to the beach at Puerto Lobos to spend the weekend."

It's about a five hour drive from Tucson to Puerto Lobos, a sleepy fishing village on the Sea of Cortez. It got its name from the Spanish tradition of referring to dolphins as 'wolves of the sea.'

Allen says "The waters there were pristine so they would take their catch back up north to Mexican restaurants.

"Somebody had a shitty house with no power, they let me stay there. They had generators and that's it.

"It's a shanty town so I'd take truckloads of stuff. I'd find what's on sale at the grocery store in Arizona and take it down – pop, candy and diapers. All kinds of stuff they couldn't get.

"The locals would dig clams for me, steam them and serve them with butter. They'd catch blue crabs while we were out on the boat and grill fish.

"They would take care of me because I took care of them."

• • •

"I met Missy at the bar, but then we built our relationship.

"I took her all over Colorado and Utah. In Taos New Mexico there's a mountain with great skiing – but there's not a lot of runs. We'd go once in a while, but only for a day or so.

"We went one time when it had just snowed a whole bunch; it took us a long time to get there.

"The name of the hardest run is 'Al's Run.' They had it closed, but the guy says 'We're going to open it and see how it goes.'

"I was the first to go down. I could not catch an edge – fell and I could not stop falling down the mountain. It looked like a yard sale.

"One night we went to a big dinner at the Westward Look in the foothills of the Santa Catalina Mountains. It was Missy's friend Marnie, Futon Ron and his girlfriend, Paulie and his cousin Nino.

"Ron took his girl in his car, so I drove the rest of us in the Bronco. I pull up to valet and I used to always tell 'em 'Just keep my car up front for me please?'

"They all knew me, all the valet guys all over. I'd give 'em $10 and they never had a problem with that, always parked me right in front.

"When we were ready to leave I came out and said 'Can I get my car?'

"They go 'Sure' – and they pull up in this brand new Cadillac.

"I said 'This isn't my car.'

"The guy goes 'No, no, no Mr. Ahee, this *is* your car.'

"I said 'Honest, it's not my car.'

"He said 'Trust me, it's your car.'

"I said 'OK, fine; give me this one and that one over there.' I pointed at the Bronco.

"Paulie and Nino took the Cadillac and we took my Bronco.

"On the way to my place Paulie decides to do donuts on the driving range. I was worried about Security.

"When he was done I said 'Well, we can't keep the car at my place and the resort's just up the hill.' I told Paulie, 'Take the car, drive it up to the resort, park in the lot and come down to the golf course. I'll come get you.'

"So I picked him up in the golf cart. Not two minutes later, BOOM BOOM BOOM on my front door.

"I said 'Hello?'

"Sure enough, it's Security. 'We have word that you guys were on the golf course doing donuts in a white Cadillac.'

"I said 'Well, you must be misinformed, because it wasn't us.'

"My truck was in the driveway. I opened the garage door and my Porsche was in there.

"I said 'These are all the cars I have.'

"So the guard goes, looks around, doesn't see any dirt or mud. He says 'OK' and they leave. There's nothing else they can do.

"We left the car and the keys up in the parking lot at Ventana Canyon."

"I took Missy to my legendary third tee and made like she was the only one I'd ever taken there.

"After a while me and Missy started having sex, sex and more sex. We'd stay in bed all day long, just having sex. And then finally we'd get up like 5:00 or 6:00, get dressed and go have dinner. Then we'd come back and go to bed.

"One night my sister was getting ready to take a load, so I had it wrapped and ready at my parents' house. Midge was going to come by and pick it up, pick up my mom and leave.

"Everything was ready to go except later that evening I was with Missy and we took a hit of ecstasy. We used to do X a lot in those days.

"The sex is really intense and it's like you can't wait to get at each other. It's just a weird experience.

"It was good X then – you knew what you were getting. It was pharmaceutical, not made in somebody's bathtub where they don't know what they're doing. These days you don't know where it's coming from.

"I realized I forgot Midge and my mom needed more money for travel and there I was high on ecstasy. *Oh God!*

"Missy and I got in the Bronco – less conspicuous than the Porsche – and tried to drive to my dad's as cautiously as possible.

"When you're X-ing all the lights are weird.

"I took care of business at my parents' and then – on the way back – I ran a red light and see there was a cop. I just pulled over and waited for him to come up behind me.

"He said 'Do you know what you did?'

"I said 'Yeah, I'm so sorry. I just thought it was yellow until I was in the intersection and went through. I totally apologize.'

"He says 'OK. Honest answer. Go home, drive safe.'

"We used to do stuff like that all the time, get high and smoke weed and go on adventures. I'd speed past the cops.

"If they spotted me, I usually tried to outrun 'em."

Did you have close calls?

"Yeah. A lot. It didn't scare me except one time.

"We were in the Porsche coming home from Phoenix with the top down. We'd both been drinking.

"Missy was driving with the cruise control set to 120. I had the seat back watching the sky and I fell asleep. She dozed off at the wheel.

"I woke up as she veered to the right and over-corrected to the left. We had just passed people we knew from U of A; we flew off into the desert and spun four or five times in a circle.

"They stopped to see if we're OK and we're in there laughing.

"We knew we had to get out of there, so we drove home and put the car in the garage. The undercarriage was fucked up.

"The next day I took it to the dealership and had them fix it."

"I took Missy to Palm Springs the day before she turned 21.

"We got up in the morning, I said 'Let's get some alcohol and lay by the pool. We can hang out, go shop, have dinner – whatever.'

"We get in the Porsche. I buy a case of beer and some alcohol and put it in the back. I've got the top down.

"You could see everything because all the cars are higher than me. I wasn't drinking, but I was smoking a joint.

"A guy in a van keeps looking at me. I'm wondering what this dufus is doing.

"He flashes a badge and yells 'Do you want to pull over or wait for the marked car to come?'

"I pulled over and threw the joint away. So they had me in the parking lot of Ralph's Grocery Store. All I had on was shorts and a tank top.

"He keeps trying to frisk me, but there's no license – only $5,000 in cash. He says 'Who are you? What's all this money?'

"I say 'It's my pocket change.'

"He threatened to arrest me until he found out where I was staying; then he gives me a ticket for contributing to the delinquency of a minor.

"He says 'I'm going to let you go as long as you show up for court on Monday.'

"I said 'No problem.' But I told Missy 'Why don't we go back to Tucson tonight? Let's get out of here.' So we took off.

"I never went to court on that and they never got me for it either.

"The cops say they don't profile, but that's exactly what they do. My family is Lebanese; we're *not* white. I'm dark, I *look ethnic*.

"One day I was driving home from Phoenix in my Bronco. I had a deep tan. My hair was jet black and my beard was heavy because I hadn't shaved for a day or so.

"Missy's in the back and I have $30,000 in my bag.

"I wasn't doing anything but driving when the Border Patrol guys pull me over. The one asked for my license and I gave it.

"I said 'What are you guys pulling me over for?'"

Like he wasn't even there … "They just asked Missy 'Are you with him of your own free will ma'am?'

"She said 'Yes.'

"That was it. That's why I would never carry anything."

"The more time we spent together, the more Missy realized I was really a good person. And I would sing love songs; so then she fell in love with me.

"She wanted to quit school but I didn't want her to. I wanted her to be a good example to the kids we were going to have.

"I was never monogamous until Missy. I still went to bars a lot, but it didn't matter because Missy would come with me. She wasn't going to let me hang out by myself.

"I'd walk into places and think 'She looks familiar. Oh wait – yeah, she should. We slept together.'

"That's how I was. But I wasn't serious about that stuff.

"Missy hated it – omigod, couldn't stand the fact that I was like that even though she was no saint. I said 'I looked beyond *your* indiscretions.'"

One old boyfriend kept a flame burning for years; he would resurface at the worst possible time.

Did Missy like your friends?

"Some she did, some she didn't.

"She liked LaMonte; he's just a good person. Ricky and LaMonte had a lot of foster kids in their home that their mom would take in, so they had like brothers that weren't. They were such good people.

"One night I was driving home from town, doing 110 on a two lane road up in the mountains and a cop was sitting there. He pulled me over and sees Ricky.

"Cop says to Ricky, 'I'll tell you what. My wife is a schoolteacher. I won't give your friend a ticket if you'll agree to speak to her 5th grade class.'

"Ricky said 'No problem.' So he didn't give me a ticket.

"The cop never called Ricky, but I know he would have followed through.

"Ricky used to get invited for the Special Olympics every year in Colorado and Durango and he'd take me.

"You'd have a Special Olympian, a professional athlete and a regular skier. Teams would get picked and they timed us. It was really a fun thing for a lot of them.

"They were kids, paraplegics and quadriplegics. They'd use their hands with poles to steer with. They had wheelchairs with skis on them. It was a great experience for the participants, to get them ready for Special Olympics or whatever they were going to compete in.

"I skied with a blind guy; he had the world record for a blind skier, 80+ miles an hour.

"He had a guy that skied in front of him and told him what the terrain was, what to expect.

"We used to go every year.

"When Ricky couldn't do it, they kept inviting me because they liked me and I brought people with me that helped *make* the event.

"They invited me back every year and put me down as one of the celebrities. And they paid for everything. It was fun."

There were a lot of good reasons to like LaMonte. Missy liked him; but he didn't like her.

Allen says "Missy went from her parents' house to a sorority house in college and then she moved in with me. When we were dating she wasn't 'full on' what she turned into.

"In hindsight, I couldn't have been more wrong about her. My friends tried to tell me. LaMonte said 'I tried to warn you; you're just too stupid when it comes to the snatch.'

"Phil moved out of state. He was wanting to sell the house we once lived in. I wanted to buy it because he said I could have it for $180,000; that was a great deal. It's on the golf course in one of the best spots in Tucson.

"Missy says 'No, I don't want to buy it. You were with other women there.'

"I'm like 'What does that have to do with anything else? That doesn't mean anything!'

"So I wound up not buying the house. It would have been a great investment. The lady he sold it to rents it for $4,000 to $5,000 a month and it's always rented.

"The years I was locked up … I could have had steady income from that."

Missy didn't like Allen's past, but she did like the way he handled himself in violent situations.

"Being with me made Missy feel safe, but I told her 'That doesn't give you free rein to do stupid things with Marnie.'

Marnie was into the action, Missy was into the drama and Allen was making a conscious effort to fight less.

Except "One night at the Flying V, Missy and Marnie were talking to some really big girl and Marnie was causing problems, jawing at her. They were both blonde. They kind of looked alike.

"This girl grabbed Missy and was mouthing off to her. She stood up on the couch, grabbed Missy's hair and tried to pull her over.

"I reached up with my left hand to grab her by the pants.

"I had a handful of underwear and jeans, whatever she had on.

"I didn't really want to hit the girl but finally I had to. I punched her soft and she fell sideways – but she still didn't let go.

"Finally I had to just whack her.

"Somebody threw a heavy bar glass that hit me right in the head and split it open.

"I said 'I gotta find the guy who threw that glass.' It would have been a problem if I found him.

"The bouncers came and grabbed me; they knew I was going to go ballistic and tear up the whole place.

"Missy was sitting outside crying. They begged her to get me out of there."

"I got thrown out of every bar in Tucson for causing trouble, fighting and what not. So when my friend Sam Fox said he wanted me to open a bar/restaurant with him, I said 'Why not?' I gave him the money.

"The place he was trying to rent was owned by the people that owned the Cadillac dealership in Tucson. My dad knew them. They rented it to us at a good rate because they eventually planned to tear it down.

"It was a restaurant before we got it. We wanted to add a big patio that would go right up against one of the main washes.

"There's a bike path and a walkway that goes all around there. It was going to be nice.

"Before it was ready, there was this campus bar I went to all the time called 'Dirt Bags.' I knew the owners really really well.

"When other bars closed, I held them hostage. I'd make them lock the door and I'd stay in there with my friends and drink all night.

"When they sold it, they told the new owners to take care of me, give me whatever I wanted.

"A few weeks before me and Sam opened our bar, I was at Dirt Bags with Missy and The Rocketman when he wandered off somewhere.

"After a while I'm wondering where he is. I walk outside and see a bunch of people huddling around like there's going to be a fight.

"I look and I see Rocketman with this guy who's about the same age but a lot bigger than he is. A normal frat boy, clean cut kid – bigger than me, stockier, in his 20s.

"The Rocketman is about to get his clock cleaned. So I walked over and cold-cocked frat boy, knocked him out. He went down to the ground unconscious.

"The new owner goes 'Omigod, I gotta throw you out. Even just for a while until it settles down.

"He said 'I'll let you know, count on two weeks.'

"It was no big deal, I knew my bar would be opening.

"A few days later I get a call. The owner of Dirt Bags says 'It's OK, don't worry about it; you can come back now.'

"I had a lot going on that day. I had gone to Phoenix because somebody needed to borrow money. I took $75,000, Missy and a case of beer. We drank the whole way up and the whole way back.

"When we got home I told her 'Let's go to Dirt Bags; they said I could come back.'

"I got all dressed up in a sport coat and tie with a long cashmere coat. We went to a nice dinner. By the time we got to Dirt Bags I'm pretty tipsy.

"Missy says 'I have to go to the bathroom.'

"I order two vodka tonics and I'm standing there waiting with one in each hand.

"The manager comes over. He says 'You're not allowed here, you're barred. You gotta leave now or there's gonna be trouble.'

"I said 'I don't want any trouble. Just let me wait until my girlfriend comes from the rest room and then I'll leave.'

"He says 'No, you have to leave NOW.'

"I said 'I'm NOT leaving now. You're going to have to wait.'

"Just as I said that Missy came out of the bathroom. I go to hand the drinks to the manager and drop them on purpose; because he was an ass.

"I walked out as he's jawing at me, shooting his mouth off. I reach in my coat like I'm going to pull a gun. I pull out my finger, point it at him and shoot – BANG!

"We get in the Carrera and I take off. I kept it 'equipped' in case of emergency. I'm driving down the road and I see cop cars going the other way with lights and sirens. There's six, seven – no, *eight* of 'em – *holy smokes* they're after somebody.

"They do a U-turn and I realize they're after us.

"I pulled into the parking lot of a clothes store and they started yelling 'Hands up, hands up! Where's the gun?'

"I'm like 'There's no gun. I don't have a gun.' They spent the better part of an hour searching my car for a gun. They wanted to know 'Where is it?'

"We're just standing there as they're trying to give us breathalyzers and field sobriety tests.

"The cops were saying 'You're going to spend Thanksgiving in jail.'

"I said 'I'm not going to jail, you got nothing.'

"I was mouthy, cocky and finally the sergeant comes. He goes 'Are you Sol's son?'

"I said 'No, Sol was my uncle.'

"So he turns to the cops and says 'You morons, these Porsches have a secret compartment on the door here.'

"He flips it open and lo and behold – there's a gun. In those days it wasn't illegal to carry guns in Arizona.

"They brought the manager back to identify me and confirm I pulled a gun on him.

"He said 'No, he just pointed his finger at me.'

"The sergeant turns to me and says 'Where'd you get the gun?'

"I said 'To be honest with you sergeant, I won it in a backgammon game.'

"So he says 'Alright, I'll tell you what. These guys are a little upset. They're going to write you a couple tickets, but you're going to go home and we'll deal with it later.'

"They wrote me a ticket for threats and intimidation … things of that nature.

"I go to get in the car and they say 'Well you can't drive. You have to let your girlfriend drive.'

"I was OK with that. So I let Missy drive and we just went home. It was only around 1 a.m. in the morning.

"When I tell my lawyer what happened, it's unbelievable. He offers the guy $400 to drop the charges and everything went away."

Except for the frat boy Allen cold-cocked.

"We were getting ready to open our place. It was a *Gilligan's Island* beach-themed bar and restaurant.

"We went to Cabo at least once a month to try to catch a marlin to hang over the bar. We'd find out who the best captains were and charter the boat for the whole day.

"If you go out partying all night it's hard to get up early for fishing. Sometimes the water's rough and you can't really drink. We'd tell the captain 'We're going back in.'

"Finally after six trips, we went out and *bought* a stuffed marlin for over the bar.

"I put LaMonte and Ricky's pictures up and some other guys that I knew.

"We booked Bob Denver to come for the grand opening. He was like 100 years old by then, but everyone had fun. All of Missy's friends came; she had a good time.

"We had a chef who made all kinds of good stuff, tortilla soup and special dishes.

"We were doing good from the start.

"Days later I'm sitting there, minding my own business, drinking a beer when this guy walks through. I don't recognize him.

"He gets behind and grabs me in a headlock. 'You remember me?'

"I said 'No, not really.'

"He starts punching me. *This isn't going to go on for very long.*

"I swing a bottle at him and he knows he's in a little bit over his head.

"He tries to run; I throw the bottle at him and miss.

"The dining room is jam packed.

"I'm at the back and he's running along the wall, headed for the front door.

"The bouncers are coming towards me but I'm telling them to go back and get him.

"I pick up a chair and throw it across the whole dining room to just trip him up. It's in mid-flight when one of the diners stands up; the chair hits him square in the face.

"I'm like *Omigod, isn't this just my luck.*

"So I hid in the back and the frat boy got away.

"The police came in looking for me and found me in the cooler. They gave me a ticket.

"The customer I hit with the chair sued me and got like $15,000. He had to have dental work, but he was OK.

"A week later I see frat boy riding a bike.

"I'm driving my Bronco and he sees me. Now he's nervous. I had a baseball bat in that vehicle and suddenly I'm chasing him, swinging at him with the bat just to shake him up.

"There were no more problems with him."

"So this guy named Bobo started coming into the restaurant all the time. Turns out he was with the IRS' Criminal Investigation Division.

"He knew what I was into and we became friends. I'd give him free meals and whatever and he'd give me tips on how to avoid audits.

"Sometimes he'd come in and say 'I gotta talk to you.' And we'd go somewhere where no one could hear us; usually I'd take him into the meat locker.

"This one time he says 'The IRS thinks you're making about $70,000 to $80,000 a year, so try to keep it in that range when you do your taxes.'

"I paid attention.

"When we needed patio furniture, I got a Home Depot credit card and it was like $1,000 for tables and chairs.

"Bobo said 'Be careful, they're watching.' He said 'Somebody's selling cocaine from here' but they knew it wasn't us."

Like Uncle Dominic before him, Allen became the go-to-guy for disturbing situations within the family.

"My cousin's son was driving on Gates Pass in Saguaro National Park at 4 in the morning. Before sunrise it's hard to see. The road gets real windey and he'd been drinking.

"There's this couple riding their bikes. He ran over the husband and took off. He knew he was dead.

"He called me, he was scared. I had him meet me at a restaurant. We sit down and I say 'What are we going to do?'

"He says 'Well, I don't know what to do.'

"I said 'Alright, leave the car here.' I had it crushed.

"By morning they had a sketch in the paper. It looked just like him. *You knew.* The cops thought it was him, but now there's no car.

"I called my attorney. He was mad at me for destroying the car. He said 'Why'd you do that?'

"I said 'Why? To get rid of the evidence! I did it – it's over with.'

"So he asks 'Is he a good kid? Is he worth saving?'

"I said 'Absolutely.'

"So he got him off. I think no charges were ever filed.

"They had no case.

"After that the kid used to bring me coke – a whole kilo to my house. He'd chop off like ¼ of it and say 'Here, this will last you for a while.'

"The coke made Missy happy, she liked that drug.

"He's in prison now. He got pulled over making an illegal turn out of a strip club; had $45,000 in cash on him – and 2 kilos of cocaine."

"Missy and me used to go to Italy every summer – Genoa, Milan and Venice. We'd go to the south of France for at least a month every year to shop. I'd rent a villa.

"I did everything; I did everything *for her*.

"When we went to Cannes I ran into my friend Slavik on the beach. I said 'What the fuck are you doing here?'

"He says 'My family has a house here!'

"When we were at U of A we were wild, him and I. When we were getting fucked up, we'd always say we were getting [Jean Claude] 'Van Dammed.'

"His family is Russian. They came to New York and lived in a one bedroom apartment. They started out with parking lots and gas stations and now they own real estate in Manhattan.

"Slavik's wife went to U of A too. All four of us became really, really close. Sometimes we'd go out for the summer and stay with them at their house.

"We were walking from the beach in San Tropez to the town. We went to the car to take off our bathing suits and change and I was tripping trying to put my jeans on.

"I never wear underwear, so people walking by were going 'Omigod.' But they really don't care over there. The beaches are all clothing optional, with topless bathing suits all over the place.

"None of us had children yet so we'd go out all day and all night. Some nights you don't eat 'til 11."

"We'd been together since Missy was 20. Now she was 23 and I was 34 or 35. She was into swimming and sports when we met. While she was in college, she drove my car to school.

"If she needed money, she knew there was cash around.

"I used to buy all my jewelry from Ahee Jewelry on Mack Avenue in Grosse Pointe. My cousin goes to Antwerp or Mumbai for diamonds every month. They work with De Beers, the world's largest diamond company.

"The engagement ring I picked out was round, 3 carats with baguettes. We had a trip planned so I kept the ring in the box in my luggage. I really wanted to get it on her finger so I wouldn't lose it.

"She knew it was coming.

"I had planned to do all this stupid romantic shit but then I decided I didn't want to do it. I was going to take her to Verona, Italy, where Romeo and Juliet was and I was going to do it there. But we got in the car in Munich and I didn't want to fucking go all around the Romeo and Juliet stuff, so we drove through Austria, stayed in the Alps and hung out.

"The next day we went all the way to Monte Carlo and stayed at the Hotel de Paris. That's where the casino is, there's restaurants, it's really, really nice.

"I proposed to her at dinner in the hotel restaurant."

She was happy; and the ring was fabulous with her diamond necklace.

"We stayed in Monte Carlo a few days, went to Cannes and stayed at the Carlton on the beach.

"We bought plates that were hand painted in Paris by some artist – they were $20,000+ just for plates. We had probably six sets of Baccarat crystal, everything they make – wine glasses, champagne glasses and tumblers.

"Whatever she wanted, she got."

Allen too. At initial launch, BMW's hand built M5 was 'the fastest production sedan in the world.'

"This was a brand new BMW, there's not many of those. I was one of the first to get one. I bought the car and we flew to Munich to pick it up.

"We got in right around 5:00, just in time. They wanted me to take a tour of the plant, but I said 'I don't wanna go on a tour. I want to go to the hotel and get some sleep.'

"I woke up at like 10:30 p.m., threw on a cap and told my wife to do the same thing. I said 'Let's go downstairs. We'll go out, check out a few beer gardens, have a few beers and see if it's any good.'

"We go to Schwäbing Street in Munich and the place is JAM PACKED!

"There was no place to park, so I parked half-assed up on the curb.

"So we go into the bar and the people don't look German. These Rastafarian-looking guys next to me are ordering beers that are really tall. They tapped 'em on the bar and chugged 'em.

"I told the fräulein 'Give us a couple of those' and tried to give her American money. This was before the euro.

"She says 'We don't take American money; you're in *Chermany* now.'

"So I turn to the Rastafarians and say 'I'll buy you guys all the drinks you want, just give me some money.'

"Turns out they're South African and we drank all night long, 'til 5:00 a.m.; and then they invited us to an after-party. We go to the basement in this place and a bouncer tells them 'You can't have white people in here.'

"And they go 'No, they're with us, they're cool.'

"So we stayed and hung out and danced.

"They said 'Want to smoke some hash?'

"Missy didn't partake, but it got me so wasted the floor was moving.

"By about 8:00 a.m. we're getting ready to leave. I go out and see my car still up on the curb, no other cars around now. It's the only one and there wasn't a mark on it.

"It was cool, we had a good time. We had a few days to drive to the south of France and turn the car in; then we were going to stay for another two weeks.

"On our last night I asked Missy, 'Do you want to go to the casino?'

"We didn't have hardly any money left on us so I go up there and start gambling and winning a little bit.

"I'm one of the best blackjack players there is. I don't count cards, I *know* the cards. I know what's coming and I play 100% right.

"A guy says 'Do you have credit in Las Vegas?'

"I said 'Yeah, of course.'

"So he goes away for a little while; comes back and asks 'How much do you want?'

"I said 'How about $10,000?'

"He says 'OK' and gives me one big chip.

"I won the equivalent of $48,000 American in francs.

"We packed the money on the plane with us. When we got back to Tucson I had my friend who worked at the bank exchange it for me."

The M5 arrived at his dealership about six weeks later.

"Missy was with me when a guy threw a beer bottle at my brand new car. I couldn't believe it, the bottle didn't even break.

"He was maybe 20 or 21, driving an older piece of shit car. It had a big back window, might have been a Pacer. Cars last forever in Arizona.

"Missy didn't even want me to get out of the car.

"I opened the door, picked up the bottle and threw it at his rear window. The glass EXPLODED as he was trying to take off, busted out his whole back windshield.

"Then I caught up with him at a light. I get up near him and he starts apologizing. I could see he was scared, so I let him go. What more can I get out of the situation?"

Was the car OK?

"Yeah, it hit perfectly, hit the bottom of the door where it's real thick. Didn't make a dent."

The M5 was perfect for his purposes.

"I used to meet Dale at an outlet mall halfway between Tucson and Phoenix. We both left at the same time to get there at the same time; not a bad drive for either one of us. Just throw the money in the trunk and drive home.

"Turk was up in Phoenix and he couldn't come down. He said to bring him some marijuana and he'll leave the money for me. He lives in a subdivision.

"I got there in 45 minutes but he was gone. I unloaded the marijuana, put it in the house and tried to get ahold of him.

"Nobody knew where the money was. I was like 'What the fuck.'

"I took off, went back to see Ozzie; he asked 'Where's the money?'

"I said 'I don't know, I didn't know where it was.'

"Finally Turk calls and says 'Why didn't you take the money?'

"I'm like 'Where was it?'

"He says 'In the backpack by the couch.'

"I say 'Well you coulda told me to check the backpack.'

"So I drove back up at 145 mph.

"I had my radar detectors, I always used them to protect myself. I made it there in under an hour and was back in two.

"I used to drive to Vegas a lot, I liked it. I could do anything and I was connected. People *act* like they're connected; I don't. I'm just a silly kind of guy – playful and I'll bust anybody's chops, make fun of them.

"People would say 'Do you know who I am?'

"They'd act like they were tough guys.

"I'd say 'I don't know – who *are* you?'"

If they were somebody, Allen would have known *on sight*; whereas average Joes only knew what they read in the papers. The relationship between Detroit and Las Vegas has fascinated people for decades; and for good reason.

John L. Smith of the Las Vegas Review-Journal reported that "…there was a time in the early 1980s when the mere mention of the name of the notorious boss of the Motor City mafia was enough to set state and federal law enforcement on the hunt for gangsters in the neon."

Back in Tucson, Allen's drug business was becoming increasingly dangerous.

"Gilligan's had only been open a couple months when Sam tells me he wants in. He was a Jewish kid, 5'10" – a little chunky. He says 'I can get drugs. I'll take the chances, the risks of making sure I get paid. Just help me out a little bit.'

Allen had to think about it.

"Things were different back then. The guy that had the weed really didn't know what to do with it; he had to give it to guys like me to get rid of it for him.

"Everybody tried to play like they were tough guys and intimidate, like – 'If you don't do this, if you don't do that, it's going to be heavy consequences.'

"Then again, some of the people that were in the business liked to hurt people; they *enjoyed* it. I dealt with some guys who were seriously mental. There were these two guys that liked to do stuff to people.

"They called the one 'Mental Dave' – he was a white dude who worked for the Mexicans. He was 6'2" or 6'3" – a big biker.

"I always used to bust his chops, like 'You're so stupid, get away from me!'"

Allen decided to give Sam a chance.

"I told him, 'You know what? OK. But don't come crying to me if something happens.'

"He says 'OK, I won't. I promise.'"

Allen told Mental Dave "The guys you work for know me, so tell them – if they have a problem with Sam – to come see me."

Sure enough, "Sam had got himself in a bind with some other guys. Something went wrong and Sam didn't get paid. As a result, his sources didn't get paid.

"There were going to be consequences. Sam was scared to death."

For very good reason.

"If you didn't come up with what you were supposed to come up with, they'd do whatever they wanted to do. They'd take crimpers and cut your tongue in half lengthwise – like a forked tongue, like a snake. Then everybody knew you were a liar.

"I've seen them burn people. They'll put a guy in a stack of tires, over his head all the way up to his shoulders. Then they poured the tires full of gas and threw a match.

"The guy can't get out. He's shrieking and the air smells like burnt rubber and roasting flesh. It's not fun to remember.

"You hate to see that no matter what. Whether the guy deserved it or not.

"I told Sam 'Get the fuck out of here, I'll take care of it.'

"I told the Mexicans I'd make it up to 'em. They were OK with that because I had a reputation of always paying people if something was wrong. I'd take care of it. I quashed the problem. They went along without the need to kill Sam."

They say no good deed goes unpunished.

"This is a guy I did everything for. Sam didn't have any credit, so I financed the bar. I financed his car.

"He knew some guys that had weed, but they wouldn't give it to him. I vouched for it and set him up with an associate who was going to sell it for him and pay him. And he did.

"I wasn't involved, I just knew they were working together and everybody was happy. He was getting paid and I wasn't getting any phone calls – but one day I happened to be there when something bad goes down.

"I'm sitting at the bar and the mailman comes in and asks for me. I have no clue as to what's going on.

"Sam jumps up and goes 'I'm his brother, I'll sign for it.'

"BOOM – it's the police.

"There's like $55,000 in cash in a blender with my name on the label. It was sent to me. It tied me in with money laundering. Even though I had nothing to do with it, didn't arrange for it and didn't sign for it; it was going to be a problem.

"Nobody said anything. They didn't arrest anybody because there was nothing they could say. I'm thinking *OK, I'm not in any danger here. Sam's going to stand up and take the heat for it.*

"Lo and behold he doesn't."

Allen and Missy were staying at Ricky's place when it hit the fan.

"He had a giant house in the foothills. La Monte was getting married, he was moving out and their younger brothers were destroying the place.

"Ricky wanted them out. He asked if I'd live there and I said 'Sure!'

"The place was big, way up in the mountains in a gated community with total views of the city and a nice big pool.

"There were no houses behind it at the time. The master wing was on one side and four bedrooms on the other.

"We moved in and everybody used to come there after hours. Ricky didn't care what I did as long as I took care of the place; and he knew I would.

"One morning Missy and me are laying out by the pool and I just got a bad feeling. *Something's going to happen. They're going to come kick down the door, I just know it.*

"A few hours later, sure as shit, here they come. We were laying there doing cocaine and some X.

"They searched and made their little comments – 'Very nice house! How do you afford this?' Stuff like that.

"I said 'This isn't my house, so don't fuck it up!'

"The prosecutor came, he knew me. He told them 'Don't break anything!'

"I told him 'There's nothing here.'

"He said 'Just don't say anything.' So I didn't. He told them to take it easy.

"They searched for a while and took me to jail.

"I need to see when they're going to get me out, so I'm standing in line waiting to use the pay phone and this Mexican guy's talking to his friend.

"He goes 'Hey man, why your sister snitched me out? That's Thirst Buster money.'

"I'm behind him just laughing. That's like 75 cents for 64 ounces of Slurpee.

"Missy called my lawyer, head of the bar association in Arizona, a top defense attorney.

"He gets me out and I'm thinking *Well, Sam, you gonna step up or what are you going to do buddy?*

"At the time my lawyer knows what we're doing. He says 'They've got you, but you're not going to have to go to jail. I can get you probation. It's probably the best thing. There won't be any blowback, any problems.'

"He goes 'Sam's not going to stand up and take his weight. He's not going to take his lumps.'

"So I said 'Alright.'

"Turns out we knew the judge. They're telling me I'm just going to get probation. *OK, that's fine.*

"But as it turns out I didn't. I pled guilty to money laundering and got 90 days' work release. That meant I had to go there and sleep every night.

"I had the bar, so I told them I had to be there at 10 a.m. and back at midnight.

"I was lucky because Pima County is here in Tucson. There were all kinds in there, gangs and a few rich people.

"A lot of guys knew who I was and if they didn't, the older guys told 'em. Nobody bothered me.

"We were still operating, I was just behind the scenes.

"I'd be gone all day. I'd go to the bar in the morning, play pinball, and hang out. Missy'd come by, she'd have lunch or go shop or whatever.

"Cocaine was the only drug I could do at that time. They were going to piss me on Monday, so I'd party Friday, stop and drink a lot of fluids so it would be out of my system by Monday.

"They're supposed to come by and check that you're where you're supposed to be. Fortunately, I knew the guy who ran the work release; I was friends with him and his wife.

"He set the schedule. He'd tell me what was going on, when they're coming by and I'd be right there every time, like I was working away.

"One night I nearly got caught. They came to Gilligan's without notice; the guy who set the schedule didn't know because they didn't tell him.

"Sam called me – it was one of the few good things he did.

"He said 'They're here.'

"I said 'Just tell 'em I'm on my way back to jail.'

"So I high tailed it back. There was no time lapse; that would have made it suspicious, but it worked out OK.

"I took my lumps and then I was out doing my thing again."

"I was driving down the street the day after I got out of jail and I look behind me and see these cops. *Same* cops, so I'm wondering *What do these idiots want now?*

"Somebody told them I used my M5 in illegal activities.

"They pull me over and ask 'You got any guns in the car?'

"It's Arizona, so 'Yeah, of course. I've got three guns in the car.'

"They say 'Where are they?'

"So I tell them where they're at.

"They take the bullets out and give me the guns and say 'We're confiscating your car.' They said it was used in a crime – delivering marijuana.

"They don't need evidence, they just took the car. It was probably worth 100 grand.

"My lawyer said 'We're not going after it. Kiss it goodbye. It would create too much of a hassle, too much of a red flag. Screw it, it's all over with.'

"I remembered *This is how it was when we were kids. This is what happens.*

"I wasn't going to drag everybody to court; it's not worth it for a frigging car."

11 Making a Life

"My partner Sam threw a bachelor party for me at somebody's house a few weeks before the wedding. They had hookers and all that kind of stuff. I'm like *whatever;* I see that all the time, I don't really care.

"Missy called and came over with friends. They didn't interrupt anything, I knew I wasn't going to partake in the shenanigans. They were more fun than the strippers.

"Then we went to Milwaukee. Her parents arranged for us to get married at the Ozaukee Country Club in Mequon. They were paying, they had money. Her father was very successful, a partner for a big silk stocking law firm in Milwaukee.

"Despite all that, her mother said it was expensive and limited how many people I could invite.

"My family tried to keep the guest list as small as possible. Peter and Paulie couldn't make it, but many others who were close to me got left out. I couldn't invite Slavik or Phil.

"The people who got left out – it really hurt me. To this day I feel like shit because of that.

"LaMonte was my best man. He stayed in his own room with his wife who was pregnant. She was having a really rough pregnancy.

"Ricky was in my wedding; he stayed with me in my suite at the hotel.

"The night before the wedding we stayed up all fucking night with some of the groomsmen, Missy and her bridesmaids. We weren't supposed to get married until evening so I thought *Fine, I can sleep all day.*

"My suite had a boardroom with a long conference table and we were playing quarters with vodka; you bounce a quarter into a cup and drink whatever's in the cup."

Did any of the groomsmen mingle with any of the bridesmaids?

"I wouldn't have known if they did. *We were so drunk.*

"Early in the morning my dad's knocking on the door. I'm like 'What are you doing to me now? I'm sleeping!'

"He says 'Your Uncle Nayef and Aunt Frieda have to leave. You've got to come down and talk to them.'

"Something happened to someone in their family in Detroit, so they had to go – but they didn't want to leave without seeing me.

"So I had to get up. I went down to see them smelling like booze. I talked to them for like an hour, had breakfast and whatever and now I was up for the day.

"They had to go back to Detroit, so they missed the wedding; which wasn't all that great. I didn't have that much fun.

"We were both hung over. I could hardly even drink the champagne. We had the open bar and everything, but I just couldn't.

"Missy seemed happy – as far as I could tell. We had 200 people, it was really elegant with Moet champagne on every table.

"It was very nice. If only I didn't go through with it, it would have been awesome."

Why *did* you get married?

"I don't know. It seemed like the thing to do. I wanted kids. I always thought I was going to have to have someone be a surrogate."

"We spent our wedding night at the hotel in downtown Milwaukee, then we left and went back to Arizona to honeymoon for a while.

"When LaMonte and his wife got home from the wedding she had to stay in bed in the hospital. It was hard for them. Their daughter was born premature, but now they have two beautiful girls.

"Rickey and LaMonte are still like brothers. The only one who isn't still married is me.

"Shortly after our wedding Missy told me that her parents would have been happier if she'd married a black person."

Not those exact words.

"I should have thrown her out then and there."

There was a long, *painful* silence before he forced a laugh. "But she was good in the rack.

"We went up in the mountains and had sex all the time – every hour – because I don't know what was wrong with me, but I could always stay hard. I banged the shit out of her.

"I made her dress up; whatever I wanted, she went along with it. She wanted money, a lifestyle, the whole dream; that's what she got."

Missy wasn't the only disappointment.

"When we got married I had some money that was owed to me, like $160,000. Someone talked Raymond into keeping the money and doing something else with it. When I got back from our honeymoon, Raymond said the money got lost.

"I said 'What are you talking about?'"

"So I went and saw him, I said 'How the fuck can you do this to me? *How could anyone talk you into this?*'"

"He apologized, paid me back and we went forward."

Missy made nice too.

"I went to a jewelry store with Dale and my wife. I had so many watches, Cartier, Tank Francais, Panther and Pasha, but I wanted this solid gold Breitling. I think it was $15,000 or $16,000.

"Missy said 'I want to buy you the watch.'

"I snapped my fingers; 'Dale – go get me the money for the fucking watch, would you?'

"He went to his house and grabbed some money for me and I bought the watch. I pretended Missy bought it.

"I bought her tits. We got 'em done in April or May and she said 'They're TOO BIG.'

"I said 'Well, let's just keep 'em for the summer. You can go topless in France, it'll be great.'

"For me it was like an e-ticket at Disney. I could go on that ride as many times as I wanted. Then she had 'em reduced.

"She was solid muscle. I wanted her to have a bigger butt, so La Monte got her a stair climber.

"When she started using it, she said 'This is a booty machine! It makes my butt bigger!'

"I said 'So? I like that!'"

In mob movies most married guys have girlfriends. Did you?

"It's true; most have a wife and a girlfriend. I was never like that. I had one wife and that was enough. I didn't need to cheat.

"It was later in my life and I wound up putting her through a lot of turmoil in her life – things she wasn't used to."

Like his parents, Allen believed in the pleasures of a well-stocked kitchen.

"I used to go once a week to buy the best caviar and a bottle of Tattinger Rosé. I'd get 00 Beluga caviar and all the fixins and just sit with my wife and enjoy.

"I'd see the butcher at Whole Foods and tell him to cut the porterhouse steaks 2" thick off the whole loin.

"I'd tip him $50 or $100. The first time I did it I said 'Take the money, I appreciate what you do.'

"Then he started charging me a lot less than what it was. He'd put some other tag on it and I'd pay like half and just give him $100 and he'd be happy.

"I didn't go in there seeking out to do that; it just kind of worked out that way. I was married, I had to buy food for home and we entertained a lot. It was like a resort."

The newlyweds started to socialize in a big way.

"We had a party at Lake Havasu every year. It's a huge, huge lake. There's everything there. We usually went the week after Memorial Day to avoid the crowds.

"We'd invite all our friends and have probably 50–60 boats. Some people would rent houseboats and we'd party all day and all night.

"We'd all go tie up in the cove where they jump off the mountain. We'd have those little squirt guns, we had water balloon launchers – we had everything and we'd bomb everybody.

"We'd drink and do drugs. We'd pop the top down on sports bottles; you could put 16 to 20 ounces of vodka in there, let it float in the water and squirt it right into their mouths.

"There was always something that happened to someone who couldn't handle it. Like these guys from Detroit came, the Locricchios. I told one of 'em, I said 'Don't drink too much in the sun. The sun is very, very strong. It's probably 110 with dry heat.'

"He goes 'Aw, I won't get sick.'

"He was puking his guts out in 90 minutes. I had to untie and take him to the dock. The water was a little rough, so the boat bounced around.

"When I finally got him to the gas station, he went in the bathroom and would not come out at all."

"Missy and me went everywhere. During the holidays we'd get a suite at the Drake in Chicago or call Dominic and a bunch of people to go out and have fun.

"Dale was dating a dancer – not a stripper, but some kind of classical ballet dancer. Her name was Jen or Jennifer or something.

"To me she wasn't attractive at all, but Dale wasn't attractive either. He's small and short with a receding hairline. Like George on Seinfeld, only not heavy.

"Me and Missy tried hanging out with them but it didn't work out. This girl wasn't very smart. Stupid people just kinda grate on me.

"We went on vacations a few times and I don't know if it was jealousy or what, but she tried to compete with Missy. They would fight, there'd be arguments.

"I was like 'I'm not doing this anymore.' It just wasn't fun; we didn't have fun with 'em. Over the years she always thought Dale was the big shot. I didn't give a shit, I just ignored her."

Bottom line – "I didn't want his girlfriend to have anything to do with our business; but he ignored me.

"I don't know if they broke up or if they were never that big a deal in the first place. As far as I was concerned, she was no day at the beach."

Allen and Missy didn't need to hang with another couple to have a good time. He didn't even necessarily need her.

"This one time we're in Carmel and I'm all ready to go, dressed in an Armani cashmere sport coat, Armani pants and a white shirt.

"I had weed on me – and pills.

"I took Missy to dinner, but after that she just wanted to go home and go to sleep.

"So I took off to meet The Rocketman at this bar. We're hanging out, having fun and there are these two girls. When we leave, we take them with us.

"I was driving the Mercedes SL 600. It doesn't have a back seat, so they're sitting on the lid cover between the upholstery and the trunk.

"We stopped at a store for beer and the cops pulled us over near Point Lobos State Natural Reserve.

"I said 'Girls, the best thing for you to do right now is run.'

"The cops come up and ask 'Are you drunk?'

"I'm slurring; 'Nooo, not at all.'

"Rocketman goes 'I'm not. Can I drive?'

"Cop goes 'If you're not drunk you can drive.'

"Rocketman opens the door and a beer bottle falls out.

"They just know we're fuck ups, so they take us to the fucking police station.

"They go to lock us in a cell, but they decide to leave the door open. We were eating marijuana, taking pills and walking around the police station, just cracking them up all night long.

"At 6 a.m. I told them we were renting a house in the area, so they said we could go."

Not what he was wanting to hear.

"I said 'This is not a good thing. We can't just go on our own, we're going to get in trouble.'

"We knocked on the door. Missy opened it and saw us with the police. She said 'You can keep him' and slammed the door.

"I had to drive all the way back to Arizona with her like that. I was hoping she'd stop being mad by the time we stopped in Santa Barbara."

"We went back to Michigan all the time.

"One summer I rented a cottage on Lake Charlevoix. We were going to hang out there for a month, so I made a big deal of it. I had Shewy drive my boat and Sea-Doos cross country.

"The first three or four days we got there it was raining all day, all night, just *raining*, so we went out to this bar called Hammering Hank's.

"My cousin Raymond and his girlfriend were with us and we got FUCKED UP at that place. Just obliterated.

"We were smoking dope and the bar was going to close, so we left and I stopped to buy a case of beer.

"There's a cop across the street.

"I put the beer in the trunk – he could see that.

"I get on the main road and he's following me. I'm smoking the last of the dope, driving the speed limit, not doing anything wrong. He follows us 15 miles to our turnoff and turns his flashers on.

"I ask him 'What did I do?'

"He said 'You went over the fog line.'

"I said 'What's the fog line?'

"He said 'The line on the right.'

"I'm like 'That is so bogus!'

"I was just SO drunk and I had a weird looking cap on. I tried to spit my gum out and it splats on the hood of his car.

"He arrests me and they take me to the police station.

"I don't know if I got a breathalyzer. If I did, I don't know what I blew. They took a videotape of me doing the field sobriety test inside. I'm laughing and making fun of everything. It's hilarious.

"After I sobered up I got a lawyer who tells me 'A lot of people drink up here. Ain't shit else to do. The jury won't care that you had a couple drinks.'

"I had to go back for trial in the middle of winter. Everybody came in to testify – Raymond, Shewy, and Missy. They all said I had *a couple glasses of wine.*

"They showed the video and the jury was cracking up. We have them. We're winning.

"After a while my lawyer says 'OK, you gotta take the stand.'

"I said 'No, I don't want to take the stand.'

"He insisted, I resisted – 'NO. Just say defense rests and leave it alone.'

"He says 'YOU HAVE TO TAKE THE STAND.'

"I said 'Alright, *fine.*'

"So I go out on the stand and go along with the story everybody else said.

"They go 'Time out' and bring in a guard from where they had me locked up. He tells them the night I was arrested he asked me 'When's the last time you had 20 drinks in one night?'

"He said I said 'Tonight!'

"They used that as testimony to impeach me as a witness. I lost the case and paid $15,000."

• • •

"My whole life was like a fantasy. I was making 1.5 to 2 million in real estate legit; plus $700,000/month selling marijuana. I had the bar. I was living well and having fun when the IRS letters started coming. *I hadn't filed my 1989, '90 or '91 tax returns.*

"The letter said 'If you need help filing your taxes, we'd like to help you.'

"I was in the process of doing them with an accountant who used to work in the CID – the Criminal Investigation Division. She was married to a bookie friend of my parents' and mine. I used to bet with him, play poker and cards and stuff like that.

"She knew something about the letter was not kosher. She goes 'No, they're looking to come after you.'

"I said 'Alright.'

"Shortly thereafter the IRS called and tried to get my file from her; the CID doesn't need a warrant.

"She made like she wasn't home, said she'd be back.

"They made an appointment to come for my files the next day, so she calls me that night and tells me 'You've got to come pick up your files NOW.'

"I remember us driving to her office with the top down. I'm singing *Let's Stay Together* and Missy's getting all weepy and crying.

"I said 'Just relax. It's going to be ok.'

"I went in and swooped up my files and records; but then I had to hide them. I wasn't going to go to Phoenix to give them to my lawyer until the next day and I didn't know if they would try to come to my house.

"If they did and I didn't have 'em, they'd go to my parents and my mom would tell them 'Get the fuck outta here.' She didn't like the government trying to push people around.

"So I left them with my parents."

"When the CID guy came to my accountant she told him 'He came and got them last night. I don't know why.'

"I picked the files up from my parents and took them to my defense attorney.

"Pic tells me I should go to a guy in Phoenix. He said 'It would behoove you to look him up. He's going to cost a fortune, but *you need to spend the money.*'

"I said 'OK, I guess that's what I need.'

"He goes 'Take some money with you.'

"So I said 'Alright.'

"I knew I was going to have to pay. He's at a big time law firm with all the bells and whistles. It's called Burch & Cracchiolo; Cracchiolo was from Detroit, the old man knew my family, my father and my Uncle Dominic because they went and visited him. His son became a lawyer and opened this big law firm.

"They sent me to this guy named Steve who was supposedly the best tax attorney in the state. They told him to take care of me.

"He's just a little fuck, pasty white. I think it was a $100,000 retainer. 'Stealthy Steve' took it in cash and put four lawyers on my case.

"Pic was busy helping one of my associates. Pic always looked out for me, he was one of the good ones – but for him to help both of us would have been a conflict; so I signed off and brought in another of my friends, Bob Hirsh."

He was known as 'Tucson's most famous criminal defense lawyer.'

"I hired Hirsh to run herd over these guys so they wouldn't screw me over.

"From the very start it was an investigation by the Criminal Investigation Division of the IRS. They're looking at me for my taxes and they don't realize how I'm getting my money in the first place.

"The CID was always coming after me, but I was selling shit under their noses. They'd look in one spot and it was in the other.

"They went back to 1989 when I had gotten the check for $75,000, cashed it and went to Vegas. I woulda had to pay $17,000 in taxes.

"The IRS kept digging. They were going to everybody that I did business with and everyone I knew.

"They'd say 'I don't know how he did all he did, he just did. I don't have any records anymore.' They said 'He paid his bills and we did business. He's a great client, a great person.'

"They couldn't find one person who'd say anything bad about me. Everyone stuck up for me, which is kind of cool.

"They're calling me and saying 'You know the IRS ...' and I'm like 'I know all about it.'"

The cartel knew too.

"I was in danger when my Mexican friends found out I was under IRS investigation. Nobody was out of bounds if they got pissed; not even me. They don't want anyone to know who they are.

"In Mexico the Federales have a list of who's wanted in the U.S. The higher you get on the list, the more you have to pay.

"Those guys were high up, they were wanted in the U.S. and had to pay dearly for their safety. They had bounty on their heads, like 5 million, 10 million – and the higher it got, the more they had to pay the Federales for protection. Sometimes it was half a million a month.

"They were afraid I was going to say something. They told Ozzie, 'Your partner's got to go.'

"They wanted to kill me, no questions asked.

"Ozzie told them 'No, no, no – he will never say anything, I promise you. You've got to trust me.'

"Ozzie was able to talk 'em into not killing me because – #1, they liked me and #2, because they *wanted* to believe us.

"If I said anything, they would have killed him along with me.

"They would have killed us both.

"I wasn't afraid. They're honorable. As long as you keep your word and do what you say, there's no problem. It's not like I say I'm going to do something and I don't do it. You've got your word and that's it.

"If your word's no good, they know. They use crimpers to crimp your tongue to mark you if you're a liar.

"When things weren't going well with the cartel, you still had to get things done. You had to make moves other ways.

"Afterwards – when they knew I didn't snitch – I could have anything I wanted. If I wanted 10,000 pounds they'd give it to me, no questions asked.

"When I would go to Mexico, they'd know and be ready for me. I'd walk across the border and they'd pick me up, drive me part of the way, fly me part of the way, whatever it took to get me to Culiacán and the grow fields.

"You go to the fields to see how it's growing. They've got to separate the males from the females at a certain point so there are no seeds. You want to know how they're drying and processing – what the buds look like and how they need to be trimmed.

"Being there then was like a movie. If I wanted to sleep on the beach they'd have guys walking around with machine guns just to watch me.

"Nobody messed with me in the United States or Mexico."

• • •

"My wife was looking for a business we could do together. She says 'How about Arabian show horses?'

"I said 'What do I care? Yeah, OK. That sounds good.'

"So there's a horse show in Phoenix at the end of February every year. It's one of the triple crown of Arabian horse shows.

"I said 'We'll go there and see if you like any horses. We'll see what's up.'

"I was sitting on the rail. There are like 60 horses in this class and Missy points at a bay colored mare.

"She said 'That horse is going to win.'

"I go like 'OK, whatever.' So when the trainer comes around I said 'How much for this horse?'

"He tells me '$80,000.'

"I say 'OK, no problem. I'll meet you at the barn after this class.'

"He says 'OK, great.'

"The horse wins unanimously, all three judges agreed.

"The trainer drew up the contract. I signed it and said 'We'll go to dinner tonight and I'll have someone bring the money.'

"I told Dale to bring a shoe box with $80,000 in it.

"We're out having dinner with the trainer when Dale brings the box. I put it on the ground and kick it over the trainer's way.

"He leans over, lifts the lid and about shit his pants. 'I like dealing with you!'

"After the show we went to Acapulco. We used to go everywhere, Cabo, Acapulco. Puerto Vallarta, Huatulco, Zihuatanejo.

"This time we met my cousin Raymond Thomas from Detroit and rented a big villa just above Las Brisas - that famous resort with the pink and white Jeeps.

"There was four couples – my cousin, a bookmaker from Detroit and some other guy, I don't know what he did.

"We get there and we're hanging out, having a good time when I get a phone call from the horse trainer.

"He says 'You want to sell your horse?'

"I said 'I just bought her!'

"He said 'Well, I have an offer for $160,000.'

"The people who made the offer had another horse who was in competition with her and didn't want her to beat their horse. They were willing to spend $160,000 so their horse wouldn't lose.

"I said 'I guess, yeah. I'll sell the horse.'

"So I doubled my money in a week. That's how we got into it. We weren't racing, we were showing and we started winning.

"I started buying horses. I'd spend $500,000 to $600,000.

"I had one truck to pull my boat and another to pull the horses. It was a big monster truck, an F-250 or 350 – 4 door, all raised up. It could go through anything and pull like a demon.

"We'd train 'em up real good and we did very well.

"Missy's instincts were good and we had fun going to the shows.

"I was driving us around in a golf cart at one of the events and Missy's mom was sitting in the front seat.

"Missy was sitting near the back wheel; it caught her dress and ripped it right off. She didn't have a bra on; just a thong.

"I was laughing so hard – me and her mom were laughing and she was *so* pissed. She wouldn't let me take her back to the hotel.

"I said 'C'mon, I'll drive you back.'

"She said 'NO! You stay here, I'll go on my own.'

"Missy's mom stayed with me. Missy didn't want *anybody* with her."

"Soon we were traveling all over the world to look at horses. When you're spending that kind of money on an animal, you better. And you better have good friends that would look out for you if there was a horse that came on the market. *We did.*

"They'd say 'Come on, we need to go get this horse.' We'd jump on a plane at a moment's notice.

"The people that are in the horse business are all Hollywood people – celebrities, everybody.

"I was in a deal with Patrick Swayze. I loved him, he was just a nice guy. He was about 5'8" – I said 'You sure are fucking tiny!'

"He was a bit of a cowboy before he got into acting. He had part of a ranch in Texas, was a horseman who really knew his horses. And he was happily married; we had that in common.

"There was a horse he wanted me to come in on. We'd be hiding in the tents at night, drinking beers and talking.

"He wasn't supposed to be drinking. He'd say 'Sneak me a few beers and don't let my wife see.'

"Everyone is just having fun. You're spending money, but who cares."

Spending wasn't a problem; but timing could be.

"My friend Vito knew all about exotic cars. I'd tell him what I wanted, he'd find it and I'd go get it.

"I told him I wanted a Ferrari. We didn't have them in Tucson, so he called the Ferrari guy and arranged for me to take a test drive. I was ready with the cash.

"He said 'I can get it maybe in a month.'

"I don't like to wait. I said 'No, I want *that* one and I want it NOW. I don't want it in a month.'

"Right then a trainer calls and says 'There's this horse you have to see, she is just unbelievable. You have to buy her right now.'

"So I bought this filly for $160,000 – and he was right. She was high strung, she could have won everything.

"I gave her to my trainer.

"If you push on them too hard you'll mentally damage them. One of the trainer's assistants did that. I was so angry. I could have sold her for over a million to an Arab.

"Another time my trainer called and said 'There's this horse; she's priced at $800,000. The guy's not going to come off of that price. Prepare to pay, but know that we're going to make a ton of money on her.'

"We flew to Chicago, then Fort Wayne – but there was a snow storm and we had to stay the night. We couldn't charter planes, couldn't get out, so we stayed at the Four Seasons.

"Somebody got there before me and bought the horse. I was so pissed at the guy. My trainer told him I was upset so he said 'Don't worry – I'll reimburse.'

"He sent me a check for $15,000 for my expenses. *I don't think he knew who I was.*"

"Finally, there was this horse Shatina that had won a national championship. This was a beautiful horse. I wanted to buy her and breed her a certain way.

"I told my trainer to offer the owners $500,000, but they turned it down. So I said 'Offer $100,000 to lease her to me so I can breed her.' They turned that down too.

"After that I wanted to talk them into breeding her the way I wanted her bred. When the baby came I could buy the baby … maybe. At least I'd have *a shot* at buying the baby, which is what I wanted all along.

"Then I got a harebrained idea; there was an auction in Scottsdale. It was in full swing and they were doing an auction of babies and stuff like that.

"I told the trainer 'Why don't you talk them into auctioning the unborn baby?' It's illegal to do ultrasounds to determine the sex, but he agreed.

"He says 'Alright' so I'm going partners; we'll pay up to $100,000 for an unborn baby, which is pretty risky.

"So the bidding comes up and there are these Brazilians.

"I'm bidding and waiting and bidding and finally some guy is bidding against me – $80,000 to $86,000.

"Finally I said '$87,000' thinking *That's it, it's done.*

"He says 'Fuck, you can have it.'

"I got the baby and we named him Shaman. He won nationals – was a U.S. National champion as a yearling colt."

"I was making a couple million a year legit all through the 90s. We were buying and selling horses for profit. I was doing real estate too, buying big tracts of land."

Allen happened upon an interesting discovery while looking at property near the Catalina National Forest.

"To the left, as you're driving up rutted road, there's this house with high electric gate all the way around and warning signs telling people to stay away.

"I knew it was witness protection, but I didn't even know this place existed. Turns out that's where they were keeping Sammy 'the Bull' Gravano. He was the guy that killed all the people for John Gotti. Later he said 'Fuck witness protection' and they let him out."

How safe is witness protection?

"If they want you bad, you can get found anywhere."

Shortly after hearing Allen talk about Gravano I was talking to A.S. about changes within the mob over time – and the name came up again.

A.S. explained "When you send a lot of people to prison, it hits the fabric of the group and things change.

"After the 90s loyalty started to turn. You had those people at the top that seemed to require a different standard of loyalty than those people that reported to them.

"People were saying 'Hey, you weren't a standup guy for me – why would you expect me to be a standup guy for you?'

"Gravano overheard a conversation where Gotti was talking about having him whacked. He's thinking 'I've done everything he's asked me to do and now he's concerned I might turn on him and become a witness - which I would never do. If he thinks that's the only way to shut me up, fuck him. And oh, by the way – give me immunity from prosecution of 19 murders which I assisted in.'

"They all became witnesses and went into the eye witness protection program.

"People you expected to have a lot of money either died broke or wound up in prison. When you're in prison, you're not a producer."

A.S. told me Gravano had no fear of being tracked down.

Intrigued, I tracked down an interview by Howard Blum.

In September, 1999 Gravano was quoted in his Vanity Fair article *The Reluctant Don.*

Speaking of Gotti's heir, Gravano said "You got to earn respect. Your father can't just give it to you." Blum added "… according to Sammy's worldview, the way to get respect is to get even when you're supposed to get even.'

When Blum asked Gravano if he was worried John junior was going to come after him, he said "I can see where he's coming from. Fine. Let's rock 'n' roll.

"They send a hit team down, I'll kill them. They better not miss, because even if they get me, there will still be a lot of body bags going back to New York. I'm not afraid, I don't have it in me. I'm too detached maybe. If it happens, fuck it. A bullet in the head is pretty quick. You go like *that*! It's better than cancer."

Allen never expected to deal with loyalty issues within his circle. Betrayal? Not in a million years.

He was enjoying success on all fronts.

"I bought 115 acres and we did the engineering work on it. I kept 15 acres on the bottom. I knew that was the only way they'd be able to get ingress and egress from the property above. They couldn't come off any of the roads on the corner, couldn't come in any way else; so I held that back.

"It was challenging to get as many homes as possible on 1 acre lots on 15 acres. You can only build so high on the mountain, you can't go up higher than is allowable. Most of the time you just can't build on top of a mountain.

"It's pretty rugged terrain. We had to spread the density because there's slope ordinances. We spread 39 or 40 condo units on the 15 acres. After all the engineering work was done, zoning and approvals, we sold it to Pulte.

"We bought another 40 acres for $10,000/acre; it was absolutely beautiful, up against Catalina National Forest. It looked out over the golf course and you could see the whole city.

"I raised money from my family, got all of them involved. We could only get five 8 acre lots. If we'd waited we could have sold those lots for probably a million apiece.

"Someone came in and offered us more than $800,000; we kept the money."

It was the last property Allen would buy and sell prior to building his own home.

"Ozzie heard about it first. He went over there and the house was already started. He was going to buy it, but we were married and he wasn't.

"He said 'You guys have to buy it, it's so quiet and private and it has a really good builder.'"

"I told the builder, 'We'll buy it but you gotta stay on and build *everything*.'"

12 Building the Fortress

"Tucson's a beautiful town, it really is. The property is way out on East Broadway and the mountains are right on top of you.

"I paid a lot of cash building my house. My contractor was Steve Ball, we became really good friends; he's very, very talented.

"We built an 8' adobe wall all along the front of the property. Nobody could come in the driveway; the only way in was through a password protected security gate between stone columns.

"I hired construction guys, pool guys, landscapers – only people I could trust to give the code to the gate.

"Once you got through you drove up and there's a giant tower with a 400 year old mission bell.

"The main house was about 4,200 square feet. We had steer skulls with horns outside and lights that were hand carved into cast iron crosses. Red chiles hung from each light.

"We had a 20' entryway, so I purchased an elk horn chandelier for $12,000. This was back in the day, when things were cheaper.

"The elk weren't killed. Every year they shed their horns, so they were all natural and huge.

"The windows were floor to ceiling. The floors were flagstone and hardwood, with carpet in the bedrooms, great room and office.

"We didn't have drapes except for blackout drapes in our bedroom so we could sleep later; otherwise the sun would rise over the mountain and come in hot.

"Everything inside was handmade and hand carved. I had old Mexican ranch doors for coffee tables, elk skin couches, Ralph Lauren furniture. I bought our antiques in France; it's cheaper to buy where they come from.

"My gourmet kitchen had giant subzero refrigerators, a Wolf oven with six burners, two ovens and a salamander grill – which is like a broiler. The fire's really hot; you can get close to the fire if you want to melt cheese. And a griddle for pancakes.

"All my cabinets had saguaro ribs that went up and down. The ceiling was inset with herringbone saguaro ribs between the beams; which are illegal to build with.

"I bought a giant dining table and put it outside under cover. If it was cold we had commercial heaters.

"My hot tub connected to the pool with a waterfall that flowed into the dark bottom pool. If I was working during the day and it was hot, I'd just take off my clothes and jump in naked.

"The 4,000 sq. ft. deck was all river rock and flagstone.

"I spent over $500,000 on landscaping. In the early 90s, that was a lot of money for landscaping.

"I had a friend of my dad's that did my yard work. His name was Abe. He had guys working for him, so my dad says 'Let your brother work with Abe.'

"I said 'Yeah, that's fine; that's OK.'

"So I come home and Douglas is in the garage smoking crack. Mind you I'm dealing tons and tons of drugs; that's all they would have needed. I would have been arrested.

"I threw him out. I said 'Get the fuck out of here.'

"I told my dad 'I can't have that here; I just can't.'"

The Fortress was nearly complete.

"I told Steve 'You gotta stay and build my barn.'

"It was about 5,000 square feet with grooms' quarters, tack room, washers and dryers. It had a hot walker and lunging pens and pastures.

"I installed infrared cameras; at night they'd go on if they sensed motion."

"I would have parties at my house all the time.

"I had a wine cellar in my basement. I would buy Dom Pérignon – 1966 is the best vintage there is. Back when I was buying 'em, they were $500 a bottle wholesale; if you could get 'em. You couldn't really find 'em.

"I had a guy that would look, he'd check for them. He'd call me and say 'I found 3!'

"I said 'Grab 'em, I'll be down to give you the money.'

"One of my friends came over. He has a lot of money. He said 'You son of a bitch, leave it to you. This fucking place is unbelievable. You've got the nicest house in Tucson. And it's decorated great. You didn't spare any denaro here, did you?'

"I said 'No.'"

Did it feel strange to have such incredible wealth?

"Everything always felt like it was just as it was supposed to be; and I took it all for granted.

"Then my lawyer told me 'The IRS likes to take things.' He said 'Get a million dollar mortgage on your house.'

"I said 'Fuck you, I'm not getting a mortgage.'

"So I went to my friend and said 'Give me a $500,000 mortgage on the house.'

"I only had a 3 car garage, but I had plenty of room outside; I had 5 or 6 cars at all times.

"My lawyer said 'You've got to get rid of all those cars, just lease them.'

"Leasing meant I'd be making payments of $2,500 a month on *one* of my cars. Most of 'em would be $800 to $900 a month. Interest rates were high at that time.

"That's lot of money for car payments. I thought *I fucking hate this.*"

On the bright side …

"I was paying taxes on over a million a year that I'm making and *everything was a deduction*; you can deduct cars, trucks, trailers, travel, hotel, meals, all that.

"You can depreciate the horses straight line over 8 years; that's why a lot of people with horses are in the horse business.

"The people that are in the business make millions and keep most of it. Sheltering a lot of your income pays for a nice lifestyle. It's work, but if they want to do it, that's how it goes.

"I only did it because Missy wanted to get into it. You buy a young horse and show it; then people get interested and they buy it. I'd buy babies for $12,000 and sell them for $100,000.

"I'd buy $500,000 worth of horses and show them; when they won, I'd sell them.

"You keep your best horses for brood mares and sell their babies. As soon as the babies hit the ground, people come to look at them so everything has to be pristine in your barn; and it was. At those times I was selling babies for $35,000 to $50,000, depending.

"If you had a colt or filly, you depreciate the mare, write off all your costs and don't have to pay much tax. If you had a colt or stud, you sold stud fees. If they produced well, you could sell *a bunch* of stud fees."

He took time to enjoy the horses too.

"I had a 7 time national championship team roper come to my house to teach me how to rope.

"I rode the horses almost every day. You use your legs a lot. My horses were trained really well. I could put just a little pressure with my knee or heel.

"The horses really liked me, especially the horse that I rode. She was trained to the nines. I'd never wear spurs or anything like that, I wouldn't do that to the animal. She had a real tender mouth, so if I just moved the reins one way or the other, or gave a little pressure from knee or thigh, she knew what I wanted to do.

"I had a refrigerator with carrots, apples and candy; when the horses heard me coming they'd nicker because they knew they were getting treats.

"I kept hard mints in my shirt pockets. They like those. They'd stick their heads out of the stall and try to nibble at my shirt.

"If I had 'em in the pasture, I'd open their stall doors and pasture door – time to come in! And they'd all run right into their own stalls; I'd shut the door and they'd eat.

"I'd call my vet to come out and a lot of times he needed help, so I did it. Who else is gonna do it? They're my animals.

"Moon Gypsy Echo was one of the horses I bought and brought home to breed. She was getting ready to foal, so one night I go out there. I had a hunch; they like to do it with nobody around.

"I went out there and the horse is starting to give birth, but the tip of the foal's nose was coming out of her ass. I looked at it and thought *Uh oh, this isn't right.*

"I called my vet and he said 'I can't get there in time. You've got to push the foal back in, find out where it ripped through the vaginal lining and pull it down to get it out the right way or else they'll both die.'

"She's trying to push out and I'm trying to push in. She's kicking, not happy about what I'm doing, so I'm fighting with her.

"I put a halter on her and my wife is holding her head. I'm pushing the foal back in – find the rip and pull him out.

"I named him Butthead and gave him a Fleet enema I'd bought from the drug store; I already knew to do that.

"After a while the vet came and stitched Gypsy back up.

"Somebody saw Butthead and bought him. I sold him for like $30,000 as a weanling; that was pretty good.

"We had to put mares under lights to simulate the time of year they go into season.

"You want to have your horses early in the year; all birthdays are January 1, so if they're born in December it's a year old. You don't want that. You try to have all your horses born February, March – the latest April.

"The next year when Moon Gypsy Echo was getting close to having a baby again, they had this newfangled thing that the vet comes and sews into her vulva. It has magnets or something, so when she goes into labor they come apart and there's this big box that calls my beeper.

"It was all about peace of mind and it was a write-off at $5,500. So I bought it and it comes a month before she's due.

"So we get this machine, sew the monitor in, test it and it works.

"I'm carrying this beeper and I'm going out to the barn to check. I reach down; sometimes you can tell they're getting close because their tits get waxy and leak.

"I go out one morning in my shorts and flip flops; I reach under to check and I guess I was a little rough. She reached around and bit me on my side.

"I swear to God I never felt so much pain. I ran out of the barn screaming 'Why did you do that?!'

"The next morning I walk out to the barn and see a baby standing up. Gypsy's all happy and everything was fine.

"Nothing worked, no whistles, no alarms, no nothing.

"I sent the equipment back. I had put it on my Amex; I called them and said 'I'm not paying for this shit. It didn't even work.'

"I was a really good customer, so they said 'OK.' Didn't bitch about it or anything.

"I had a bruise for a year."

"One year for my birthday Missy and Sam bought me a Dalmatian puppy. I named him Otis. He was a great dog, I loved him.

"There was plenty of room for him to run. The only problem was he could be a pain in the ass with the horses. He'd come up from behind and nip at their heels until he got kicked in the face.

"We bought a female Dalmatian two years later. Otis and Toby got along good but we were gone a lot. We traveled for the horse business, went on buying trips and stuff. Depending on the time of year, we were gone at least a week or two out of every month.

"We'd leave the dogs with my parents.

173

"One time Toby was in heat. I told my parents 'Don't let them get together!'

"Sure enough, she was pregnant when we got back. LaMonte took one puppy, Nadra took one – we found homes for all of 'em."

"I'd cook and people would come over. If they wanted to ride horses, they could ride horses. We'd have a blast.

"My wife had this friend and I was kind of friends with her husband. They'd come over on Sundays and she always wanted to ride. She said she knew how.

"I put her on the easiest horse I had and she yanked the reigns nearly hard enough to break 'em.

"I said 'The horse is trained, you don't need to do that.'"

She wasn't someone he wanted to deal with again.

"Slavik came from New York and stayed with us. We had a big party, we were all going to go riding in the national forest. It was me, Slavik, a couple people I knew and my wife.

"Missy said her friend wants to go. 'Would you try to take her again?' Her husband was going but he could ride.

"I said 'I don't want to take her.'

"Missy talks me into letting her get on the horse.

"I warned her. 'You have to listen to what I'm telling you when you ride a horse, especially in the desert.'

"So we saddle up, get 'em all tacked up, and head out.

"I'm riding Ivan, this giant Friesian I had bought for my wife; my friend Slavik is riding my horse, Lady Cash, and there's a bunch of other horses we had. Everybody's riding.

"Out the back gate, there's a trail head where it's all fenced off before you get into the park. We get out there into the forest a couple miles, we're all walking along and I said 'Is everyone comfortable?'

"They wanted to run, get a little bit of up and down. We run for a little while and I stop and say 'We'll walk now.'

"We're like 4 or 5 miles into the national forest and they want to run again and I said 'OK.'

"So we start running and I'm in front.

"I have Slavik in the back so he can see if anybody's having trouble. Everything's going smooth except for Missy's friend. Slavik said it looked like she took a dive – face and stomach first – into a cactus plant.

"Chollas are the worst kind. They call 'em jumping cactus because if you get close, they *will* get you.

"She's just unbelievable. All you have to do is follow the trails. The horse turned left and she went right. Now she's rolling over and she's just covered from her neck down in needles.

"I looked at her and said 'Omigod, we've got to get an ambulance.'

"I gathered everybody, we got off our horses and got her out of there. Then we lay her on the trail and her husband starts picking the cactus thorns out.

"I have to go to the ranger's station all the way back at where we started. The rangers will get somebody out there to help her.

"I said 'Slavik, please take everybody else back to my house and I'll meet you there. I'll take my horse, you take Ivan.'

"I took Lady Cash because she's really fast. I could go the whole way in a couple minutes; I knew it would be the best thing to do.

"I take off all the way back and tell the rangers what happened. They call an ambulance and I head back to the house. I'm pretty pissed, thinking *She said she could ride.*

"I get back and everyone else is already there. They had unpacked the horses. I had the grooms clean them and put them all away.

"Later we're outside partying and I hear somebody at the gate. I'm like *Who the fuck is out there.*

"So I look down and see the ambulance. *Can't they just take her and leave me alone?*

"I go to the door and she says 'Well, they got all the thorns out that they could, but I have to get pain pills. I know you've got 'em, so I had them drop me back off.'

"I let her back in and gave her pain pills; but I was always pissed at her."

She wasn't the only guest to land in the cholla.

"My cousin Raymond knew this guy who was an ex Mr. Universe. He was a big guy, but he had developed stomach cancer from all the shit he'd done to his body.

"He said he wanted to ride Ivan. That horse was beautiful.

"So I said 'Alright, I'll take you for a ride.'

"He did the same thing … big tough Mr. Universe. Only he didn't whine about it. I took him back home, used duct tape and pulled out as many thorns as I could."

175

From caring for the horses to managing his fleet of vehicles, the responsibilities were growing in direct proportion to his wealth. It could be overwhelming.

"The first thing I used to do when I got new cars was I'd get the Dinan engine performance chip to make 'em go faster.

"And I'd get new tires and wheels, even if the car was brand new. I'd just store 'em, in case I needed 'em, like if I buy something else or trade it. I don't want to give the next owner my good tires and wheels.

"So I have probably 4 sets of tires and wheels at this guy's place.

"He says 'I can't store them anymore; you can't buy any more cars.'

"I said 'Well SELL 'em.'

"He said 'Well, if I can, I will.'

"I had to have guys come to my house every month to detail my cars. In Arizona it's really important to use a lot of wax on the paint so it doesn't oxidize in the heat.

"I'd make sure they were clean and nice, but to me cars are just cars. I don't particularly think that they're the end all be all of your life.

"I had six cars. I didn't want to lose my keys so I *always always always* left them in the car; most of the time still in the ignition. That way I knew where they were.

"I don't want anything in my pockets but cash.

"This one time I told Dale I needed $300,000 for something. He says 'You gotta drive up to Phoenix.'

"I was in a hurry. I said 'You fucker!'

"So I had to go up to Dale's house, I was just going to run in and out. I wasn't in his house a minute, I'm saying 'See you later bro' – BOOM – I come outside and the car's not there.

"I said 'Which of you guys is fucking around. Where's the car?'

"They're like 'Not us, honest.'

"I said 'C'mon, I don't have time for this shit.'

"They didn't have it. Some kid had stolen it and took off. I'm like *what the fuck!*

"I said 'Well you guys have to take me to the rentacar place.'

"I rented a car and drove back to Tucson.

"When I got home I told Missy 'Well, somebody stole the car.'

"She goes 'Surprise, surprise. Where were the keys? In it?'

"I said 'Yeah.'"

"When the insurance company asked where the keys were, I told 'em the truth.

"They said 'That's not a good thing.'

"I said 'At least I knew where they were.'

"I had cars stolen – easily 6 or 7 times. Not to mention the cars that I gave to the Mexicans and said were stolen.

"In the 90s the cartels were willing to do anything and everything to take over the drug business. The old school guys said 'No!' But when the old guys died, their kids took over.

"They knew me. They still know me. They gave me whatever I wanted."

Allen was generous in return.

"My friends in Mexico liked new American cars and trucks and I always had new cars. I'd say 'Here, you can have this one. Just give me 3 days.'

"So you give 'em a few days and report it stolen and that's great for them, they love that. That was all the time."

His father was a fine accomplice.

"He was old and looked good, so it was pretty funny.

"I used to make him go to Costco. He'd be wheeling out a big basket of stuff and 'find out' the car's not there. And he'd call.

"I had him do it a couple times. He could pull that kind of stuff off."

Usually the 'stolen' cars were never found.

"I had a Denali. I was out of town and one of my Mexican friends says 'Can I borrow it?'

"I said 'Yeah, I don't care.'

"So while I'm away these guys get raided and they take off in my Denali. So now I don't know.

"I said 'You know what? I'll give you four days and then I'll report it stolen. Do whatever you have to do, it doesn't matter. I'll give you enough time to get wherever you have to go across the border.'

"They said 'Cool!'

"So I had somebody take me to the mall and leave me there. I bought some stuff to make it look like I was shopping and then I called the police.

"They came and I told them my car was stolen. They said 'OK' and did the report.

"A couple days later they called and said 'We can't see it on the film anywhere.'

"I said 'Where I was parked I thought there was camera access; it's possible there wasn't, but I know the car is gone.'

"The guy says 'OK, I guess it's no big deal.'

"The insurance company paid in full but then 30 days later I get a call from the people down in Mexico, on the border. They asked for me.

"I said 'This is he.'

"They said 'We have your car.'

"I said 'What car?'

"They said 'Your Denali. It's in the impound yard. You can pick it up whenever you want.'

"I said 'Well, it's not my car any more. You've got to call the insurance company, they already paid off the claim. They own it.'"

• • •

"When the U.S. government feels the bad guys are getting too bad, they try to get them. If you got El Chapo Guzman in the U.S., you'd get $25 million; but you'd be dead.

"I was his biggest distributor in the United States.

"Tucson is only 45 miles from the border. When product got here, some guys knew me well enough to come and say 'Take a look at this. I think you'll like it.' They might have 400 or 500 pounds.

"The growers work for people, but some are independent growers who do what they want. To me, those were better than dealing with the cartel. If the product was good I'd say 'Sure, I'll take it' and they'd be happy."

Didn't working with the independents get you in trouble with the cartel?

"No, because it's their dope anyway. They didn't care. They were supplying the bulk; but if I needed 400 or 500 pounds, it was much easier for me to get it that way.

"Then they'd want us to come down there and hang out with them and party. Usually I'd tell them 'Just leave it for me.' I'd give 'em money and they'd hold it.

"The independent growers were just crazy people. They were way far out in the mountains with no power or water.

178

"They'd be out in the fields for so long that when they got away, they usually kept to relatives or someone that they could trust.

"It was always violent. In the early 90s I'd be in Mexico and they'd roll up with five or six Suburbans with guys with guns. They bring their fighting cocks and they're ready to fight, drink and do drugs. They just want to display how much power and strength they think they have.

"*OK, whatever.*

"I saw the cartel violence. It's not cool. It's not something that I want to see or talk about.

"In the 90s the cartel violence kept escalating and escalating. If you're somewhere where a rival cartel is, they just stop the Suburbans. They're wearing masks. They get out and start shooting at each other.

"They kill each other on the street and leave the bodies where they fall. You don't want to be around that.

"There's parts of New Mexico that the independent guys used to take the dope in the middle of the desert and just leave it. And then you're supposed to send somebody there to pick it up.

"There's so much action and activity on the border, you can be in the most remote spot – no fence, no nothing – but there's cameras on the telephone poles. You've got to imagine they work.

"If the dope didn't have a GPS on it, they'd give you specific coordinates where it was. There'd be 300 or 400 pounds rolled in like an old rug or something. You'd just throw it in the back of a pickup truck, drive off and hope you don't get pulled over.

"I didn't do that though. That wasn't in my job description.

"When you'd send people out to the desert to pick up drugs, we'd have a specific drop where they could back up and unload. Usually they brought them back to the houses in Tucson.

"We had houses full of dope, floor to ceiling, every room. And more than just one. We rented them and sometimes we had Mexicans live there.

"They're not supposed to leave. We'd load 'em up with food and stuff. They'd come and get it and we'd move it to the staging area.

"You move the stuff and then you collect later. Could be the same day – depends on how well you know the buyer.

"They could owe as much as 4 or 5 million. If it's somebody you deal with all the time, you give them the stuff.

"Then, when they have the money together, it got brought straight to me and I'd keep it in my closet. Nobody knew it was there but my wife. If she wanted something, she'd just take some money out of the box. It was a pretty big box.

"It would take my guys a month to come for it. They knew I had it, they weren't worried. They'd take their time.

"The guy I dealt with would always come to my house. He'd show up in a nondescript van and ring the gate. My driveway was almost a quarter mile long. I could see who it was and let him in.

"He'd drive up and we'd take a box out to his car. He didn't stay very long. He just got back on the road and left.

"One time my probation officer asked me for the code to the gate.

"I said 'Fuck you, you're not getting the code. You want to come see me, you've got to make an appointment.'

"He didn't like that. He said 'Do you have a gun in the house?'

"I said 'Yes I do. I don't even know where it is.' Which was a lie.

"They said 'You know you're not supposed to have a gun as a felon; that's prison time for sure.'

"I said 'It's my wife's gun. It's in her name. I travel a lot, so she feels safer having the gun in the house.'

"They said 'Would you be willing to ask her to get rid of it?'

"I said 'Fuck no! If you want her to get rid of it YOU ask and see what she tells you.'

"They never asked.

"We were all watched like hawks, but that was part of the thrill for me – trying to outsmart 'em. Get around 'em.

"Sometimes I'd go outside my wall at night. One time there was a chair mysteriously there. I'm like *Who the fuck has a chair by the wall. Are they trying to listen to me?*

"You always had to assume your phones were tapped. I didn't have gas or cable TV at the house – but I DID have 5 phone lines, 1 fax and an intercom in my house; and 1 phone in the barn. I had two phone numbers, one regular number and one just for special people; it was private.

"I had my house swept by an ex-CIA guy recommended by my attorney. Paid him $1,200 a month to sweep for bugs and make sure the phones weren't tapped.

"I trusted him to know what was going on in terms of new technology.

"Sometimes my cousin would tell me 'Give me 90 minutes and call me at this number.'

"I'd say 'OK.'

"There was a 7-11 a pretty far piece away from my house. Whenever there was enough time, I'd have my horse saddled and ride her there.

"I had these saddlebags that you could put ice in them. I could fit 10 beers in the ice; she didn't mind at all. I drank and kept the empties in the other saddlebag. I don't litter.

"So I'd ride down through the wash – this way I knew nobody would follow me. And even if ATVs were trying to follow me, there was no way. You couldn't drive them there because there were so many trees and things. An ATV couldn't get through.

"On horseback, you just gotta go carefully. When there's low trees, you just put your head behind the horse's; she's not going to run into anything.

"I'd ride over there, make the call, empty out the beer cans – and get another 12 pack for the ride home.

"You *can* get a DUI for riding drunk.

"I hate the police. Not the regular policemen, they're fine. Those are the guys you see, the guys that give you traffic tickets. It's the guys you don't see that are the most problematic for you.

"The guys that think they're helping society by ridding the world of marijuana. People went to jail for it.

"In the beginning there were no problems for us; but when cocaine came on the market, there was more scrutiny. It's almost a police state now. It really is disgusting. I call them the alphabet boys. FBI, DEA, ATF ... ICE.

"You always have to be mindful that somebody could be following you. You have to make sure that you know that they're there, know where they are and what they're looking at. Concentrate on that. You don't know if they're going to take shots at you.

"When somebody gets pulled over and they find dope, their typical procedure was they want you to continue the route and deliver the dope so they can catch *all the people*. They'd just follow 'em to the destination and bust 'em.

"So you live your life in your rear view mirror. You time the light before anybody behind you can get through. That way the light's red; if they want to run the light, they're going to expose themselves.

"They switched up to try to fool me. It wasn't always the same guys, but I wasn't so easily fooled. You just knew. If you run into a guy a couple times during the day, it's not a coincidence – it's a legitimate threat.

"I used to tell them 'This is the second time I've seen you today. If I see you again today, somebody is not going to be happy, let me tell you that. If I see you a third time something is going to happen.'

"I was never scared. If somebody had to be dealt with, we'd take 'em out to the desert with our big truck and a back hoe on the back and dig a real deep, deep, *deep* hole and throw 'em in there. Throw some acid on 'em and cover it up.

"Alive or dead, it doesn't really matter. They're not gonna matter."

"In the mid-90s pay phones were getting harder and harder to find. They came out with cheap phones called burners. You buy 'em, you buy the card and put the minutes on 'em, give 'em a zip code and that's where your phone says it's from.

"You could set 'em up for anywhere in the country and they wouldn't know who it was.

"I used to buy 'em and I'd just throw 'em away after I used 'em. Just throw 'em in the trash.

"If I had to see my guys face to face, we'd pick a destination time and city to make the flights. And we'd go and we'd meet, spend a day and fly home that night.

"We picked obscure places people would never expect, places that wouldn't draw any attention. Not any place where we would have fun, just a place to blend in – fly in and fly out.

"You always worry. You always have to always be cautious. If we had to stay at a Holiday Inn for the night, that's OK; I'm just gonna sleep there.

"Without 800 thread count sheets, there's no other reason to go there."

Allen was cautious about who he hung with; Missy wasn't.

"I always kept my circle small. You've really got to know and be careful of who's around you. People will approach and you question yourself, *Why is this guy coming to me? What do I have that he wants?*

Whereas "Missy became friends with the woman who lived on 15 acres kitty corner to us.

"Just before we moved in we heard this woman's husband was dealing some weed.

"The dealers he dealt with told me he was a decent guy. They said she set him up by putting a significant quantity of weed in his trunk. She started a fight and – when he stormed off – she called the cops and they nailed him.

"He wound up in jail for a long time. She divorced him and got *everything*.

"She used to put her horses on the ground and bang pots and pans to scare them so they wouldn't spook so easy, so they're perfectly well behaved.

"But they remember that shit.

"One time when she was in the stall the horse kicked and trampled her. She was fucked up, in the hospital for a while. She got hooked on oxy.

"We all went camping one time and she was just a piece of work. She said something to me and I said 'Who the fuck do you think you're talking to bitch? I'll kill you and your kids and leave you here and nobody will ever know.'

"Later Missy wound up befriending a couple that lived in Tucson a few miles away from us. They came to my house sometimes. I don't know how she became friends with them.

"They flew airplanes for Fed Ex and they were into horses. I didn't know they were ex CIA.

"We were sitting outside one day having beers. I must have said something about Detroit because they said something about Jimmy Hoffa.

"I said 'The place he disappeared wasn't far from our house. We used to go by there once in a while. I know what happened.'

"They go 'Yeah, right.'

"So I said 'Whaddya mean, *yeah right*. You want to hear the story or do you not?'

"I told them the story; probably it was one of the theories they heard in the CIA. Their faces went white as ghosts.

"From that day forward they were scared to death of me. They knew that was the true story; that I associated with dangerous people.

"That's pretty much the last I had to do with them."

Well, nearly.

13 Surviving the Cliff

"Missy was worried. People kept wanting more and more and more product; she knew anything could happen with me, so we spent all our time together. She didn't work *with* me, but she was around all the time.

"We were good friends; and we were trying to get pregnant.

"My friend Ray came out to see me for his bachelor party; he brought his brothers and all these people and she knew. We were going to go to the strip club. I did that all the time; I love 'em.

"The next day she calls Ray and says 'That was great last night. You can take him any time you want.'

"Then she'd pee on the stick. If she was sitting on the toilet I'd make her spread so I could pee between her legs.

"Every time I got in the shower I had to pee, so I'd pee on her leg and she'd squeal like 'What are you doing!'

"In the shower it's OK. I'd always pee in the pool too. I'm drinking – I'm not getting out every fucking time.

"We finally got pregnant at the Cloud 9 Motel in Globe, Arizona. It's dumpy, but we didn't want to drive all the way home after a day at the lake.

"Her friend Marnie was in the bed next to us. I don't know if she was asleep; maybe.

"We both knew we were pregnant. That's where Jo got conceived."

Missy quit taking drugs while she was pregnant and Ella was happy to serve as their nanny. She and her daughter became an extension of the family.

"After Jo was born, Missy worked out really hard and bounced back quickly."

"She only gained 19 fucking pounds; I gained 25. I'm like *What the fuck*? I had just been eating and eating and I went from 160 pounds when we got married to 195 or 200 by the time we had the baby."

Fortunately, "LaMonte got me back in good shape."

"Before the baby was born we went to Mexico all the time. I would always rent a villa. A lot of times it was in Cabo or Puerto Vallarta. It was very romantic.

"I'd have 'em set up a table on the beach and we'd have dinner with nobody else around. We'd stay out there until the tide started coming in and we got water on our feet. It was nice.

"Jo was only six weeks old, but Missy was ready to go again. I thought it was too soon, but I said 'OK.'

"We reserved a house on a hill near this place I would always go to – the Palmilla, one of the top resorts in Cabo. All the movie stars go there.

"It was Dale, Missy's brother Scotty, and Sam's girlfriend Carey – she was a nice person, a friend of ours.

"We'd been there about a week. We had an open air Jeep Wrangler and we drove out to spend the day swimming at a beach 30 or 40 miles from Palmilla.

"By 5:30 in the afternoon we were ready to drive back to the resort, have dinner and drinks and party.

"There's a dirt road that goes along the back way from Cabo San Lucas to La Paz. It's really mountainous and the beaches are deserted. At that time there was nobody there, no resorts, only a few homes that were few and far between.

"This particular stretch of road was on the edge of a cliff. The sun was going down over the ocean and it was just beautiful.

"Missy was sitting on the floor between the two front seats; nobody was wearing seat belts.

"I was driving a little too fast and the road was banked the wrong way. I tried to correct, but we just kept slipping toward the edge.

"I told everybody to jump before we went over and started rolling sideways. I tried to hold Missy down so she wouldn't get tossed out, then we flipped headlong towards a giant boulder a couple hundred feet down.

"The steering wheel was bent into a V from me holding on. I didn't want to get thrown, but there was no denying centrifugal force.

"When the Jeep hit the boulder, I got thrown out first. It was like an out of body experience. I kept flipping down the mountain, landing on my back in slow motion – tumbling and hitting and praying to God 'Could you please just make this stop!'

"There was nothing I could do, the momentum was so strong. When I finally came to a stop, I remember the cliff was so steep I couldn't see anything above. My only physical sensation was pain.

"Our passengers were OK.

"I could hear their voices - but not Missy's.

"I could hardly talk. I was laying there for a while before I could finally say 'I want to hear her voice.'

"They kept telling me 'She's OK.'

"I knew there was no help for me and only one way out – up. I had to climb back up the mountain with a broken hip, shoulder and back. It took me a while.

"Turns out Missy got thrown out and up into the air; then the Jeep landed on her. She was in bad shape.

"Two Mexican guys in a Chevy Blazer happened to be driving by real slow drinking beer. When they saw us they stopped to pick us up.

"We're still in bathing suits; I'm in swimming shorts, no shirt. We all had scrapes and cuts from the rocks and terrain. We squeezed in and were bleeding all over their seats.

"They took us to the hospital. We limp into this place and it's like a pet hospital with Abbott and Costello x-ray machines. I had to stand up so they could take x-rays; my back was broke. They wanted to strap me to a board and I said 'There's no way. I'm OK.'

"They took us all to a room with a big shower and used a wire brush and water to sweep the cuts and get the gravel out. I could hear everybody screaming.

"They took x-rays of Missy but didn't catch the fact that her ribs were broken and her lungs were punctured.

"Missy's brother tore his meniscus; he was supposed to play soccer that summer in Argentina. That didn't happen. Dale got a little banged up. Carey wound up with her arm in a sling.

"By this time it's evening. I told the doctor I thought he was in over his head. I said 'We gotta get outta here; there's nothing you can do for us.'

"He says 'I know – but it's expensive; $25,000 for a Lear jet and you would need two.'

"I said 'Well hook it up doc, I'll pay. I have no problem with that.'

"He said 'OK.'

"I gave him my Amex platinum card and he made the call.

"The Lear Jet air ambulances couldn't be there 'til 5 in the morning. I said 'I'm not staying here.'

"Palmilla is in San Jose del Cabo – south of Cabo, closer to the airport. They hooked us up.

"We originally had the house on the hill but they gave us a room with two king sized beds right by the front of the hotel so when the ambulances came they could just take us right out – Missy, me and her brother.

"They got us a nurse to give us morphine shots. I stayed on morphine all night. Every time I needed more I said 'Hey, I need another shot!'

"Missy says 'Are you having a hard time breathing? I can't breathe!'

"I didn't know what was wrong, I just said 'Get another shot; they're helping me.'

"The others stayed in the place we already had. They stayed behind.

"At 5 a.m. the ambulances came to the hotel to take us to the private airport.

"I couldn't move, so Missy went to our safe deposit box to get our stuff. I had probably $10,000 to $15,000 in cash. Everyone that wasn't hurt so bad helped.

"Then I told Missy 'You go first.' She got in the ambulance.

"They wanted to put me on a board in the ambulance, but I said 'I'll stay still. Just get me a Valium or something and get there fast.'

"There was ambulances waiting at the airport in Tucson. They realized Missy was in bad shape, her lungs were punctured; in another hour or two she would have drowned in her own blood. They put a tube in her lungs and it helped them drain.

"They fitted me for a cast. I couldn't get out of bed. I had the morphine drip and I was taking all kinds of pills.

"I wasn't eating and I was so blocked up I went almost two weeks without taking a shit. I was just too embarrassed to pee and poop in the pan.

"After Missy stabilized, I said 'Why don't we get a room together?'

"She tried, but I'd be on the phone chattering and she said 'I gotta get outta here.' She got her own room.

"Until the accident I'd only had a few concussions, but I never had a broken bone. Which was kind of weird because I always lived life on the edge.

"I went from never having a broken bone to being a bag of bones. I believe the only reason I didn't die is because LaMonte was training me.

"When we got home Missy's mom moved in and took care of us for months.

"Ella was there taking care of the house and helping with the baby.

"Missy was pretty bad, I was pretty bad. I had to wear a body cast that was like a suit of armor. It went up to my chin and had to be strapped tight; I couldn't move, couldn't bend.

"After a few months I stopped wearing it. *Screw this.*

"The pool wasn't done yet. That pissed me off. Being in the water would have helped.

"I was taking OxyContin; they call it 'Hillbilly Heroin.' This was a new drug on the market at the time. It knocked you the fuck silly. If somebody had never taken one and wanted to try it, I'd just give them a piece of one and they'd be fucked up for days.

"They were made in 160 mg. tablets and I was getting 400 a month from a doctor who finally got in trouble. I took six in the morning and six at night.

"They had the time release coating, but that's not my style. I used to wake up in the morning, peel the outer shell off, chew four or five, drink a beer and I was off to the lunar express.

"I was taking any kind of thing you could think of, any kind of narcotics. I was drinking too. It did help with the pain.

"In those days I never knew how to fall asleep; I only knew how to pass out.

"Months later I'm in my 12 cylinder Mercedes convertible. Missy and I were going to party, so I had to go meet the coke guy. It's already dark.

"When you're driving in Arizona, you never know what's out there. We have the mule deer; those fuckers can jump. They'd get in my yard and take off as soon as they saw someone.

"One time I'm driving and I stopped for one; I didn't know a fawn was following and accidentally hit her. I shot her to put her out of her misery.

"We have a ton of javelina too.

"So I'm driving about 80 mph on my street. I had a pocket full of pills, ¼ oz. of cocaine and there's no shoulder, no street lights, *nothing.*

"All of a sudden I hear BOOM BOOM, BOOM BOOM and my mirror is hanging off on the right side.

"*Omigod*, I thought; *I better back up and see what that was.*

"It was a girl in a black track suit on a black bike at night with no reflectors on the bike. No way I could see her, especially at 80 mph. Fortunately I just clipped her.

"I called my wife first to come and get all the drugs off me. I said 'You have to come get the stuff, hurry up, I have to call the police.'

"I called 911 while Missy was on her way.

"The area where I lived was so exclusive if the police pulled you over they wouldn't usually give you a ticket. They'd just ask you to slow down. I didn't even get a ticket."

Was the girl OK?

"Yeah, I checked and made sure. The next day I called the hospital and they told me she was OK.

"I found out she was trying to stay near the white line because there was no shoulder; it's all sand and she drifted into my lane. I hit her with the right front end of my car and spun her around.

"She got hit pretty hard, tore off the mirror. I felt like shit about it. She sued me, got $35,000. They said it's easier to pay her than to fight it.

"When I ran over that girl I realized *I'm addicted to this stuff now.*"

He was still in serious pain when Jo neared her third birthday.

"I was somewhere out of town. I came home and my dad was at my house with my daughter. I took some OxyContin and asked him to make me a BLT. He gave me my sandwich and left.

"In the morning my daughter woke me up saying 'Daddy, daddy!'

"She was sleeping with me and I'm all turned around, in a daze still. I look down and the BLT was still on my chest. I hadn't even taken a bite of it; I just passed out.

"I'm like *Oh God!* I thought about what would have happened to her if I had died.

"A lot of people die of opiates one way or the other. You get cancer because you can't shit. I have friends who died like Elvis because they did opiates for so long.

"I realized *This is not even worth it. I'd rather have the pain.* I slowed down, I cut way back and my wife started taking my medications."

Was the accident the beginning of the end?

"Not at all. I was under investigation from the IRS and I knew that, but the car crash didn't affect anything but my ability to work at that time; and probably even now."

Physically he would never be the same.

"I had spasms so they put me on Valium and all kinds of muscle relaxers. I can't even tell you how much shit I was taking.

"I had a seizure, so my doctor told me to go to this really great neurosurgeon. So I walk in there, this big fancy office. The nurse is a total 10, just absolutely gorgeous. She comes in and she tells me to take off all my clothes.

"Now I'm thinking somebody is playing a prank on me. I'm kind of embarrassed, but I take off my clothes.

"The doctor comes in and he tells me 'OK, hop like a bunny.'

"I'm like *WHAT?* Hop around buck naked? What the heck! But I did.

"He said everything was alright. He said if I stop taking some of my medication, I will have seizures again.

"After a while they went away; *mostly*.

"The last time it happened at home I broke my nose. We had 4 x 4 beams going into the bathroom, so when I had a seizure I hit my nose on the beam, broke it and was knocked out.

"Jordan came in and saw me laying on the floor bleeding. She went and got her mother and I went to the hospital.

"My neurosurgeon told me 'Don't stop taking your Valium!'"

14 Providing for Family

"After all that time investigating me the IRS just couldn't figure it out. They just knew I had this beautiful home right next to the mountains with views of the mountains and city.

"My lawyers thought they were going to try to hang the Kingpin act on me, but the IRS didn't know I was dealing drugs. They had no idea."

What's the Kingpin act?

"It's in the U.S. law; they have a special category for a drug kingpin. You get 25 to life. That's what my lawyers were worried would happen if they found out what I was doing.

"I would go up to Phoenix at least once or twice a week to meet with my accountant and lawyers at the law firm. I'd be there for at least 5 hours; they'd have lunch brought in.

"They'd ask 'Where'd you get this, how much was it, how did you pay' and they'd see my clothes – which were over the top expensive. We'd go over all the money I spent and how I spent it, where it went, so they could put it together.

"Bobo – who worked with the IRS' Criminal Investigation Division – continued to check in on the activity from his end. Then came the day he realized he was being kept out of the loop.

"When Bobo punched my name in the computer, it automatically set off all the alarms.

"As soon as he did that, they were 100% sure he was feeding me information; but he wasn't, he really wasn't. Years before the investigation started, he only told me little tidbits on how to avoid an audit.

"When Bobo punched my name in the computer, they raided me; they raided everybody.

"I'd been up all night partying with my wife. We used to have kinky sex, do drugs, do cocaine and stuff like that. We were up pretty much all night and she took off because she wasn't tired.

"I went to sleep and all of a sudden the phone rings at 6 a.m. Anybody that knows me knows not to call at 6 in the morning.

"I don't answer so they call again. I'm like *Well fuck, I better answer. Somebody really has something to say.*

"It was my wife. She says 'THEY'RE COMING IN!'

"She saw them trying to get in the gate, they were taking it down to get through.

"I said 'OK.'

"I got up, I was completely naked and my hair was all messed up. It was kind of long.

"I had some coke left; I don't know how much, because I used to get it for nothing. I mean pure, pure coke. I took it and flushed it down the toilet.

"They came to my house with 60 to 70 people, vans full of people, every agency – all the alphabet boys. They're ringing the doorbell and they have one of those battering ram things – and my door's all French glass.

"I yelled 'WHOA, WHOA, WHOA – I'm coming right now!' They were complete asses. Nobody can control them fuckers.

"I walked to the door – still naked – and let 'em in. There were some female agents; they showed me the warrant and I said 'OK.'

"There was a woman in charge of the investigation; her name was Eva. She had dark hair. She wasn't bad looking, but she was no dime piece.

"My daughter was still in her crib. I said 'Let me go get the baby.'

"Ella was there, she was cool; she knew the shit could hit the fan. She said 'Let me take the baby and leave. She doesn't need to be around for this shit.'

"She took the baby and left, which was OK with those guys.

"So they start searching my house up and down, in and out.

"I had the commercial kitchen with a huge vent over it. They might have found some joints because I used to smoke and turn on the vent so it would kill the smell. I would put the half smoked joints on the top of the vent pan.

"Same thing with my outdoor kitchen – I had half joints out there.

"There was a piece of plaster in one of the vents. They said 'What's that right there?'

"I said 'It's a piece of plaster you moron.'

"They took the computers and documentation for properties I was looking at. There were books and other reference stuff I had that were all horse related.

"There was one book on the IRS, something like *How to Stay Under the Radar from The IRS and The Government.* Somebody gave it to me, I hadn't even read it.

"They searched my house for nine hours and never found any of the joints. They were unbelievable.

"My Halliburton suitcases were in the barn. One of 'em says 'What do you use these for?'

"I said 'Luggage idiot.'

"They made me take the horses out and put 'em in the corral so they could take up the floors in the barn.

"The stalls had rubber matting topped with a mix of cedar and rosewood chips; it made them easy to clean. They took up this, took up that. The girls had to redo it all.

"They expected to find a lot of shit, mostly dope and cash; they were visibly upset. They went through everything and found nothing except for $17,000 in my sock drawer. They took it.

"I was pretty lucky they didn't come the week before; they would have found a box with 4 million bucks. I was waiting for my guys to get it and they had just come.

"Finally my wife came home like nothing had happened. She knew I could take care of it. She knew the baby would be fine, knew the maid took her.

"I didn't get arrested that time. 60 agents raided my house and nothing happened except for the $17,000 that was in the house.

"They went to my parents' house and Midge's house because somehow they knew she was involved with me. They wanted to know 'Did you give him money?'

"She just told them 'That's my brother. If he needed money and I had it, I would give it to him.'

"My phone kept ringing. My lawyer called. My in-laws called because they raided their house as well; they raided my father-in-law's law practice.

"It happened all over the country, all at the same time.

"Bobo got fired the next day and they tried to take his pension. I got a lawyer for him, helped him get his job back; then he retired and took his pension early."

"Later I told my accountant 'I'm spending half a million dollars on landscaping. I'm spending $600,000 to $700,000 buying horses.' I said 'They're looking all around and they see all this shit?'

"He asks 'Did they go in your closet?'

"I said 'Yeah but they're too stupid to know what anything costs.'

"After ten years my parents closed The Sheik. Business never went bad, they made the best food on earth; but the guy that owned the center sold.

"To that time he had never charged them dues. He told them they didn't have to pay because they were friends. But when he sold, the new owners wanted my parents to pay all the back dues.

"It was a lot of money. I didn't pay because they needed to retire. That was enough. Let them enjoy their lives."

And they did.

"In Tucson there's olive trees everywhere. My mother would take a ladder and pick them off the trees. She's an old lady and the police would say 'Ma'am – what are you doing?'

"She didn't care what anyone thought. 'I'm picking olives.'

"She'd bring 'em home and cure 'em. They would always come out good. She used to make prickly pear jelly too. It wasn't that good, I gotta tell you. It wasn't sweet enough for me.

"Now that my dad was retired he wanted to drive all the time. He said 'Let me and your brother go.'

"I'm like 'Dad, you're killing me.'

"He was a very nervous kind of guy. He knew Douglas had serious drug problems, so he always tried to coddle him.

"I used to tell him 'That's not the way to go. You guys baby him too much, give him too much.'

"My dad and Douglas wanted to make a trip one time, the two of them. So finally I let them go.

"So they're driving on the highway and they need to pull over to the side of the road for something. They decided to stop right *on the shoulder* like two dufuses.

"A cop car pulls up behind them and puts the flashers on.

"The cop says 'What's the emergency?'

"My dad says 'There's no emergency, we were just going to switch.'

"Cop said 'Well you have to get off the highway, you're not supposed to do this. Can I search the car?'

"My dad remembered what I told him. He said 'No, you cannot.'

"The policeman searched the car anyway; he found drugs in the trunk and arrested them.

"So they called me and I said 'Alright, I'm on it.' I bonded 'em out and they came home.

"When they had to go back for trial I had representation for 'em. I told 'em I wouldn't be there; I would never be there.

"The judge asks the cop 'Did he give you permission to search his car?'

"The officer said 'He told me *no*.'

"Judge said 'If he told you *no*, you can't search the car. What part of *no* do you not understand? Case dismissed.'

"Then he told my dad, 'We're sorry for your inconvenience.'

"All charges were dropped. I lost a couple hundred thousand dollars, but there were no payoffs.

"There was a record of his arrest, but it was Illegal Search and Seizure. That was the law."

One night in March Allen used his connections to rescue Missy's brother.

"Around 3 a.m. we got a call from Michael, he wanted to talk to me. He went to Cancun on spring break and got arrested.

"Sometimes they do that, round up college kids for smoking dope, throw 'em in jail and hold 'em until their families pay to let them out.

"Michael was scared; fortunately he knew who to call. I called my guys and they let him go right away. Nobody had to pay anything."

Did your father-in-law ever find out about that?

"No, I don't think so. He didn't know what I was up to."

Allen and Missy continued to live like celebrities.

"There was this nice restaurant in Telluride and it was our anniversary. My wife and I took her parents, brothers and Jo; she was still quite young.

"The couple at the next table was Darrel Hannah and JFK Jr. We weren't paying any attention to them.

"So my mother-in-law gets up to take pics of my wife and myself and JFK Jr. says 'No pictures!'

"We were like 'Who wants a picture of *you?*'

"My father-in-law says 'You can't even pass the bar exam!'

"In Telluride, nobody cares. We weren't there for them."

"In 1994 we went to George Foreman and Michael Moorer when Foreman was an old man fighting this guy for the championship. Missy and my sister Midge were with me; I got us a huge suite.

"I had a feeling Foreman can beat this guy.

"I bet a bunch on him to win by a knockout.

"He just kept punching on him and punching on him and he won by knockout – so I cleaned up. I took the money, went to the tables and won more. It was like I couldn't lose.

"After a while Missy got pregnant again, but we lost the second baby. I didn't understand how she reacted. I was trying to be patient, but we knew the child would have had something wrong with it. The miscarriage was better in the long run."

Did you have second thoughts about having another child?

"No, not yet. We had money, we were traveling, we were doing well. But we were having trouble getting pregnant again and she started looking for answers.

"Of course it was going to be my fault, my sperm count had to be low. I needed to drop off a sperm sample.

"My dad is driving us to the airport. We're going to a horse show and the doctor's office is on the way. I'm in the back seat beating off to Penthouse; I squirted into the cup, lidded it and took it in.

"The doctor checked it out. He says 'You've got a very high sperm count. It's not you.'

"We went for in-vitro bullshit; that cost me a fortune.

"Then we started doing it when she knew she was ovulating. I used to prop her ass up on pillows. I said 'That shit's getting in there. I'll see you later.'

"Finally we got pregnant again.

"Missy was pretty disciplined about not taking any drugs while pregnant, so I've got two really healthy kids.

"I started calling our little one 'Pajamas' because when I would tell her it was time to go to bed, she'd say NOOOOOO, I don't want pajamas!"

Allen went to great lengths to keep *all* his girls happy.

"I had bought Missy a Bulgari ring when we were in the south of France. I think I paid around $12,000. It was really beautiful. It had diamonds that swirled around at all angles; it just looked cool. There weren't too many like it.

"When her cousin got married in Vermont, we took the kids and stayed at a bed and breakfast with her parents. Our youngest was still a baby. It was all of us – her brothers, our kids, me and her sleeping all over the place and she lost the ring. She was really, really bummed out about it.

"When we came back home to Tucson I got on the phone. I called Bulgari in Los Angeles, told them who I was, told them where I bought the ring and asked them if they had it.

"They did, so I asked 'Can you get me a deal on it?'

"She gave me a small discount, like $1,000. So the one ring cost me nearly double – like $23,000.

"Missy had it good. She didn't need to take care of the girls because we had the nanny.

"Ella was awesome, she loved the kids." Like his own Carrie, "She fed 'em, made 'em whatever they wanted. She didn't live with us, but she'd stay late; sometimes she'd stay overnight. She got paid well.

"I bought her a car. I didn't want her to drive my kids around in a crap car, I wanted to know they were safe.

"She had a daughter who got pregnant when she was 15. She came to my wife to get an abortion and Missy took care of it. She could be nice to other people *sometimes*."

Allen believes "All life is about is making money, taking care of your family and being with people you care about.

"Before the girls were born, I was closer to Paulie than Peter because Peter didn't want to have anything to do with 'the business.'

"As I got older I related more to Peter. He was always above board, even when he knew what I was doing. He was like another voice of conscience. His children were pretty much grown already; but through the course of your life you realize who you want your kids around.

"Brian Williams decided he wanted to come to Tucson for a visit. He was living in Chicago then, playing for the Bulls and he was going to retire.

"I hadn't met his girlfriend yet and he really wanted me to meet her. They came to stay with us and brought their whole entourage.

"My wife freaked out. She walked in to find all these people and was ready to tell them to get out."

Allen defused the situation, assuring her "Brian's just a really nice, nice person. A gentleman, big and handsome – just a teddy bear."

They'd had some good years, but "Missy was getting so that she liked to create problems.

"Missy was into the drama. She was like 'So and so said this and that.' I just said 'Who gives a fuck.'

"I told her 'You get everything you fucking want, leave me alone.'

"She'd want to go shopping and I had all my cash in clips of $2,000 to $4,000. She'd say 'I need four or five clips.'

"So boom – 'Here. GO. Knock yourself out.'

His main concern was the children.

"I was in Arizona, so I was confident they were going to have a good childhood.

"At first I didn't have a childproof fence around the pool cuz I thought it would look ugly; but there's a lot of kids that drown in pools, so when the girls were born I put one in. It came out pretty nice. It was like weathered steel and it had a gate only an adult could open.

"I made sure they could swim as soon as they could walk. I made sure they knew how to get in and out of the pool."

"My house was like a resort, so people came to visit. I always had friends' kids over.

"I'd let my kids bring field trips from their school. It was fun. They'd come to the house and see the ranch and see how everything was done.

"The girls were safe around the horses. They could walk underneath and I knew they weren't going to get kicked or anything like that. I took my oldest riding with me all the time.

"One winter we were in a huge wash full of melted snow that was coming down off the mountain. It's freezing cold, her horse is running and her reins broke.

"My horse was faster, I had her run as fast as he could go. I caught up to her, grabbed her off the horse, rolled off mine and let her fall on top of me.

"We fell in the water and it was freezing. Both horses kept going. I thought 'These goddamned horses!' I was so pissed.

"It was a four mile walk back to the house. When we got there, the horses were standing at the front gate like 'What took you guys so long?'"

Beyond caring for his family's physical security, Allen took pains to plan for their *financial* security. That involved stashing money safely outside of the country.

"I never wanted the girls to have anything to do with my business. I just wanted them to have money and be happy. And to this day that's my goal.

"I had a friend who used to ship yachts to the south of France in the summertime. I'd meet him with a box, like a luggage box. I'd have 3 or 4 million dollars in there.

"I paid him pretty good, so he never looked in the box; he never cared.

"I told him I'd meet him in St. Tropez or Monaco or wherever he was taking the boat. And then I'd put the money in the bank.

"I would have liked to have more kids, but things started to go sour. It got so that Missy didn't want me to be close to my family.

"She didn't want them to come over, she didn't want me going over there and she didn't want me to do anything without her.

"She even made my parents feel uncomfortable, which I hated about her.

"They were getting older, but they were still doing good. They cooked every day at home. My dad still had the pizza oven in the garage. He rigged it with extra gas to make it extra hot because regular heat doesn't get it hot enough.

"There was a Lebanese guy that they knew a couple houses down on their street; sometimes he'd come over and try to get some of my dad's pita bread.

"My oldest still remembers helping my dad make the bread. When it would come out of the oven, he would put butter and honey on it. It was unbelievable.

"Imagine, for a kid – fresh hot bread with butter and honey. There is nothing better than that. She loved it."

Whereas at home "Missy was addicted to working out and not eating so there was never any fucking food in the house. How can you not have food in your house?

"I told my girls, I said 'Your mom's anorexic; always has been, always will be.'"

"When Missy said she wanted to leave, I said 'Go ahead.' At that point I've had it, I've had enough.

"Except" – as he confessed – "I was no day at the beach."

During monsoon season flash floods come out of nowhere. They could be deadly; in 2015 twenty people died near the Utah-Arizona border.

"It was monsoon season and I was going to get my kids from school.

"They had Road Closed signs on both sides of the road, but I didn't pay attention. There was a wash flowing, but I wasn't worried. My truck was jacked up way high. It had four wheel drive and a winch, so I knew I could go through.

"I got stuck in the middle of the wash.

"I put it in four wheel drive and couldn't get it out. I wasn't sunk in the water, it just wouldn't move.

"I look up and there are police on the other side; I know I'm going to get a ticket.

"I got out and pulled the winch out to tie it onto a tree. I just needed a little traction to get out, but the sand on the road gets slippery so my tires wouldn't grab.

"I get within earshot and the policeman says 'You know I gotta give you a ticket.'

"And now there's a news crew. The camera guy is filming me and he has his camera right in my face.

"Finally I got mad, I said 'That's enough. I don't want that camera in my face! If you do it again I'm going to fucking knock you out!'

"The police tell the cameraman 'You should probably get that camera out of here.'

"I had to call Missy to go get the kids.

"My cousins saw me on TV; they had a big laugh."

"And then I was going to teacher conferences for my kid and my doctor had just given me these new drugs. I took them and during the conference I'm drooling and trying to stay awake.

"The teacher had to be thinking 'No wonder this kid's a mess.'

"My wife's yelling at me 'What the heck's the matter with you?'

"I said 'I didn't know what they were going to do to me!'

"I was still into the Quaaludes too. I loved those things; they made me feel goofy and relaxed.

"My cousin came over with some pills, but he warned me 'They're really strong!'

"I'm like 'Yeah, yeah, *blah, blah, blah.*' I took one and drank a beer.

"Next thing I know it's 4:30 in the morning and my wife is shaking me. I'm face down on the cutting board in my gourmet kitchen. She woke me up and took me to bed.

"My cousin had given me rufies. Missy used to get so disgusted with me it was unbelievable."

15 Telling the Truth

"Raymond had been taking care of everything in Detroit ever since I told him his brother George wasn't competent. With Raymond we were going gangbusters; until he started doing coke and taking shortcuts.

"So he's out here at the horse show with me and we've got 15,000 tons in the warehouse.

"I'm thinking *When we get rid of this 15,000 tons, I'm retiring; I'm done. I'll have another 6 or 7 million in cash. I can put that away and do the work that I do that is legit.*

"Raymond's thinking everything is copacetic, everything is going great. He left another cousin in charge. He didn't think they'd be needing anything because they had loaded him up.

"Except one of Raymond's contacts was dealing dope to people he shouldn't have trusted.

"While Raymond's in Scottsdale with me, the cousin calls and says he needs 300 or 400 pounds, 'something minimal.' Raymond had given him permission to do that.

"They go to the warehouse and it's a sting – they set him up. They arrest him, lock him up, take all the dope and raid everyone's house that's related to Raymond.

"The Macomb County Sheriff's Department or whoever was so overjoyed about the amount of dope they confiscated and the money that they got that they didn't turn it over to the feds. That's 15,000 pounds plus – *5.3 million dollars.*

"They didn't make it a federal crime, they made it a county crime. It was very fortuitous for me that they didn't turn it over to federal. If they had, they'd probably have got me then.

"They're thinking Raymond's cousin is Raymond, so he's not saying anything yet. *But I know him, so I know he's gonna.*

"I was just devastated. I had to beg Raymond to turn himself in. It took two days to talk him into it.

"I'm like 'How in the fuck could you do this bro? I cannot even tell you how mad I am at you right now. You think you're going to go on the run and leave us all hanging? I don't think so. You made this mess, you're going to go home.

"I said 'And – by the way – your cousin's locked up and they think he's you. When they find out he's not you, he's going to tell. What do you think is going to happen to you?'

"I told him 'I'll do whatever I can to get you out of this, but you have to go home and turn yourself in so they'll let your cousin out.'

"I had to pay a judge. If it had gone federal, I would have been in trouble. But since they kept it local, I could find out what his price was.

"We paid the judge $100,000. It was a lot of money at that time, but it was peanuts compared to everything else."

"So now it's 1998 and there's this big article in Detroit. I flew to Chicago, met with Dale, got the newspapers and read 'em.

"My family is reading 'em too and they know they're talking about me. Everybody who reads it that *knows* me *knows* they don't know who they're talking about. 'Someone who once lived in Detroit, now lives in Tucson.'"

"Cindy's like 'What are you, Keyser Söze from *The Usual Suspects*? What are you, that guy? What's the matter with you? This is unbelievable. How do I explain it to your nephews and nieces?'

"Nobody ever knew what I was. I never told anybody anything. There's no reason for anybody to know. Unless I need something, they're not going to know about me.

"My business in Detroit was running OK until the fuckup with Raymond. When he got arrested he knew he had to do his time and he said he was finished.

"His little brother George was taking back over then; he couldn't fuck it up any worse than what Raymond had done. The others went with him and I got out."

There was a problem with the way it went down.

Allen explained. "It's a business. If you bought my business, you gotta pay me. *They just stole it.*

"Ozzie was saying he wasn't working with them anymore. That's what he'd always tell me. I'm like 'OK, whatever dude.' I always suspected it, but I didn't have any proof."

It was coming.

"When Raymond fucked up he lost a lot of money, so we all came up with a figure to cover the loss; it was 3 million each.

"But then George didn't want to pay. He had an attitude towards me. He was mad from before, because I threw him out. He was *snippy*. He says 'We took care of it; *ask your partner.*'

"That's how I knew Ozzie was with my people in Detroit.

"He went back with my cousin and Dale.

"Over the course of years, Dale had gotten to know the Mexicans. So they just kind of basically took what I had done and kept going with it.

"The people that I know from down there and their nephews up here say Ozzie told them I was too reckless, too wild, too flamboyant; something had to be done.

"Whatever their reasons were they wanted me out, it was still my thing and I should have gotten paid something. I should have gotten a percentage of what they were doing because it was my business. It should have been like a buyout.

"But it's better that I didn't because I probably would have been arrested then and thrown in. So it kind of worked out for the best.

"I was just so mad that we had lost pretty much all I had worked for all those years. I was going to retire with 20 million dollars cash. I really was going to be done and just relax, live a happy married life and spoil the girls.

"There was no reason for me to keep going. What more could I do? How much is enough?"

He paused.

"It would have never been enough."

"The judge went light on Raymond, gave him a good sentencing – 10 months' work release; but he continued to fuck up.

"Doing cocaine always brings out the worst in people if you keep doing it. It's just the way cocaine is.

"Most people can't do cocaine and stop. They do it the first time and it's 'Wow – this is a good rush!' But then you're always chasing that initial rush and you can't ever achieve it at that first intensity. That's how people got hooked.

"When Raymond pulled a gun on The Rocketman, I said 'We can't have that.'

"So I flew there, had a meeting with Raymond and told him 'You have to go to Betty Ford because you do too much cocaine.'

"I sent him, I paid $30,000 for it.

"I figured maybe that'll help. He met stars and other addicts in there that were getting high.

"So three days later he calls and says 'I'm cured.'

"I said 'OK.'

"I'm thinking *You either want to do it or you don't want to do it. You can't force somebody to do something.*

"So after he leaves Betty Ford he meets this born-again guy named Bud. He knows Raymond has a problem.

"Somehow some way Bud and his friends convince Raymond they're going to have a ceremony that will cure him of his drug addiction. They prayed over him and laid hands on him.

"They told him he started talking in tongues and he believed them. All I know is, to this day – *so far as I know* – he doesn't do drugs."

•   •   •

"As time went on, the cartel always wanted more money, always wanted things their way.

"The Sinaloa cartel is the biggest criminal organization in the country. They come up in black Suburbans and they've got ten guys with guns. They have pistoleros, body guards and machine guns. They have the 50 caliber guns so they can shoot down helicopters if they come overhead.

"They'd roll up with their cock fighting roosters and they're ready to gamble.

"We had horse races at Rancho Sandario, a small town on the border. It was a little quarter mile track with a photo finish that was set up right.

"They could just come across with their horse and jockey and I'd get a horse and jockey in the gate and they'd run. We'd bet from $40,000 to $50,000 a race."

Allen was granted a rare honor; he was invited to ride their dancing horses. According to *telesurftv.net*, "Sinaloans, especially drug traffickers, are known to breed dancing horses to show off at parties and gatherings."

Allen says "It's pretty cool when you're on them. Some, their mouths are sensitive, but some aren't and you have to keep a tight rein.

"Lady Cash was sensitive, she knew what I wanted. If I pulled hard she knew she had to do a slide stop.

"I was a pretty good horseman, skilled with the horses and riding. The cartel respected that, it's a macho thing to them.

"And then, once you're in with them and they like you, they don't ever want to let you go. They just keep sending more and more; and you sell it.

"I was getting good weed, the top stuff.

"They'd call. They'd come and meet me at the border towns and show me what they had. *Los Jefes* [a Mexican film] and *Sicario* – that's kind of what it's really like on the borders.

"They have cameras on every power pole in border towns now. Some of the bigger towns like Juarez, Nogales and Tijuana, that's where all the high tech stuff is. It's not easy getting it in.

"When you're coming into the city of Nogales by Tucson, you come over a rise and you can see down into the city. The border is a port of entry with trucks backed up for probably four or five miles.

"You think they search all those trucks? Once in a while they check one, here or there. With NAFTA now, they don't really check the vehicles coming through that hard. They'll put maybe 8,000 pounds of cocaine in the front of a semi.

"To get the bigger loads across, a lot of times the cartels will set their own guys up. They'll arrange to have a young kid cross with like 20 or 30 pounds of dope in his car. They know he's not going to do a lot of time, only a year or so.

"The kid knows he's going to go away for however long, but they'll take care of him either before he goes in or when he gets out.

"They'll call in an anonymous tip and tell the cops a guy in a certain car has drugs. That distracts the guard so they can get their big loads through to a staging area, stash house or whatever.

"We would take all the dope out to the ranch and load it into whatever vehicle we were going to use to transport it."

"There's other towns all along the border that you could go to. You could just be in a car on one side and not even go through a port of entry. There's some like that in California, Arizona, New Mexico and Texas.

"If a cartel sees another cartel in their area, they'll stop their vehicles.

"Usually three or five guys with machine guns will get out and start blasting away. They think *They shouldn't have been in our area* and they don't care who gets hit. It happened – it *happens* a lot, mostly in the border towns.

"Or they'll put a hit on somebody that wasn't playing ball. On the streets, when they get out of the car they'll have a bandanna from their nose down and something to cover their head.

"They can see you, but you don't know who they are. You only know that shots are going to get fired. They would kill anybody, they didn't care.

"People that live there know. They hear shots ringing, they get their kids, go somewhere and try to hide because these guys have Uzis and everything else.

"One time the cartel sent word that they wanted to see Ozzie. He didn't want to go, so they sent some guys up here, threw him in the trunk and took him down there.

"He thought *This is it*. He gets word to me, 'Well they need money.'

"So I got them money and they let him go. I think they needed it for their payoffs.

"That's how they are. It was all brutal. It's not good dealing with them."

There aren't a lot of options.

"You stay with one cartel. You get in big trouble if you deal with one cartel and go to another cartel; you're going to get killed – plain and simple. They're going to put a hit on you."

"Gary Triano was a pain in the ass. He kind of liked to welch on his bets and he was doing business with the cartel. They didn't ask my permission to do what they did to him.

"We're playing golf one day at La Paloma. He couldn't golf for shit that day. Me neither. That was what it was; we golfed.

"Afterwards we're sitting there in the men's clubhouse; it was me, Ozzie, Freddie Krueger and maybe Futon Ron.

"When Triano went out to start his Eldorado, we heard a huge explosion. It blew up right in the parking lot, just blew to pieces; he burned to death.

"I got outta there quick."

The hit was never solved.

The Tucson Citizen reported that "The pipe bomb, containing at least 1 pound of black powder, was powerful enough to blow the roof off the car and shoot the windshield over 40-foot trees and into a swimming pool more than 70 feet away. A 500-foot radius around the car was strewn with debris."

Allen says "They came and questioned a few of us. I said 'I have no idea, the car blew up; what the fuck do I know.

"I said 'He doesn't owe me enough money to blow his car up.'"

The Associated Press later described Triano as "a developer who made millions investing in Indian bingo halls and slot-machine parlors in Arizona and California before Congress authorized tribes to open full-blown casinos. But after the real estate market declined and he lost control of his gambling interests, Triano went broke. That's around the time Phillips filed for divorce, prosecutors say, because Triano could no longer support her expensive tastes."

According to Allen, "He had his own contacts, like a lot of people in Tucson do. He was a friend of Donald Trump for a little bit. And he was doing his own thing. From what I understand, he wasn't paying."

CBSnews.com reported that "Triano's sister and children all took issue with the defense characterization of their father as a mob associate and swindler."

The press said that at the time of his death Triano was a defendant in at least 54 civil cases, accused of 'nonpayment to business partners or defaulting on loans.'

The Arizona Daily Star said he owed lenders and associates more than $9 million.

Allen says "He wasn't a mob associate, but he was definitely a swindler. He owed everybody money. He had a zillion enemies."

•   •   •

"The IRS had been on me since about 1990. I was never charged with anything, but they were investigating me to try to charge me for *something*.

"They couldn't really get me except for I had a check from a real estate deal I had done in '89. I cashed it and went to Vegas and never paid taxes on it.

"It took them 11 years to find that check.

"In 2000 a $17,000 tax bill turned into a $250,000 penalty. I was ready to pay and plead guilty to filing a false tax return; but before I did, my lawyer insisted the U.S. Attorney give me immunity.

"My lawyer was good friends with this U.S. Attorney. I was in his office when he called him.

"He kind of went to bat for me, told him I was a good guy. He made it seem like I knew something and would tell them.

"He told him 'Let's make a good deal for him and the next one, I'll do you a favor.'

"I got blanket immunity. That meant anything I had done previously, i.e. selling drugs for all those years, I could have murdered people, whatever; I was immune from prosecution for it.

"When I got charged with a tax violation I had to go turn myself in to the U.S. Marshalls. I did it the day of our meeting at the U.S. Attorney's office in Tucson.

"I walked in the front door of the U.S. Marshall's office, got photo and fingerprints and walked out the back door. I didn't spend a minute in jail for any of this. Usually they'll arrest you.

"The lady that did the background checks – she wanted the U.S. Attorney to put me in jail and not let me out until everything was over. I heard him tell her straight out, 'That's not happening.'

"A few months later, before my sentencing, it's mandatory that you go in there and answer their questions. It's part of the Federal Government taking responsibility for what their actions were.

"So I'm in a meeting room with my lawyers and all the alphabet people, every one of 'em, every agency. My attorney had established the meeting rules, told them which questions they could ask.

"They couldn't ask anybody's names or anything like that. I told them up front, 'I'll tell you what I did, but I'll never talk about anyone else.'

"They wanted to know about Bobo. They were willing to eat their own young if they think they did something wrong. They had already fired him and tried to take his pension in '93.

"I told them 'We didn't talk the year after they raided me. I ran into him in the airport in Tucson and he asks how I'm doing.

"I said 'Good.'

"He said 'Thanks for everything.'

"I said 'No problem.'

"I told them he never gave me any information.

"I said 'I haven't talked to him for two years. When you guys were investigating me, we thought it was best that we don't talk. So we hadn't talked.'

"They didn't know I was dealing drugs, they just knew I was making a lot of money.

"They said 'Well then, we see how you were making this much money in the horse business. What were you doing other than what we have here?'

"I told 'em 'You know what? I was selling marijuana.'

"They said 'Oh, OK.' They didn't think anything was abnormal about that.

"I had already told them 'I will never tell on anyone I did business with. I would get killed, it would be a death sentence.' I said 'Whatever you do to me doesn't matter.'

"So they asked 'How much were you making?'

"I said 'I dunno, seven or eight hundred thousand dollars.'

"They want to know – 'A year?'

"I go 'No, a month.'

"Their jaws hit the floor. They were looking at the horse business and they were totally off course.

"They were fuming. That's why they kept coming after me. They didn't stop 'til this year [2016] when all the liens and stuff go off my records.

"After the meeting my lawyer said 'Telling 'em about the money was the best thing you coulda told 'em. They can never do anything from this point forward. You've got immunity; you've got everything.'

"When I went in for my sentencing in front of the judge – we weren't even in the court room yet – my attorney said 'Don't worry about it, you're going to get probation.'

"How do they know already? They must have made a deal with the prosecutor and the prosecutor went before the judge. They recommend the sentence.

"I pled guilty to filing a false tax return.

"My attorney said 'Make sure your fines are paid because they could put you in jail otherwise.'

"I was going to get an armored car, drive it to the IRS and pay in quarters.

"My lawyer begged me not to do it, so I took good old American greenbacks.

"All my taxes were done and audited and the government signed off on them. I'm all caught up and I get put on probation for three years.

"On the way back down you get more paranoid, but you are also kind of in denial a little bit. *They can't get me. They're not going to get me.*

"I'm thinking *I'm protected from every angle.*"

But they could and they would.

"Now I'm on probation and I have to go to El Paso and handle a situation for numbnuts Rocketman. By this time he was in his 40s; he looked like his dad. He was Sicilian, short and stocky as a brick shithouse.

"I'm like *Goddammit, how will I get to El Paso?* It's over 300 miles. I couldn't fly and I wasn't going to drive my car.

"I had somebody rent a car and I drove through the checkpoints no problem.

"El Paso used to be a good border town, one of the best; it's shit now because of the violence.

"I get there, meet the guys, and it's good; they're going to transport product to Detroit for me.

"I said 'Alright' and then I went and smoked some really good dope at my friend's house. I was so fucked up I walked out, tripped over a cast iron fence and split my head open at the hairline.

"I was bleeding profusely and I couldn't go to a hospital because I wasn't supposed to be there.

"Strangers were trying to help but I told 'em, 'Just give me a towel or something – I'll go to my hotel and get the bleeding to stop.'

"When I got to my hotel I had to walk through the lobby with a bloody towel around my head. I kept telling people 'I'm fine, I'm fine – leave me alone.'

"One guy saw I was bleeding pretty badly and asked me if I needed help.

"I told him 'I'm perfectly fine' – but he called the paramedics anyway. I got back to my room and I'm bleeding through towels, there's bloody towels everywhere.

"The paramedics knocked on the door and I said 'No, I'm fine. It's nothing.'

"They said 'You don't look fine.'

"I couldn't stop the bleeding even when they were at the door.

"I insisted 'It's not that bad.' *But it was.*

"Somehow I managed to survive the night and drive home the next day. That's how I was. Go big or go home.

"If you can't run with the big dogs you gotta stay on the porch."

16 Going Legit

On 9/11 the first plane hit the tower at 8:45 a.m. New York time. It was 5:45 a.m. in Tucson.

Allen remembers "Missy saw the news on TV and she kept trying to wake me up.

"I said 'I don't want to look at anything.'

"When I realized what was happening, I started watching and calling my friends to see if they were alright. It personally affected people I cared about.

"Slavik owns apartment buildings in Manhattan, he was in midtown. Ray's office was near the Intrepid Museum on the west side of Manhattan.

"I called those guys and we were all glued to the news."

After 9/11 the government started spending millions on 'drugs and terror' ads that accused recreational users of supporting international terrorism.

We talked about it. Allen was having *none* of it.

"Why would al Qaeda have anything to do with cocaine? They don't work with the Colombians. The people in al Qaeda think they're the best thing since sliced bread. Why would they even consider working with infidels? They *wouldn't*."

But they could follow their example. In July 2015 Don Winslow, author of *The Cartels*, wrote an article for The Daily Beast; *What ISIS Learned From the Cartels*.

He wrote "In May 2005, a cartel boss associated with the Beltran-Leyva branch of the Sinaloa Cartel captured four Zeta hitmen sent to kill him. He took them upstairs in a safe house, lined the floor and walls with black plastic bags, and then 'interviewed' them on a handheld Sony camcorder. After the prisoners confessed their various crimes, he shot them in the head—on camera—then mailed copies of the tape to various television outlets...

"The television stations didn't broadcast the tape in its gory entirety, but it soon went viral on the Internet ....

"The images—decapitations, immolations, disembowelment, torture—were truly terrifying, and that was the point. Like the present-day ISIS, the cartels were trying to seize and control territory, and to do that they needed to intimidate the local population.

"The videos were a statement of pure power, a way of proclaiming, 'Look what we can do. Look what we're *willing* to do. This could be you.'"

Allen believes "That whole al Qaeda spin was bullshit, just something they said so the government could put the Patriot Act in to know what everybody is doing.

"They put the patriot act in to keep track of us. They want more power over us. Once they changed the law and went to the Patriot Act, they could charge us as terrorists smuggling drugs. We had to tweak how we did things.

"They started listening to everybody's phone calls. They have trigger words that will automatically tape your calls. We had no privacy any more.

"It was a good time to get out of the business.

"I'm sort of coasting at this point. I had money and Raymond's born-again friend Bud had an idea for some kind of software involving banking and travel. It was a good idea that Bud said 'Just came to me from The Lord.'

"Tom Ku of Silicon Valley was working him, he was one of the first guys at Sun Microsystems. They had a team of guys working on coding.

"Raymond was paying him money out of our proceeds, $300,000 to $400,000 at a time. By the time me and Ozzie found out what he was doing, we were into it for close to a million dollars.

"He needed more money, so we had to take a trip to New York. I think we brought him $300,000.

"We stayed in a hotel while Raymond stayed in his apartment overlooking Central Park; $25,000 a month rent I'm paying for that apartment. Liza Minnelli was living in that building.

"At this point we're funding the whole deal and looking for more investors. Bud sets up a meeting with us and Michael Hammer, the sole heir to Arm & Hammer. He happens to be one of these Holy Roller born-again Christians as well.

"So we go to Hammer's house and Bud walks in with a brand new Breitling watch, probably $15,000 or $20,000 at least – and a solid gold Cartier pen that he didn't used to have.

"Oz and I both noticed. It was a bad situation.

216

"I wanted to say 'You use our money to buy shit like this for yourself?'

"Hammer is waffling and all of a sudden I realize we don't have anything in writing. I want to know what we own. I'm not going to continue to fund this if I don't have my stuff in writing.

"Later Bud comes to my house with Raymond and it was just weird. They were weird. They start talking about 'You have to do this.'

"I'm like 'I don't have to do shit.'

"I wanted my stuff and the percentage we owned in our name – I wanted a contract. Everybody's supposed to get their fair share, it's just the way it is.

"Bud wasn't willing to give us a contract for what we deserved, so I told him 'Go fuck yourself.' I said 'You're not getting any more money from me' and I threw 'em all out."

While weighing his options, Allen convinced Ku to come over to his side.

"I took him away as CEO. I knew Hammer was living in Grand Cayman and I can't trust this guy Bud who's supposedly 'with God,' so I tell Ku 'Here's money. Fly down there and see if Hammer wants to do the project with us.'

"I told him to explain that we have a good product and everybody loves it. The software scheduled things, like if you need to go on a business trip, it did everything for you. It made your reservations.

"If there was anything you requested – like a book you wanted to read while you were in the hotel – it would be there in your room. Anything you wanted to see or do, it would arrange. We were working on scheduling tickets for NHL games and sports events.

"We were very fair and generous but Hammer didn't want to come."

"I didn't have money from drugs anymore, but I thought I was OK because the U.S. Attorney had told me 'You can take your money you have stashed and put it in the bank.'

"That's how I funded the dot com.

"We were told 'We won't tax you. We won't come after you.' Which was a total lie because they were stealing money from me the whole time.

"*Only I didn't know that then.*

"My older brother got involved; he put a couple hundred thousand in it. He knew there was a chance it could go bad.

"My sister Cindy got involved.

"Nadra and her husband are schoolteachers, so I didn't ask them. Nadra was upset, 'Why didn't you ask me? How do you know I don't want to invest?'

"I said 'Nadra you're more than welcome but teachers don't make a lot of money. I just didn't want to put you in a position that could hurt you.'

"She said 'But I want in.'

"So I gave her some of my stock and she gave me $25,000.

"I was putting $250,000 to $400,000 in the bank a week *cash*. I'd go in, they'd see me, they'd go in the back, count it with the counters and I'd just deposit. It went into my business account.

"I'd send checks or wire the money to where it had to go.

"We opened an office and I hired a payroll company to handle the details. Tom hired code writers and people that he knew in San Jose and Silicon Valley.

"We got a money guy from Price Waterhouse; he was a vice president there. We even hired the top guy from Morgan Stanley.

"My father-in-law was negotiating the deals. Some of the people we hired were already making $300,000 to $400,000 a year – why do they want to come with us? Because we're paying big salaries and they see an opportunity to make *more* money and have stock.

"All this time we're paying these guys our nut was $300,000 *a month* – not including legal fees.

"We were doing SEC stuff, but we had it all pretty much under control. Our CEO knew how to do this."

"After a while I finally told my father-in-law what I'd been doing. I had to take him with me for a meeting up in Silicon Valley and he was wondering how I had all this money; so I told him.

"He suspected because we were talking more than 20 million dollars. Between real estate and horses I was doing well, but not *that* well.

"I told him how it was, how nobody's in danger and I'm very well respected. Everybody takes care of me.

"We ran into a situation where $150,000 in cash was needed on a Monday. I didn't have it at home, but I had it in San Diego.

"So I drove up to Phoenix, contacted my friend Shewy and said 'You want to go to dinner in San Diego? I just gotta pick up some money.'

"We got on a plane, got the money, had dinner and flew back.

"We used to pack cash in big manila envelopes with computer discs and carbon paper. Then we put the envelopes in a bag of clothes in the trunk.

"We had a few drinks at Shewy's house and I said 'I'm going to stay here for a little while tonight. I'll sleep on the couch and get up and go when I wake up.'

"So I try to sleep. After a couple hours I got up and started to drive home. It was 3:30 in the morning; I wanted to be home in time to get cleaned up and go to the bank.

"On the way home I *am* speeding, there was no question about that. I put all the windows down and was trying to put the moon roof back to help me stay awake.

"I swerved a little bit because I was tired.

"In Pinal County, close to Picacho Peak, two cops pull me over. The one asks if he could search my car.

"I said 'Fuck no.'

"He tries to anyway and I said 'FUCK NO, you have no permission! Absolutely *under no circumstances*, get the fuck out of here!

"I said 'You want to write me a ticket, write me a ticket!'

"I'm getting lippy so he throws me in the back of his car; but I still have my key fob. He unlocks the trunk from inside and as he goes to walk back around, I lock it with the fob. Finally he figures out I have the remote and he's really pissed.

"He takes my keys and looks in the car. Then he takes my fob and opens the trunk. He finds the bag with the clothes and envelopes, starts tearing open the envelopes and finds all hundreds.

"He says 'Hoo-ee boy, lookie here! Where'd you get all this money?'

"They take me to jail. The police station was still under construction. It had a teeny tiny cell; they just threw me in and locked me up.

"Him and his partner said they pulled me over for drunk driving, but I wasn't drunk at all because I slept. I knew I wasn't drunk but their office didn't even have a breathalyzer.

"There is no way I was drunk.

"They count the money. 'This is a lot of money.'

"They can take the money because that's their jurisdiction; you have to prove the money is legit. Even when you prove that it's legit, it's up to the county to make the final determination whether they're going to keep it or not.

"I called my lawyer. He says 'Don't worry about it.'

"He calls the U.S. Attorney.

"U.S. Attorney tells the cops 'This guy is legit, that's his money.'

"They said 'It's drug money. We're keeping it.'

"He said 'He's a business man, he's not up to anything.'

"But then some IRS agent went to the cops and told them 'This guy's a big deal, a very big deal and you should investigate him further.'

"This is after they heard my immunized testimony, which is completely illegal. It's a crime. They broke the law on several occasions with me.

"It didn't end there. I got my license suspended. The judge said 'I tend to believe the officer more than I believe you.'

"I said 'Alright, whatever. Nothing I can do about that.'

"I had to get special insurance for people who've had their license suspended. Got all that, but I didn't stop driving. I didn't give a shit. What are you going to do to me? Suspend it longer?

"My attorney managed to get $30,000 back. He took it for attorney fees, so I got zero.

"Later on one of those cops had the cojones to come to my house. He came in the back road and Missy happened to be in the barn. The Dutch windows were open so the breeze could come through.

"She was getting ready to go riding, backing up a horse when he came up to the window and tried to talk to her.

"He tells her 'You know, your husband is a very bad man.'

"She says 'You know what? You're on private property and I'd like you to get the fuck out of here.'

"She was good that way."

"That year Missy got some kind of sickness where she couldn't get out of bed all day long.

"My oldest would come in to see me; she was just like me with the sarcasm. She said 'Is mom having a bad hair day?'

"I'd say 'Yeah honey' and we'd hang out.

"I took Missy to the Mayo clinic in Scottsdale and they couldn't figure out what was wrong with her.

"At first they thought maybe she had some kind of cancer, but turns out it was a recurring infection. They'd get it under control for a little bit and it'd come right back.

"I thought *If they can't fix it here, we'll send her to the original Mayo Clinic in Minnesota.*

"Fortunately I had really good insurance. After the accident they'd paid $50,000 for two Lear Jet air ambulances to get us out of there

"So I put Missy on a plane to Minnesota. Her mother was going to meet her there."

Allen stayed behind with their daughters.

"We had two young kids. We had maids and nannies and whatever, but if both your parents are gone – that's not cool. I stayed home and took care of the kids."

I didn't understand why he felt the need to explain until he told me about the complication.

"There was this guy who was in love with Missy since high school. He happened to live in Rochester, Minnesota – where the Mayo Clinic is.

"We had a little history with Brad. I called him 'Brad the Buffoon' – he's an agent for big time golfers. He makes a lot of money.

"When Missy was in the clinic, he'd go every day and say things about me. He told her 'He doesn't care about you, he's not even here.'

"He wrote her love letters. He even started calling my house.

"I said 'Look motherfucker, don't call here anymore' but he kept calling.

"I told Missy about it and she said some things. Maybe she started believing him, that he loved her and I didn't.

"I said 'Are you out of your fucking mind?'

"Buffoon and I got in a little argument one night in the small town where he lives. We were with a bunch of people, so we went outside.

"My friend Magoo was with us, he went to school with Missy.

"The Buffoon was there trying to talk to my wife and I said 'Why don't you just get the fuck out of here.'

"Magoo slapped him like a little girl.

"After that he wrote a book and said that he took on the mob. It was the funniest thing I ever heard.

"When Missy finally got better I said 'You want to leave? I could give a fuck less. Leave.' I wasn't going to stop her at that point.

"I said 'If you want to leave GO.'"

"It was 2002 and we were just getting ready to take the dot com public. Ozzie and I owned 35 million shares. Pre IPO they thought we'd open in the 40s and go to $90 per share.

"I figured *if this goes through I'll never have to work again.* I'm like *I should be set for life.*

"I didn't know Missy was only sticking around because she thought we were going to get a huge payday.

"Bottom line was the market crashed in 2002 – but it did a correction. While we were bickering back and forth with Goldman Sachs and Prudential as to who's going to take us public, the NASDAC dropped from 4,000 to 2,000.

"Prudential was ready to sign. I told our CEO to 'Just take the deal.'

"The next week the market went back down and both Goldman Sachs and Prudential pulled the plug on us. They weren't going to do an IPO in that environment.

"We would have done well had the market not had that correction. I knew it was over with then. We lost $20 million dollars.

"Another company that was trading at $14/share was going to buy us out because they liked the product. We structured a deal where we were going to get their stocks at value.

"It took the lawyers 10 months to negotiate the deal. We had a 6 month lockout where we couldn't sell our stock; we would have crippled the company because we owned so much of it.

"By the time the deal was negotiated their stock went from $14/share to like 60 or 70 cents.

"To this day I don't remember the name of the company. I wound up giving Missy all the stock. I don't know what happened. I don't know if they got any money out of it or went bankrupt.

"I had another potential business deal in the works, so I borrowed money from Futon Ron and put him as second on the house."

Did you have any sense of foreboding?

"Not at all. We'd been friends for a long time.

"We were always straightforward with each other.

"Obviously everybody that got involved in the dot com lost their money.

"Now Nadra's husband says I'm the worst. We don't really have a relationship because of him. She can't talk on the phone to me, she can't do anything. She texted me 'Happy Birthday' on my birthday – which is nice. But, I mean, that's our relationship? That's bullshit.

"Both of her daughters got married and she didn't tell me about either one. Her husband and The Rocketman get together and jerk about me."

David was a different story.

"There was such an age difference with my older brother that we never spent a lot of time together. When I had a bunch of money he'd come and stay with me and we'd golf every day. We'd joke around and got along well.

"We had a good relationship until my wife was getting ready to leave me. I knew she planned on taking the kids.

"We had a $2,500 electric bill. Missy had maxed out all the credit cards and I only had cash. I called David and said 'Put it on your card and I'll get the money out of the bank tomorrow.'

"So he called and put it on his credit card.

"As soon as the bank opened Missy went in and took the money. I couldn't even pay him back.

"I said 'Why did you do that?'

"She just didn't say anything.

"I told him what happened, that I would get it to him, but his wife said I was just a liar and he believed her. She never liked me anyways. I didn't lie, so it was just like she took him away. It was exactly like something Missy would do."

"While Missy was dating The Buffoon we still had sex.

"After she left him he got violent with her. He punched her and she had a black eye. She called the cops and they arrested him, but nothing ever really happened to him. I don't think she went through with the charges.

"And then somebody fucked up his car. He thought for sure it was me. I'm like 'Why would I beat up your car? I don't even care about you, you're nothing to me. If I'm going to hit something, it's going to be you.'

"It was just a stupid thing. She left him eventually."

"After all that my probation officer was worried about me. She kept telling me 'You don't have a job! You *need* to get a job!'

"I said 'What do I need a job for?'

"She says 'Go be a greeter at Walmart. Just do something. I can't have you laying around screwing college girls all the time.'"

17 Dropping Dirty

"Kevin Porter – 'KP' we used to call him – used to work for me as a bouncer at Gilligan's. I was in Arizona when he called and told me Brian Williams was missing.

"Then Brian's mother called me. She asked me to look around and see if I could locate his brother in Tucson. Him and his brother Kevin [a.k.a. Miles Dabord] never got along; I don't know if it was jealousy or what.

"Brian was almost 7' tall, but basketball wasn't his thing. He was good at it, but that wasn't the end all be all with him. He used it as a way to make money.

"I used to say 'Come play with me' and I'd take him to pickup games at the Jewish Community Center.

"Most guys that are playing college basketball at that elite level wouldn't just come play at a pickup game with some guy. They just wouldn't do it. He'd do it and the other players would say 'That's not fair!'

"In the last three years of his Pistons contract he walked away from a $30 million contract. He didn't care, he had enough money. He had a big yacht, he had a captain; he took his girlfriend and they were going to sail to the South Pacific."

On July 7, 2002 all three vanished west of Tahiti. In September Miles showed up in Phoenix.

The New York Times reported "The police in Phoenix detained Dabord on Sept. 5 after he said he was Brian Williams and signed receipts with that name while trying to buy $152,000 in gold. The police did not have enough evidence to arrest him, a police spokesman, Tony Morales, has said. Dabord also had credit cards and a passport belonging to Brian Williams, the police said."

On September 13 arrest warrants were issued for Miles. On September 14 the boat was found in Tahiti; the boat's name had been changed and investigators found blood inside and out.

They learned Brian and his party – including his brother – stopped on an island near Tahiti with plans to continue to New Zealand and Hawaii.

On September 25, 2002 the search was called off.

According to the New York Times "The ocean is nearly 10,000 feet deep in the area, Prosecutor Michel Marotte said Tuesday, and investigators suspect the bodies were weighted down before being thrown overboard. Continuing the search at this point would be futile, Marotte said."

As Allen remembers it, "The brother made it there by himself. Everything happened at sea, so it's hard to say how it all started. He killed everyone on board, took Brian's ID and tried to buy rare coins. The dealer knew it wasn't him.

"He took off to Ensenada and OD'd."

At the time the story came to press, they reported that Brian's mother intended to have her son's apparatus removed soon.

Allen says "Their mother called me. She lost both sons. It was just tragic. The funeral was in L.A. I didn't even go."

The losses – financial and emotional – were piling up.

"I pled guilty in 2000, but they were still trying to investigate me in 2003. My lawyer said 'Let's wait and not file returns.'

"The IRS didn't do it right away, but suddenly in 2003 they started filing returns FOR me and charging ridiculous fines and penalties.

"Then, towards the end of my probation, they kept asking me for paperwork. I really didn't have it and I didn't know where it was.

"I told my probation officer 'I don't understand this at all.'

"She said 'Nobody here understands. Your case is so complicated, with the IRS asking for this and that.'

"I straight out told her 'I'm not giving them another piece of information so they can continue to fuck me.'"

At this point Allen had little to look forward to.

"My friend Ray came from New York to Tucson for his bachelor party and we went out with friends. I was supposed to be in his wedding. I'd be able to see my kids while I was out that way.

"My probation officer told me I *could not go*. She says 'You're *not* going to New York.'

"I said 'But my best friend's getting married.'

"She says 'I don't care, you're not going to New York.'

"Normally I would have just taken off; but this time I didn't."

"I'm just living my life when she calls and says 'You have to come in and see me in the morning.'

"I said 'Alright.' So I went and saw her.

"I had six months left on my probation when they violated me. I just didn't understand why they chose to do it at that time.

"My probation officer said she had nothing to do with it. She said the order probably came from higher up."

How did they violate your probation?

"Two ways. First, they told me they *could* violate it because part of the terms of my probation was to cooperate further with the IRS. I wasn't about to do that. They knew I knew everything but I wasn't going to tell 'em.

"And the second thing, they used that I dropped dirty. They just called me in out of the blue for tests and there were drugs in my system.

"Usually you have to go see your probation officer once a month and they do it then. The drugs that were in my system were legal prescription medications.

"They knew about the accident. They had all my records. They can't stop you from taking prescription medication. So I never had a clean UA [urine analysis] with them. Finally they stopped testing me because I was always dirty.

"And the next time they did it was right before they violated me. They used that I dropped dirty. I was pissed at that time, so I smoked weed. That could have been part of it too.

"She tells me 'Well, I have to violate your probation, but while I'm doing the paperwork, there are some people here that want to see you.'

"I say 'Who wants to see me?'

"She took me to this private office and two DEA agents were there waiting for me, an older guy and a younger guy. They say 'We know you're not doing anything, but we also know you've got money hidden all over.'

"It was true. I wasn't doing anything, but I had money stashed in places like Monte Carlo; they were trying to find it.

"I made it clear I didn't give a shit about what they were saying, but as soon as they started telling me details of things that were going on behind the scenes, I knew there was a snitch. And I knew it could only be one of two people; Dale or my cousin George in Detroit.

"They were the only ones that were always involved in the day to day stuff.

"In order to get to us – meaning Ozzie and I – the DEA would have to go through them.

"The grilling was nearly over when one of 'em says 'Do you know Dominic Corrado?'

"I remember thinking *God that's a weird question for them to ask me.* I don't know if they were trying to connect the dots that I was part of that family and that's how stuff was getting done in Detroit.

"I said 'Yeah, he was my uncle, but he's been dead a long time. Why don't you just leave him alone.'

"The younger agent was getting agitated.

"I said 'Who the fuck are you? I have socks older than you!'

"They said 'We also know somebody owes you over $3 million and we can help you collect.'

"I started laughing. 'The last time I checked, I don't need help collecting.'

"The rookie threatened me, he said 'We'll take that immunity and fucking tear it up.'

"I lose it. I said 'What, are you a *newbie?* If you think you can, why don't you just go ahead and try you stupid motherfucker.'

"The older agent said 'No, he didn't mean that. We were just having a conversation.'

"I said 'The conversation is over.'

"I got up and walked out. I said 'You know where I'll be. I'll be in jail.'

"They violated me and arrested me right there, threw me in the holding cells underneath the court. I sat there all day before they took me to jail.

"I was wearing a $28,000 Bulgari diving watch. My probation officer says 'Why don't you give me that, something could happen to it. I'll give it to your dad.'"

"I had to come back for a sentencing hearing with the judge. When they violate your probation, you've got to do whatever time they give you; they won't let you bond out.

"When I got to court, my attorney said I shouldn't have to do more than three months; they wanted nine months.

"The judge split the difference, so I got six."

Florence Correctional Center

"I was locked up from April to October.

"When I was locked up for those six months *I was pissed.* I shouldn't have been locked up, I didn't do anything wrong.

"When they violated my probation, to be honest, if somebody needed something, *I planned on making it rain pounds.*

"The problem was, I never knew consequences. Then, when they did finally hit, I'm on a 15 year down slope."

"Jails and prisons are profit centers. In Florence the federal prisons are CCA – Corrections Corporation of America – a publicly traded company. The more people in they have in jail, the more money they make."

CCA is the second-largest private prison company in the country. In *The Corrections Corporation of America, by the Numbers* – from the July/August 2016 issue of Mother Jones – it was reported that "In 2015, it [CCA] reported $1.9 billion in revenue and made more than $221 million in net income – more than $3,300 for each prisoner in its care."

In October 2016, CCA 'rebranded' as CoreCivic.

"Florence is kind of like a mid-max place. They've got guys that would shoot you dead if you tried to get out.

"You had 3 people in a cell. There's a lot of Mexicans, Chicanos and Latinos that are American. Half of 'em don't speak or understand English. They don't get along."

"Now that I know there's a snitch, I can't talk on the phone because every call is recorded. I can't get a message to anybody because they read your mail.

"I don't know when they got to the snitch, but he filled in all the blanks, the cocksucker.

"While I was in jail the DEA got ahold of my lawyer and said they wanted to talk to me. He came and saw me about it.

"I said 'I'm not talking to those motherfuckers.'

"He said 'That's what I told them.'"

Still in pain from the accident, jail meant going off OxyContin cold turkey.

"If I had brought them with me, I could have taken them until I ran out; but I didn't.

"The first week I didn't come out of my cell, I was sick.

"I would give my trays away and just eat fruit. Bananas, oranges, whatever they had. Then, when I got off of them, I went through the withdrawals and everything was fine."

"Missy served me divorce papers while I was in jail. I wasn't surprised. Some officer of the court comes in and says 'You're better off signing and not fighting.'

"They went off my IRS records which were accurate. But now I don't have a job, I don't have a company, I don't have anything.

"While I was locked up Missy came back in town and cleaned out the house. Her parents came. And her brother. They rented a big old U-Haul, loaded up everything that was of value in my house and took off.

"I don't know what she did with all of my stuff. I had probably $250,000 worth of clothes. I bought the best you could buy.

"I had jackets, coats – a full length shearling, a $12,000 coat. I think I bought it on sale for $7,500. It was warm as could be. I don't know what she did with it; probably sold it on eBay. Just such a bitch.

"I had French furniture from the 14, 15, 16th century – original paintings from every period. I had a $36,000 couch made out of elk skin and cars up the kazoo.

"She gave our nanny the antler chandelier and some hand painted pieces from Mexico.

"I had custom made saddles with marijuana leafs on 'em. They had sterling silver all over. These saddles are like $10,000 and she takes 'em all, 26 western saddles.

"She doesn't even ride western. Where they live *nobody* rides western, they ride English. They're probably still in storage."

What happened to the horses?

"We were getting out of the business, so she sold most of them. The ones that were with trainers, they bought or got buyers for."

Some of what she took had *no* financial value.

"I had pillows since I was a kid, down pillows. She took all of those. Featherbeds, 600-800 thread count sheets and 15 duvets. Just silly things that she could have left for me. Now I have none."

Worst of all "She takes the kids out of state – totally illegal. You can't do that no matter where I'm at. My kids are born there.

"After it was over, Ozzie told me Missy told him 'If the dot com doesn't work, I'm leaving.'

"So that's what the thing was. It was all about money with her.

"Douglas took my Bulgari watch to the pawn shop to buy crack cocaine while I was locked up. My dad was trying to cover for him. He told me my nephew Rodney stole it.

"I said 'Dad, don't even go there. I know who stole the watch. You don't have to fucking pretend.' He protected my brother so much.

"While I was in jail I had hundreds of thousands of dollars' worth of furniture in a storage unit – this is just the stuff that my wife didn't get.

"My little brother didn't pay the storage fees. I lost everything."

"People have no clue what to do if things go bad for them. No matter where you are, you have to make the best of it. Even when I was in jail, I was always smiling and happy.

"It doesn't make sense to be depressed. It's a waste. Live for now, do what brings you joy each day.

"You can't really sleep in jail; I always wanted to get up and go out. I got up early and took a shower when nobody was around. And then I'd go to work at the dry cleaners, that's the best job there. You work for 45 minutes a day and get paid $75/month.

"A couple guys that I met there, I made friends with. They used to joke and say 'You're the richest guy here and you get the highest paying job! It doesn't make any sense!'

"I said 'Well, I don't know what to tell you.'

"These people that are there are like small time people. If I were to say who I was they would laugh. So I wouldn't tell 'em.

"I thought *Nice to see you. If I never see you again, so what?*

"I just said 'I'm not rich anymore.'"

But he knew how to find and finesse available resources.

"The police had their own kitchen and they got special roast beef. I knew somebody who worked in there, he was from Jamaica. He'd get me bags of roast beef, fresh vegetables off the dock, cheese and loaves of fresh bread every day.

"I'd give him phone time to call home.

"We didn't have refrigerators, so I used to pay a guy who lived in my housing unit to keep everything on ice in a garbage can in my cell.

"He'd change the ice and make sure it was in order for when I got back."

"I happened to know the guy who was the shrink at Florence. He always used to come into my family's restaurant. He saw me in the hall one day and he says 'Hey Allen, what are you doing here?'

"I said 'I'm here for taxes. I'll be here for six months.'

"So he said 'If there's anything you need, let me know.'

"He liked my parents, he liked me. So I got a job with the captain and I could move anywhere I wanted to go. The captain gave me a note so the guards would just let me go outside to the yard whenever I wanted. When I wasn't going to my job I went outside.

"Regular jails are state penitentiaries; federal are federal. You can do a lot more in a federal jail as far as work-wise, taking classes, finishing a G.E.D., getting a degree.

"I taught math and did a bunch of other shit to help the teacher. I helped people to get jobs.

"They've got people locked up for drug crimes that shouldn't be locked up. There's been overzealous prosecution on marijuana; that zeal should be directed towards harder narcotics.

"As far as the federal government is concerned, marijuana is considered a Schedule 1 drug like all the other drugs."

According to *DEA.org*, "Schedule 1 drugs have a high potential for abuse and the potential to create severe psychological and/or physical dependence."

Drugs.com lists DEA Schedule 1 drugs and substances as follows:

- Heroin (diacetylmorphine)
- LSD (Lysergic acid diethylamide)
- Marijuana (cannabis, THC)
- Mescaline (Peyote)
- MDMA (3,4-methylenedioxymethamphetamine or "ecstasy")
- GHB (gamma-hydroxybutyric acid)
- Ecstasy (MDMA or 3,4-Methylenedioxymethamphetamine)
- Psilocybin
- Methaqualone (Quaalude)
- Khat (Cathinone)
- Bath Salts (3,4-methylenedioxypyrovalerone or MDPV)

"Heroin started coming back onto the scene probably about 20 years ago. The reason was OxyContin; it led to heroin, which was cheaper. Then heroin became a big thing."

It bothered Allen to see all the kids in jail.

"Kids were trying it and they were instantly hooked. They weren't stealing to make money, like robbing a bank; they were stealing to get high.

"They do anything to do heroin. You have no idea how many young kids were locked up because they stole TVs from Best Buy just to buy heroin. Hundreds and hundreds and hundreds of 'em.

"I'd say 'What are you here for?'

"They'd say 'Retail theft.'

"I saw a lot of that in jail. There's no reason they should be locked up. Locking them up does nothing to solve the problem. They have to get them help. They should be in rehab."

"I had a seizure after I got locked up. I'm standing there all shackled up getting ready to get on the bus with 30 or 40 Mexicans just out of the desert.

"I call them 'chapulines' - grasshoppers. They're mules, they get paid to carry a 40 lb. bail of marijuana on their backs and walk over the mountain, across the desert and into an area just east of Tucson. That was their staging point.

"There was a lot of people that went through there. I knew some of 'em. One of the guys knew who I was and we became friends.

"These guys just spent at least 4 or 5 days crossing the border; they're all sweaty and stinky and the smell is so overpowering I had a seizure. With a border crossing like that, there's no preventing it.

"The guy I knew helped me when I started to seize; he made sure I didn't fall and crack my head on the concrete.

"I'm laying on the ground all handcuffed up and they called the guards. They unshackled me and called the ambulance.

"I'm mumbling 'If I go to the hospital I'll get my medication.'

"One of the guards said 'No you won't; you're in federal custody.' The hospital couldn't give me any medication. They said 'We have anti-seizure medication at the jail, you'll get it when you get there.'

"I said 'Why should I go to the hospital instead of going to jail? I'll go to jail.'

"I went back to jail and they gave me the seizure medication.

"I didn't have any more seizures after that.

"I called these kind of mules 'chapulines,' but for most people that name refers to someone you use to get around whoever you've been dealing with. You can get in big trouble for doing this.

"The cartels have layers, this is a lower layer. If you haven't discussed it and made arrangements, it will piss them off and they'll kill you."

What happens to mules when they're arrested?

"They're not citizens, but they get locked up here. Depending on how many offenses, they usually spend time in Federal, get taken back to the border and are deported."

"In prison you have a couple of people that you know and trust and you keep it that way. You only associate with people that were checked out, guys that were decent guys that were there for DUIs and stuff like that. It just depended.

"There were a lot of child molesters there and I did not like that. I had to have 'em checked out to see if they were because nobody's going to tell you who they are.

"When you know, it's weird. They were more creepy than you'd expect they'd be. And they won't change, they won't stop doing it. It's just sick.

"I had guards that – if I asked – they'd tell me because they felt the same way.

"The guards liked me because I wasn't a child molester; they knew I was a big time drug dealer. I worked up front, so sometimes they'd let me go on the computer so I could look things up if I wanted.

"When their uniforms were damaged or too worn, they could order new. If they turned one in that had holes or worn out, I just ordered for them. When it came in, I'm like 'Here; fuck that other uniform.'

"I cooperated with everybody. Why not?"

"While I was in Tiny became a friend of mine. Tiny was not tiny, he was 350 pounds – a Mexican, a likeable guy.

"He went to jail when he was 18, was only supposed to do a year or two, but he ended up stabbing his black cellmate 19 times. Tiny doesn't like black guys.

"I go 'Tiny, why 19 times?'

"He says 'He was persistent.'

"Tiny was on death row. I don't know how he got off. He wasn't the kind of guy who would have ratted someone out.

"He was getting ready to get out after 58 years and 6 months. He had to be about 70 years old."

"After 6 months I was *off* probation.

"Usually when they violate your probation they like to extend your probation again, so when you get off you're still on probation.

"The judge even asked the prosecutor 'Are you OK with this?'

"He said 'Yes.'

"The day I was getting out I called my lawyer to say 'What time are we getting out of here?'

"He said 'They're supposed to process you in the morning.'

"I should have got out at 10 a.m.; instead, I got out at 10 at night. Ozzie said he'd come get me, but I didn't want him to be seen with me, so my dad came.

"Ozzie came and got me the next morning. He gave me an envelope full of money. I told him, 'Bro, I know you don't want to hear this, but there's a snitch. I don't know if it's George or Dale, but it's one of those two.'

"I felt telling him was the right thing to do. If he wants to go down that road and get busted, it's on him now. I did what a good friend is supposed to do. I could have let him dangle and get busted.

"I stopped talking to Dale, but Ozzie poo pooed it, which was a shame. If he'd have got his ducks in a row and listened to me, he might have not had to do 15 or even 7 years.

"I told him that the bus was coming. I told him and he didn't listen. He thought I was jealous because I wasn't making any money.

"He goes 'You're just upset that you're not making money now.'

"I said 'No I'm not; I'm happy. I don't give a fuck about that. Somebody is *snitching*, I know 100%!'

"Things were never the same after that. I kind of stopped cuz I knew they were watching every step I made. I absolutely knew they were investigating me so I was careful.

"Bad things happen to people who aren't careful."

18 Issuing Warnings

"Getting out was just weird. Everybody was gone. My kids. Who I thought was my wife. My house was very comfortable. I didn't want to leave but I didn't have anybody there.

"My dad goes 'Come on, you just come live with us.' I listened to him, which was a big mistake. I should have just left all my things in the house and stayed.

"I gave the house to Futon Ron for the time being; I didn't know what the fuck else to do. I had about $800,000 worth of equity in it. I told him to take it, I said 'Just give me $250,000 or $300,000 and keep the rest.'

"He said 'Fine, no problem.' He said he'd pay me later.

"When we were moving everything out, I sat a bottle of Dom '66 next to the door and figured *I'll drink this tonight.*

"There was still a lot of stuff. My bed was huge, Missy had to get on a step to get on the bed. I still had the $16,000 Italian couch in my great room.

"Somebody took the wine. I'm sure they didn't even know what they were drinking. It was the best vintage, 1966 – worth maybe $800.

"I took my Dalmatians and went to my parents' house. They cared about me, but it wasn't about that then. My mother had fallen in the shower, hit her head really hard and spent some time in the hospital. They had to do surgery and she got dementia after that.

"I still had to travel and do shit, so I had to leave both of my dogs with my dad. He doesn't like animals, dogs or whatever.

"While I was gone he had them put down. I got back and I'm like 'That's just fucked up.'

"He says 'They were old. What are you going to do with them?'

"I said 'I would have liked to have had the choice.'

"That was not good. And then all the other stuff that was going on with me.

"The IRS kept going through my file and they came to see me after I was out. I said 'What do you guys want?'

"I had a lady doctor that was prescribing my medication. They knew that I was getting drugs for the right reasons, not for recreation – but she would do that too. I sent people there.

"She charged them $100 or so and wrote their scripts. She didn't really care, she was making so much money.

"They came to me to ask if I would testify against her. I said 'I'm not going to testify against anybody.' I think that kind of pissed them off too.

"You just do what you gotta do, keep pushing on. That's it. There's no extra, *nada*.

"The feds tried to get to me after I was divorced. They'd send hot chicks to befriend me, to try to find out what they could.

"I knew it was the feds. I don't know if they were agents or whatever, but I knew. You can tell.

"One of my friends asked 'How do you know?'

"I said 'I just do.'

"Or some guy would come and try to start a conversation by starting with generic questions.

"I'd just sit there and laugh."

"Tiny and I got out around the same time so we hooked up and hung out. He had been away for so long I took him to some nice places and he was kind of enamored by everybody that knew me and the power that I had.

"He goes 'I don't know anybody that can go into a clothing store and walk out with $4,500 worth of clothes without paying.'

"I said 'That's because you don't know me – and he does.'

"He was just a friend from Iran. He went to Italy to buy the best clothes and shoes.

"I told Tiny 'I've been buying clothes from him since I was in my teens. I brought him a lot of customers over the years.'

"Tiny was a good guy too, he would do anything for you. We used to take his mother for pancake breakfasts and stuff.

"He introduced me to this guy he liked and trusted. Whetto was chubby, average height, brown hair – light skin. That's why we called him 'Whetto' – because he's Mexican but he looks white.

"I knew him, but I really didn't want to work with him. I had a thing … I have enough trouble with the friends I have, I don't need new friends.

"I would always push certain people away and not be part of anything that they were about.

"People are either good or bad, not half good or half bad.

"I think initially most people are good; but then something happens along the way. Something happens in their life where they think *Maybe I could rob a bank or come up with some stupid white collar scheme.*

"If they're going to fuck you for $100, they'll fuck you for $1,000. You've got to not be around them.

"But Whetto kept calling me, begging me.

"We started meeting for lunch and Whetto always had this guy with him; I don't know if he was an agent or not. Tiny wasn't always at these meetings.

"Whetto's guy pretended he didn't do drugs and didn't drink. I don't know if it was a setup, but Whetto's guy pretended not to speak English. I knew enough Spanish to get a bad feeling from him.

"I'd be drinking and doing lines of cocaine and I didn't really give a fuck. What are they gonna do to me? All the things I did … they're not going to arrest me for that. They're not going to make a case out of that."

After taking time to see his kids, Allen went to Chicago to see The Rocketman.

"Midge used to bring him product from Detroit. She'd load up the car with 200 – 300 pounds and take it to him. He'd give it to his guy who sold it for us in Chicago. Some he kept.

"So I go over to see The Rocketman and we're partying, doing cocaine and everything else. We had girls over and sent them home about 10 a.m. Gave them cab fare and 'See you later.'

"All of a sudden we hear the buzzer; somebody's trying to get us to let them in.

"I say 'Who is that?'

"He goes 'Holy shit, it's my mom.'

"He never told me that his mom's coming. Dominic didn't want to let her in at first. I think she had drugs.

"I said 'She's got something for you, don't be an ass! Just let her in, tell her we were out and we partied.'

"The house is kind of like a little messy and we had a big dinner plate *piled* with cocaine. He tells me to hide it. Where am I going to hide it? She's like 5' tall, so I put it on the top shelf in the cupboard.

"So his mom comes in, 'Hi, *blah, blah, blah.*'

"I hadn't seen her in about six months, but now I'm tired.

"Later me and Rocketman are just hanging around upstairs and all of a sudden she yells 'DOMINIC!!!' She started cleaning the kitchen and found the cocaine.

"Rocketman says 'I told you to hide it!'

"I said 'I didn't know she was going to clean house!'

"She says 'What are you guys doing? What's the matter with you two!?'

"So I went down and said I was locked up and we just partied, harmless fun, it's all my fault. So I kind of took the blame for it.

"I *wanted* to say 'Dominic's always fucked up on cocaine and stuff like that. You can't always blame it on me 'cuz I'm not always here.'"

"Me and Ozzie were talking at least a couple times a week while I was in Chicago. According to him, 'Our guys stole tons of money. They have offshore accounts.'

"I said 'Well what do you want to do about it? What can we do about it now? There's nothing we can do.'

"He said 'They're not going to give it back; they kept stealing.'

"I said 'We can make our own money and be happy or we can start a war. In a war there's no winners.' I told him 'When I come there we'll do shit together.'

"We were figuring stuff out, legal stuff. He was all into it, but then I left my phone on the train one day and lost half of my contacts – including him.

"I couldn't get ahold of him after that."

"After working for me for all those years, Midge was good at what she did. I warned her 'It's over with. There's no more money. Whatever you have, live nicely. You're done.'

"I said 'Don't do anything for anyone. You have got to stop NOW.'

"I've seen money change people. They swear up and down that they'll never change, but once they get real money they change as quick as they can.

"My mom once told me 'Be careful of your sister Midge.' For my mom to say that about one of her kids – she knew. She knew she was no good.

"I had told Midge 'You have your house paid for and everything is good. Just relax, enjoy your grandkids and don't do anything.'

240

But sure enough …

"My cousin George calls Midge and asks if she would drive $375,000 out to Las Vegas. They were going to pay her about ten grand.

"They said the money would be hidden inside a Cadillac Escalade. They took the console out and hid money all over. They told her if cops took the car apart, they weren't going to find it.

"So she calls me and asks me 'What should I do?'

"I said 'Don't under *any* circumstances – do not do it! Do not go!'

"When I was first starting out Midge worked with somebody else who was a friend of George's. I had him fly some money to me on a plane.

"I don't know how they found out he had money on him. It was around $70,000 or $100,000 – and they took it. I said 'You know what? You're done with me. That's it.'

"I told George, I said 'I don't want to see that guy; I don't want him involved in *anything*.'

"Everything about this new deal stunk. The car wasn't in her name; she had no say that she had permission to drive the car.

"My cousin George – fucking piece of shit – he wrote a note saying she had permission to drive the car. You could wipe your ass with that.

"I told Midge 'This is so stupid' – but The Rocketman convinced her to do it.

"She told me 'Dominic said you just don't want me to make any money.' Like I would begrudge her something.

"But my nephew Dipshit Dominic was going to *get* some of the money. He was going to get the money and pay her; so he pushed her.

"She was good. She knew how to keep her calm and they convinced her if she got pulled over, the cops would never find the money.

"Lo and behold, she gets pulled over in Kansas. She's thinking they hid the money so well it's not going to matter.

"When they asked, she said 'Sure you can search.'

"You should never do that – I told her that a million times!

"They took the car apart on the side of the road and found the money. It's not illegal to have money, there's no charge, but they will seize it because they view all big sums as drug money.

"Nobody carries $150,000. *Although I used to do it every day.*

"They find the money, they seize the money. They give her a receipt and let her go on her way.

"She doesn't have to go to Las Vegas now. She doesn't have anything left to deliver so she goes back to Detroit.

"She calls me and I said 'I TOLD YOU NOT TO GO!'

"She says 'Well, Dominic said it would be OK.'

"I'm like 'Well, good thing you've got your son Dominic; let him help you.'

"Then George gets some casino to say the money's legit – which only made him look worse. I think that's how their eyes were wide open now to what was going on. They were putting the dots together.

"Later the snitch told them 'She used to drive loads for me.' So now she falls under 'ongoing criminal enterprise.' It's a RICO charge."

"Six months after I got out of jail they raided everybody.

"The Rocketman was in Chicago when he heard. He called me and said 'George and those guys got raided!' so I jumped in the car and ran over to Ozzie's.

"They had already been there and taken him."

On February 23, 2004 the DEA published a press release to *dea.org* – 'DEA investigation halts huge marijuana ring.'

It named twenty individuals, including Midge, Ozzie and others and stated that "The indictment alleges that from 1991, until the date of the indictment, the above defendants engaged in a conspiracy involving numerous locations, in which 40 tons of marijuana were transported to the Detroit area for distribution. U.S. Attorney Collins called the case *the single largest drug conspiracy indictment in Eastern Michigan history.*"

As Allen remembers it, "They say we moved 180,000 tons worth – over $4.9 billion from '84 to 2004. We did more than that even.

"They couldn't get me because I had immunity. My name was never mentioned.

"Midge had been out for so long they couldn't have arrested her no matter what the snitch said; but because she drove, they put her back in. That's how RICO works. They labeled her part of an 'OCE' – ongoing criminal enterprise.

"I told my nephews to get their mom a good lawyer.

"The Rocketman says 'Oh yeah, we got her a good lawyer. We got her a public defender.'

"I said 'You are a complete fucking asshole.'

"He's making money and he didn't even get her a good lawyer. I'm like 'You gotta be kidding me with this.' That pissed me off to no end. Those are her kids and they can do no wrong.

"If Midge hadn't driven the money, she wouldn't have gone to jail for a minute. But she drove the money and that's how they caught her with the RICO act, the ongoing criminal enterprise.

"It's not illegal to have money, but my cousin George tried to prove the money was his from something that pissed off the government worse.

"It made them look even harder at what was going on.

"So when he got arrested, they were able to tie her into the case because it was an ongoing criminal enterprise.

"She never stopped, they said; which was true. If her idiot son hadn't encouraged her, she would have never gotten in trouble. But since she did, she had to do three years in a federal prison.

"She was sixty-seven when she went in. She felt that if I came forward and told on the others they would let her go. Which would have probably been true, but I'm not wired that way.

"When I was a kid, we'd hear 'That guy – he's a snitch.' So the thought of me telling on someone to save my ass was never an option.

"The way we grew up, it's a matter of honor to do the time and save the others. I'd rather try to fight and do what I can do through the legal system than tell on someone else to get off.

"I believe in dealing with it by getting as much information as you possibly can. Like my lawyer would hire a lawyer for the person that got caught; so if he was telling, I'd be the first to know. You just do things that way, protect them and protect yourself.

"Now Midge doesn't talk to me. It's part my fault because when she went away I never went and saw her. I was under indictment.

"I could have written her but I'm not like that. I don't write letters. Even when I was locked up, people would write me, but it was rare for me to write back. It's just not my thing. I can pick up the phone and call you; *it's not 1863.*

"I was talking to my other sister and I said 'Midgey did it to make money and maybe help her family. I don't know.'

"She said 'You know why she did it. To make money, that's *all*. She knew what she was doing.'"

"Fifty-seven people went to jail." To Allen's surprise, "Everybody was like it was no big deal. I'm like 'OK.'

"Everybody went to jail; people are still in jail for it. It is what it is. We had a long, long, long run at the top. Even though we dodged a lot of bullets, when the bullet hits it always strikes true. The bullet's always right.

"When people get caught it's always scary. You always think but you never really know – *Are they going to tell?*

"It's amazing how when things start going wrong that people just start to tell. They can only think of themselves.

"They say they're honorable, but they're young and they've never been faced with having to go to jail or do time. They just say 'I'm gonna tell.' It's the first thing to come out of their mouth. Like 'What do you want to know?'

"We used to have a guy that had check cashing places. He converted our bills from small to fifties and hundreds so it would take up less space. It was very convenient for us. That much money gets really bulky in a hurry.

"He couldn't convert it all, it was just too much.

"My cousin snitched on him to get his sentence lightened. To me that was kind of shitty."

"After the big drug bust I'm thinking *They think they got everybody. I'm good because they're not going to be looking at me or for me.*

"I didn't know Dale was the snitch. He started wearing a wire the month I got out of jail. I'm sure they offered him witness protection.

"Later I found out Dale had told them all about me. He gave them *180 pages of testimony* on me and how I started the organization. I didn't know that they were paying *extra* attention to me because they knew who the real boss was and I had gotten away.

"They were willing to do anything to nail me."

Allen and Dale had been close friends for so many years it was hard to understand the depth of his betrayal.

"Dale didn't have to drag my sister into it.

"There was no reason for it; she wasn't working for them.

"I don't know *how* Dale's deal went down, but I think I know *why* it went down the way it did. He was still in love with his ex-girlfriend.

"She used to do deliveries and she was good at what she did, but we had to help her out all the time. She got in trouble for drugs, for using. She'd get pulled over.

"At first Dale would ask me to help. I had a friend in L.A., a lawyer, so Dale started going straight to him. I didn't know how bad it had gotten because he wasn't talking to me. He didn't want to keep coming to me with those problems. I didn't want her around anyway.

"He kept doing his stuff and she would get caught up in not major things, but enough small things that she kept drawing attention to him. Then he'd go to my friend in California and he'd get her off.

"Somehow something happened that she decided she would work with the government. She told on him and set him up for controlled delivery of 2,500 pounds.

"In those days we were so brazen. You know those big rolling containers people use for trash and stuff? You can really put anything into 'em. We used to put 'em in places on corners or off the corner so the truck could back up and load it really quickly.

"Nobody ever expected anything like that. We had someone keep an eye on 'em.

"Then we got so big we had to use semis. We had a connection with Allied Van Lines and their storage facility in Detroit. We were using their trucks; we'd unload there and move it out.

"The DEA wanted them to deliver the load so they could have all the evidence they needed.

"When Dale's driver came to the stash house, they were waiting. From there it didn't take them long to convince him to wear a wire. He had been wearing a wire for six months when he snitched.

"At that time I wasn't involved, really. I just sat back. My cousins and everybody kept going, but I was done. Dale brought everybody down but me. I don't think he felt bad about anything.

"He told on some of the Mexicans. I wouldn't want to have his life right now.

"In the end his girlfriend wrote a book, but she doesn't mention me except in some weird reference.

"She knew not to."

"Supposedly Ozzie was the only one that kept his mouth shut. He got convicted for 15 years but did 7, he got it overturned on appeal. They ruled that it was some kind of illegal setup with Dale. I don't know the whole story on it.

"Ozzie's best friend had two kids with this girl; then I don't know what happened, but she and Ozzie started getting close and they had one kid together. It was a mess.

"Ozzie told her to tell me not to kill Dale; maybe because he thought it would create more problems."

"I had $17 million in an overseas account at ABN AMRO. I shipped it with the yacht guy, then I'd fly to Monaco and spend a month there – or the whole summer.

"I was watching the account. I had been making deposits all through the 90s; it was in a safety deposit box.

"I was afraid I'd lead 'em right to it, so I had a lawyer make inquiries. They told him 'He has no account. He has no box – no boxes here.'"

The money was gone.

"I don't know how they found it. As soon as they figured out where it was – maybe because I made inquiries – I think the IRS called Interpol and they went and took my money.

"Or maybe they could get it because ABN AMRO opened a branch in Miami.

"I wasn't informed of how they did it. They knew how I was making the big bucks so I didn't matter to them one iota. They just took my money. 'Fuck him.'

"$17 million dollars could have gone a long way. That was my retirement fund, that's what I was going to use. I was so depressed I can't tell you.

"And then Missy's attorney was a total bitch. They both forced me to agree to $5,000 a month in child support for two kids.

"$5,000 a month is a lot of money when you're not working. I knew the dollar amount was out of whack and everything, but I didn't bitch about it because they're my kids. I'd do anything for 'em but it got to the point that I couldn't keep up.

"She told the kids I abandoned them. I couldn't even have my own place to live because I was giving them everything I had.

"I sold Gary Triano's widow an original painting for $12,000. I never met her before. An art dealer that I used to buy art from introduced me.

"I sold Freddy Krueger my Tank Francais for $18,000. Still, I'd wind up in the hole.

"I'd miss a couple months of child support and every time I'd go up to see my kids they'd throw me in jail. Bond was $15,000, so someone would have to come get me.

"They threw me in jail three times for going up to see my kids. I didn't have money to even get a lawyer. I thought *Fuck this, I'm not going to court up there.*"

"My horse Ivan – the Friesian I imported from Holland – there was one like it on a novella, a really, really popular Mexican soap opera.

"The star of the show rode it, so all the drug guys wanted that horse. They would have given me any quantity of product for him.

"Missy gave Ivan to her friend, the ex-CIA agent – the lady that was deathly afraid of me.

"Ivan was not titled, was not registered to her. I told the police 'These are my horses, my wife had no right to sell them.'

"The lady and her husband were both ex CIA, both pilots for Fed Ex and they worked all the time, so they had enough money to satisfy her.

"She sold 'em a $75,000 vaisselier. She tried to tell me 'It wasn't worth much.' And the 15th century armoires. I know she didn't give 'em to 'em. She probably made 'em a package deal."

Missy's final sweep of all he owned – combined with her ongoing financial demands – put Allen in an impossible situation.

"I kept digging a deeper hole. I started taking chances I shouldn't have took."

An unexpected oversight on Missy's part put Allen back in the action.

19 Moving 1,000 lbs.

"Missy had a *lot* of jewelry, including that $40,000 necklace I bought wholesale from my cousin Greg for our first Christmas. I don't remember how I got it; I think it was at the jeweler being cleaned when she packed to leave.

"My Mexican friends said 'We'll take that.'

"Missy was already gone, I didn't need it and I'm not giving it to another girl. I gave it to them and got paid in product.

"Then the cartel called me and asked if I could come to Tijuana for a meeting. I said 'OK.'

"While I was there I had meetings with them; but they timed it so I'd be there when they had their vengeance. The mayor of Tijuana wasn't acting right. They didn't tell me why. They just killed him and 13 other people.

"I said 'WHY? Why while I'm here?'

"They said 'It had to be done.'

"After they shot those people I had to get home. I thought *Why did they have to do this while I'm around; why didn't they wait until I leave?*

"I had to cross the border and maybe get searched. I didn't have anything on me, it was just the mentality. They run the country. They don't care.

"Another time I'm down there and some guy had betrayed them. I didn't know anything about it. We were out by the pool talking. We had a real special bottle of Tequila.

"We toasted, he drank and BOOM-BOOM – somebody came up and shot him in the side of the head.

"I was just across the table. It didn't blow his head off, it just went in and out. And I'm thinking OK. *Should I run or just stay here with poop in my pants?*

"I just sat there and El Chapo looked at me and he goes 'He was a fucking piece of shit.'

"That was it. They took him ... wherever they take them. And I sat there by myself. It kind of made me ..."

He chose his word carefully.

"You're always *scared* – kind of. I knew I hadn't done anything, but they can misconstrue anything you say. Fortunately – when somebody's making money for them – it's different.

"It's all about respect – in a twisted sort of way. I earned them lots of money."

Culiacán – home of Mexico's drug trafficking industry – is only 67 miles from Mazatlán.

"The cartels weren't a problem in resort areas; but nobody goes to Culiacán unless you're asked or invited. That's where Chapo's headquarters were. There's no white people there.

"You never knew if Chapo was there or was gonna be there. I usually met with the guys that would report to him. They liked the honesty that I had.

"When you go to Culiacán and see somebody it's usually a good thing. Unless you fucked up; then you're marching to your death.

"If you fucked up, it depends on who you are and what you did; they'll kill you wherever you are. They've got guys in Chicago, they've got guys everywhere.

"Even now - just because Chapo's caught doesn't mean they're not working."

Allen was invited back before the holidays.

"My friend called and said 'We have to go.'

"This trip was different from previous trips. I went to meet him at Agua Prieta, the border town across from Douglas, Arizona. I got a ride because I didn't know what was going to happen, where we were going to end up, or what we were going to do.

"I walked across the border in my $150 pair of jeans and Gucci shoes with my Louis Vuitton bag.

"My friend Roberto was waiting for me in a truck and he starts driving. It was just him and me. We were going to a field they wanted me to look at in the mountains.

"He says 'First we go to Hermosillo' – which is kind of a long drive from there. Before we head out he takes me to the pharmacy so I can get whatever I want."

Allen mentions something that sounds like 'roaches.' He explains; "Roche manufactured a date rape drug; they're downers, sort of like Valium. This was four or five years after the accident, so I got a bunch of other stuff like pain pills.

"I didn't need a prescription for the narcotics, my friend knew the pharmacist. I'd get like five different things, give him $400 or $500 bucks and say 'Thank you.'

"They loved me because I didn't care about money.

"When I went I saw that the kids I knew from before had grown up. They said 'You don't have to go there; you can get whatever you want here.'"

Grateful for his past generosity, they said "You got my hair cut, you got me clothes."

Allen appreciated the offer. "I remembered that I took care of them; but now I have to go because the cartel guys are expecting me.

"I'm the passenger in the front seat and I'm going to be there for the next five or six hours.

"We stopped at the Tecate store and get like a 12 pack and off we go. We start driving and drinking and that's perfectly legal where they come from. We're talking and having a good time.

"We'd stop at the roadside taco stands. The best food is from those stands; a million flies can't be wrong. It was somebody's home and they just set up outside and when you come, they cook inside and bring it out with every kind of condiment – jalapenos, radishes, cucumbers and onions.

"We'd eat, get back in the car and one of us says 'Tecate' or 'Pacifico' and we'd stop and reload.

"In Mexico you just throw the garbage out of the window. I said 'This is not good. This is your country, it's messed up.'

"If they don't care, I don't care. We'd throw everything out the window. If you have to pee, you'd pull over and pee on the side of the road."

"Finally we get to Hermosillo and meet up with Carlos, one of my growers. That night we partied a little bit.

"He goes 'You want pills?'

"I say 'Of course!' I used to always laugh, 'Por que no!' Why not!

"So they'd laugh. We'd be doing cocaine and my little drugs. We'd get girls in but we had to get up early, so I'd shower.

"Carlos says 'Come on, we must shop for tomorrow.'

"I said 'OK.'

"We'd eat breakfast at another outdoor market where they had different taco stands. I'd try 'em all.

"We'd go through the hardware store and get what they needed for his brother there at the grow site. He needed PVC pipe and stuff. I'd pay for it, of course. I took at least $7,000 or $9,000.

"A lot of times I'd burn through that, so I had to have someone send me money.

"And then we'd go and get all fresh food, as much as we could. We'd buy chicken, fish, this, that and whatever they don't have at the site. They don't have much out there.

"We continued the journey with me and Carlos sitting in the bed of the pickup truck; we had a ton of supplies back there and we're just bouncing around doing cocaine the whole way.

"We made a stop at this guy's house. He had cocaine called lavada; it's washed, it's flavored, it's white flake – omigod, the best cocaine ever.

"They wouldn't take money from me for that. I'd get piña colada, pineapple, bubble gum. Usually piña colada was my favorite. It's unbelievable. It's really clean and you have no aftereffects. You could snort it and go to sleep.

"It doesn't make you jittery, it's just so good. I said 'Omigod, I'll get in trouble with this shit.'

"We took off and we'd drive ten hours to get up to the mountain.

"There's other growers to the left and right and they have gates – and pigs. The pigs are good if you gotta kill somebody. I saw it happen.

"Some guy betrayed us and they told him 'C'mon, we have to go.'

"I didn't really watch. I was going through the crops and he was just sitting there. They cut his throat. He didn't see it coming. He didn't know.

"They'll take the guy's teeth out, cut their hair, shave their heads and chop them up. The pigs will eat them."

Why take out the teeth and cut off the hair?

"Because the pigs can't digest those. It would make them sick or die."

"There's so much weed growing there and nobody says anything about it. The government doesn't know where it's at, first of all. I'm sure if they flew over with a helicopter they'd see it.

"Their 50 caliber bullets for shooting down helicopters are almost as big as my penis.

"We'd get up to the growing field and they'd be all happy to see us. We brought gas for their generators. They'd unload the truck and fire up this ginormous wok on coals.

"While they're cooking my guy took me on a tour of the fields to see what I want to pick. They've got some stuff still growing, some drying.

"I'm like 'OK.' I tell Carlos 'I'll take the whole field, just bring it.'

"The fish were fresh; they'd fry the fish. We'd eat. I'm telling you, it was delicious.

"That's when one of the guys was telling me about the headcheese. I'm like 'headcheese'? 'What the fuck *headcheese?*'

"'Muy bueno' he says.

"I said 'I don't know, *no sabe.*' Finally I'm like 'Yeah, fine. Headcheese.'

"So the next thing I know he's got a ball of *hashish.* Like a big half of a golf ball. They make it off the top of the bud, the very top of the plant; grind it and press it together.

"He broke it in half, stuck it with a paper clip and lit it; took a couple puffs and gave it to me. He gave me so much and it was so powerful, I'm just inhaling it.

"Nobody else is doing it. I'm sitting in a lawn chair and the ground moved. I was stuck like Chuck.

"I felt so good, but I had no will. I was full from eating, all I could do was drink more. They'd keep you in beer and I didn't even want that. Once I eat I have to go to the harder stuff; like vodka or something.

"So we continue on our trip with Carlos and catch a flight from Hermosillo to Culiacán. We land and everything's great.

"Culiacán is close to Mazatlán so they have all fresh seafood, giant glass bowls filled with oysters, clams, everything from the ocean.

"They give you a spoon and crackers, hot sauce and lime. I can't even describe the flavors, it's like the ocean, it's so delicious and so fresh; everything fresh that day.

"And then we'd party and go out and meet girls. My wife was gone, I needed el sexo.

"Me and Carlos shared a room. And I kept screwing this girl, she had a great body, rock hard; and her friend was with Carlos. And he did it maybe one time and he was done.

"I'm like 'Hey, can we switch? Let her come over with me.'

"The girl that I was with was kind of jealous, even though she knew she was getting booted in the morning.

"*I just don't understand that.*

"I kept going over to the other girl, putting my penis on her forehead. I said 'I just want to see if you're warm.'

"In the morning the girls got booted and my friend had to go back home to his family."

Allen was ready to go back to Tucson except "I didn't realize I'd lost my passport. I tried to get on the plane to go home and it wasn't there.

"The route I took, they had no idea who I was or what, so they wouldn't let me on the plane. I had to go to the U.S. Consulate and they sent me somewhere else. They needed to give me the right passport number.

"I was thinking about going home for Thanksgiving and I thought *For what? Fuck Thanksgiving, I'll stay here 'til Sunday.*

"My Mexican friends called a hotel in Mazatlán and told 'em to take care of me. It was just me but they gave me a four bedroom penthouse, the whole top floor; it had like 5 balconies and 4 bedrooms.

"They gave me a driver to take me wherever I wanted to go. He'd be there in the morning no matter what time I woke up. If I wanted to go sit by the pool for a few hours, he'd wait.

"He would take me to the place where they had girls. I'd just pick a couple and buy them clothes because they didn't have much. I said 'Take me to a nice store and pick whatever clothes you want.'

"I had girls in all the rooms and we'd go out to dinner and the clubs and go back to the hotel.

"When the girls were gone I'd usually just hang out at the pool. The valet guys figured out that I was somebody of some importance; they said 'Well, we've got girls too.'

"I said 'OK, must be fine!'

"They got me a really beautiful girl and she'd come over and we'd make love. She called me 'muy guapo' – very handsome. Her and I would do it all day and then I'd go out to dinner with the other girls and do it all night.

"And I'd always sit on the beach. Sometimes it's hot, so I'd always wear a decent shirt with swim shorts. I'd take off my shirt and the ocean was right there. I'd go swim and come back.

"They'd give me a towel and I'd eat again.

"For dinner I liked red snapper; they take the whole fish and fry it and it's – omigod – so delicious.

"At 2 or 4 in the morning I'd tell the driver to take me to the bakery. They make this cake that I adore called 'tres leches.'

"It's made from three types of milk and whipped cream. It's unbelievable. I'd buy like 2 or 3 of 'em and put 'em in the refrigerator.

"I had a full kitchen at the place and I'd eat a whole cake in one sitting."

Problems in Chicago interrupted his good time. The Rocketman was in a bind.

"When I had money I got him set up with a condo in Lincoln Park in Chicago, a million dollar place at the time; it was 3 stories with a rooftop deck and a private elevator that opened up into his family room.

"Now he's saying 'I can't pay my mortgage.'

"He's not working, he needs to work. I know he's always just partying, so I say 'Well I'll go home, I'll see what I can do.'

"The Rocketman was a drug addict and an asshole and I took care of him. I would have never gotten in trouble if he would have done what I told him to do."

"The pain from the accident kept getting worse and worse. It was hard for me to work and my mother was in bad shape. She got dementia after her surgery, forgot all the other kids but she remembered me.

"They flew her back to Michigan. She was on the airplane and the guy in front of her had dark hair like me. She started hitting him on the head like it was me.

"She was in hospice in Detroit and I went to see her. It was bad. She was going down quickly.

"I had a lot on my mind. I wasn't thinking clearly, not taking everything as seriously as I had always done before.

"I go back and get the 1,000 pounds I got in Culiacán and tell The Rocketman what we have to do.

"I said 'I need you to get a nondescript van – a plain white van, that's it. Get a driver and I'll be there with 1,000 pounds That will last you and me through the summer.'

"At that time everybody else was already arrested. My normal guys weren't around so I had to improvise.

"For a year Whetto kept begging and begging me to transport product. He had driven loads for me before, but it had been a long time since I'd done anything with him.

"He said he'd give me a discount on the price, so I finally said 'OK.'

"Plan was – Whetto would transport the product to Illinois. It had to be taken to Joliet, which is far from the city, because it's hard to drive semis in Chicago.

"So Whetto brings this giant box truck to me in Tucson. I had my car, so I had my nephew Rodney drive the truck up to some parking lot in Chandler.

"We left the key under the mat for my guys, but they called and said 'We can't use the truck. We can't take it down into the subdivision, it'll stand out.'

"My guy at the stash house says 'We'll give you our van and we'll load it.'

"I bought moving boxes and tape so my Mexicans could wrap the weed and put it in the boxes.

"When they gave me their van I was so pissed. Do you know what these stupid motherfuckers did? They cut the boxes and wrapped them *around the bails*. I don't know why they did it like that.

"The van was FULL OF WEED and it was stinking. I'd have to deal with that later.

"I took Marcos with me and we parked it at his friend's house overnight until I could get it to Whetto the next day. I knew it was safe, nobody would say anything.

"I told Whetto I left the big ass truck at one of those big box stores; I put the key under the mat thinking he rented it and would need to return it.

"So turns out he goes 'Oh, I can't take it out of the van and put it in my truck.' He said 'No, you have to put it back in the truck because it lines up evenly with the semi.'

"I'm like 'You stupid mother fucker, what's the difference between loading it from the van to the semi or ....'

"Whetto says 'The truck I gave you backs up perfectly; nobody can see and I can just move 'em. Just put 'em in the fucking thing.'

"He persisted so I said 'Alright.'

"So I had to go back and get the truck; it was a fair distance away.

"I had to buy a padlock and we had to throw 1,000 pounds of dope from the van into the truck.

"I didn't have any place to do this. I didn't have no cover spot like a garage or warehouse so no one could see. I had to wing it.

"I got in the truck and we did our thing behind a grocery store. It was 10 or 11 in the morning, kind of quiet back there.

"We would never do anything at night because that's when it's expected and police are out. I like to do things during the day when things are bustling and everyone's out and about. That way there's no reason for them to be looking around.

"We did the transfer so fast it was unbelievable. We backed up the van, opened the truck and within probably five minutes threw the thousand pounds into the box truck.

"We found a place that had three big box stores all in a row. We took the truck, locked the back and left it there.

"I met Whetto for drinks and gave him the keys to the truck and the padlock. I was still upset about the smell, so I told Whetto 'I'll give you 25 grand to rewrap this shit.'

"He said 'No problem.' He told me he'd see me in Joliet Tuesday. I tell Rocketman I'm going to fly in on probably Friday or Saturday.

"I'm relieved, thinking *OK, great. FINALLY*. So me and my friend go to a strip club.

"I took 140 pounds to Marcos in Tucson and told him it was 'In case I need money while I'm up there.' He had a guy who was going to buy it. I said 'That's great, I can use that while I'm waiting for these other guys to pay off the 1,000 pounds.'

"140 pounds is a pretty good chunk of change, somewhere between $70,000 and $100,000; I'd have money to do what I want to do. So I went back to Tucson and Whetto took off.

"Everything's good – except I didn't know Whetto was working with the feds."

Whetto had been using Tiny to get close to Allen.

"When I land in Chicago on Friday The Rocketman's not there. *I'm furious*. I call him on his phone; 'Where the fuck are you? I can't get in the house!'

"He goes 'I had to come to L.A. for a party.'

"YOU HAD TO GO TO L.A. FOR A FUCKING PARTY? THAT'S MORE IMPORTANT THAN THIS?"

"I said 'You know what? This is not gonna work out. I have a really bad feeling now.'

"He goes 'Pick me up on Sunday at the airport and we'll work it out.'

"I get a limo and pick him up at the airport on Sunday.

"I ask him 'Who've you got for a driver? Where's the van?'

"He says 'I don't have a van. We don't need a driver, I'll drive it.'

"I said 'OK tough guy. What are we going to do about a van?'

"He says 'Well my girlfriend will rent one for me.'

"I said 'Do you know how that stands out, a U-Haul rental van? It says U-Haul all over!'

"I give the van to Whetto, I tell him 'Here – call me when it's loaded and ready to be picked up.'

"We go back to Joliet and he calls me in two or three hours. He goes 'Alright, I'm ready for you guys.'

"I tell my nephew while we're on the way 'I don't feel good about this. I think this guy might be a cop. He might be fucking setting us up. I don't like how this thing has gone down.'

"He says 'You're just paranoid.'

"I said 'You know what? I've done this a long time. I get paranoid for a reason.'

"He goes 'Well don't worry about it.'

"I said 'Alright.' He was going to drive the van anyway.

"So we went and met Whetto at a Cracker Barrel in Joliet. He stayed next door at the Holiday Inn; that's where the van was.

"Whetto takes us over there. Rocketman sees 1,000 pounds in the van and he panics. 'I can't do it, I'm scared.'

"I say 'Give me the keys, just go in front of me. Show me where I'm supposed to deliver this shit.'

"When Whetto realized I was going to drive he turned white as a ghost.

"I got in that van and it stunk *so bad*. But at that time you gotta go, the clock's ticking. I get in the van and take off. He's in front of me.

"As soon as I get on the freeway I see three or four of those black cars and I know Whetto was working with them the whole time.

"I know I'm toast, so I'm on the phone while they're chasing me, making calls, probably made three or four calls. I knew I wasn't going to be able to call once I got to jail.

"I tell Marcos, the guy in Tucson; 'Dude set us up. I'm gonna need that money for the 140 pounds.'

"They pull me over.

"When the cop comes up to me, he says 'Smells like you've been smoking dope.'

"The smell of smoking dope and raw dope, it's two different smells.

"He says 'You been smoking weed?'

"I say 'No.'

"They open the van and it's full of it.

"While I'm getting pulled over, my nephew the retard – who was driving in front of me – starts acting all crazy, like he can distract four fucking cop cars away from a van they know has 1,000 pounds of dope in it.

"They grab him.

"I say 'He's got nothing to do with it. He didn't know anything; he just gave me a ride out here.'

"They separated us when we got to jail, kept him away from me. Rocketman was in a holding cell and I was in the cell block.

"In the morning I told him 'After we go for the bond hearing, I don't know if the feds are going to try to tie me into the other case with the 57 people who went to jail or if my letter of immunity will stand up against that.' I told him 'Let me sit. If the feds don't come within a week, come bond me out.'

"I had bought him all kinds of shit. I told him 'Sell your car, do whatever you gotta do to get me out.'

"He says 'OK' and they let him go."

At that point Allen had time to think about out how it all went down; starting with why Whetto insisted on using the truck.

"I would never let anybody know where the stash house was, especially somebody that's just a driver/transporter. I wouldn't tell him anything like that.

"I realized maybe the truck had a tracker on it so they could find the stash house and snag those guys. It would look like I set them up and my life would be in danger.

"When we moved the 1,000 pounds from the truck to the van and then back to the truck, that's probably when they realized they can't get me like that. They had to improvise.

"And then Whetto thought my nephew was going to drive the truck and get arrested; they'd make a case against him and he'd tell on me. He wouldn't have to testify against me.

"When he sees me get in the van to drive, he gets nervous. He knows I'm going to get busted and he'll have to face me."

"Two weeks later Rocketman came and got me out on bail.

"Turns out Marcos wouldn't meet me with the money I knew I was going to need. This is when I needed it more than ever because I had to pay lawyers and everything else.

"In fact, Marcos never talked to me again. He got scared that I'm going to set him up."

Allen wasn't upset. "That's a natural reaction."

Allen didn't know the *full* extent of Whetto's treachery until after everything went down.

"Months before Tiny had wanted to work for me taking stuff, so I said OK. I had a friend in NY. I did a load and Tiny was going to take another load with 300 pounds.

"So I loaded him and I told him 'Don't tell anybody. Don't say anything, just get on the road.'

"He stayed in a hotel the night before he left; and he called Whetto and told him what he was doing. I don't know why. That's not something you tell anybody.

"Tiny got on the freeway and in less than five miles the DPS [the Department of Public Safety] pulled him over. They got a tip."

NOW Allen was angry.

"Tiny had been in jail for all those years and Whetto put him right back in.

"So now my Mexicans wanted to see me. They asked if I could come down. I took a flight from Chicago to Tucson and talked to 'em.

"I said 'Look, the guy that set me up was working with the feds. We used to call him Whetto. He told the DEA and FBI where I was and that's when they got me. I knew it was fishy because they don't just do that; they're not going to just pull me over. There's no way they could catch me if he didn't tell.'

"They said 'Don't worry about it. You go back and take care of your case and we'll take care of Whetto.'

"I never heard about Whetto again."

"I met my guys from Chapo in Juarez a few times after that. He was going to be there. He and his brothers were running everything down there.

"My guy called and said he wanted me to come down and shop. I decided to take The Rocketman.

"I told him 'We're going to go to Juarez.'

"They made reservations for us at some hotel and my guy would be there.

"I flew to El Paso. The taxi guy drove me and The Rocketman across the bridge and they had a hotel for us, a real nice suite ... as sweet as a suite can be in Juarez.

"So I check in, we had breakfast with my guy and he says he's got some things to do.

"I had guards, so I told Rocketman 'Don't say anything. Just look and learn and some day you can do this.'

"My guy put me with some other guys with machine guns in Suburbans and we started going around to houses, warehouses and whatnot looking at dope.

"The police are in front and in back of us. I remember they used to take me around to where all the dope was.

"On these trips you go into private homes and the people are just very gracious; they offer you drinks, whatever you want. They know that if I'm there I'm somebody. They don't do that with insignificant people, they just don't.

"I met with Carlos, one of my guys from Culiacán. Carlos and I always had fun together because he liked to party; they couldn't believe how much I could party all day and all night.

"We went up to where they were growing the weed and it took us probably 10 hours to get there.

"This one small town had no power, so they had generators. We had to bring gas and tubing in case parts broke, so that the plants could get watered.

"I'd walk through there to look at all the plants and see how they're coming and tell them what I wanted. They had some drying.

"I'd walk through the creek that runs through. They have like boards over it so you can get across.

"I had The Rocketman with me and he was a complete idiot. He disliked everybody. He's kinda short, has that Napoleon thing going against him. Outward Bound didn't help.

"He said stuff that was out of line, that was disrespectful. 'This stuff is garbage!'

"I had to tell him 'Shut the fuck up! Just SHUT UP!'

"The first time I went I took Dominic. After that I wouldn't take him again.

"The second time they stashed me in a house with 5 or 6 guys.

"They said 'You want to play cards or *do this or do that?*'

"I said 'No I want to go out.'

"They told me 'We can't go outside.' They didn't want me to be seen."

He laughed. "I did have the best Lobster Thermidor down there."

20 Bending Under Pressure

"At first the feds said they pulled me over because I was speeding in a construction zone. My lawyer tells the judge, 'You think he'd be speeding with 1,000 pounds of marijuana in the van your honor?'

"If the feds had a witness, they would have had a case and I would have been in the Fed again; but they didn't, so they turned it over to Will County.

"I got a lawyer Rocketman knew from college – some kid. And then right off the bat he's telling me I'm going to do 7 years.

"I said 'Fuck you and 7 years; I'm not doing 7 years!' They don't have a case!' I told him 'The feds are involved. You gotta get to discovery.'

"Later he comes back with 'They came down to five years.'

"I said *no* again. I kept after him and he said 'I got it down to 3 years. They're not going to come down any more.'

"I was going to do three years, less six months good time that everybody gets. I would have been out in under a year; with good time, probably 8 to 9 months.

"I called a friend of mine that's a big time lawyer in New Jersey, ran the scenario by him.

"He says 'You know you're going to win. It's just up to you if you want to take the time right now.'

"I was seriously considering that. But then I talked to another guy who was out on bond and he said he had a really good lawyer in Chicago – Joe Lopez."

Allen told his friend in New Jersey "I'm going to talk to him."

I googled him. Burnstein's headline on *gangsterreport.com* read "CHICAGO'S 'SHARK' MIGHT GET BIT, MOB LAWYER COULD BE IN HOT WATER."

In the story Burnstein describes him as "Famously flamboyant Illinois criminal defense attorney Joe (The Shark) Lopez, a mouthpiece and litigator for numerous high-profile Chicago mobsters and underworld characters...."

Burnstein says he was "Nicknamed the Shark for his aggressive courtroom tactics."

Allen says "I told Joe they offered me three years on 1,000 pounds which – in retrospect – I probably should have took.

"Joe said 'This is easy,' so I fired the kid. I felt he really wasn't trying to help me.

"I gave Joe $25,000 in cash and explained 'They're hiding what really happened.' I said 'You've got to subpoena them to come to court. Get to discovery from the feds.'

"Joe keeps asking for the discovery. Finally we get it and it's all blacked out.

"They had a 20 team task force trying to get me. So I said 'Subpoena them.'

"He subpoenas the DEA, goes to court and tells the judge and everybody that we had an informant; we gave them the information.

"The local police kept saying they had no information, they just 'happened' upon me. They kept saying it was just happenstance that they pulled me over for something else.

"I knew from the get-go that that doesn't happen. I don't *just get caught*. Their case is bogus; it's bullshit. They could never win, never in a million years because they had no witness and they lied."

"All this time I'm flying or driving back and forth from Tucson to Illinois for court appearances.

"Sometimes I'd stay up in Wisconsin with the kids. You're not supposed to do that, but what the shit. What are they going to do?

"I'm on a tight deadline heading back in a cream Escalade when I get pulled over in Texas. I was going one way on a road close to Amarillo; the cop was coming the other way.

"He saw me and he's thinking 'Oh, *a big shot*.' He made a U-turn, pulls me over and says 'Can we search the car?'

"I say 'Fuck no; you're not searching the car.'

"So he says 'OK, just wait right here. I'm going to get a dog.'

"You could tell there was nothing in there. They said the dog alerted. *Yeah right*. Dogs always alert. So now it's going to take probably 3 hours.

"They took my car apart. Took everything out – the seats – didn't find anything.

"I'm on the side of the road just sitting there. I think I had half a joint in my pocket. He patted me down and found it in my cargo shorts.

"He said 'This is it? Why didn't you just tell me? It would have saved us a lot of time.'

"I said 'Fuck you, I wasn't doing anything wrong!'

"He gave me a ticket for misdemeanor possession and took the joint. No big deal.

"I get back on the road. I'm not stopping, I need to make up time. So I drive and keep driving. Finally I get close to where I'm supposed to go to court, which was in Joliet.

"It's the middle of the night, like 2 a.m.

"In Springfield I get pulled over again. This time the guy has the dog in his back seat. I'm like 'What the fuck.'

"He goes 'Mind if we search your car?'

"I said 'Yes I mind, I have to be in court tomorrow in the morning.'

"So he goes 'Well, I'm going to run my dog around it.'

"The dog alerts. There's nothing in the car, not a thing. I didn't even have the joint any more.

"He says 'We're going to have to take it to the shop where they take 'em apart.'

"I said 'As long as you put it back together as it was.'

"We're in a Podunk town and he had to call a guy to open the body shop.

"I'm sitting there for three or four hours and they find nothing. Well actually they found a pocket knife.

"They're like 'What is this?'

"I said 'Fuck if I know.' It wasn't mine, the cop in Texas must have dropped it while he was searching.

"They find nothing, so finally they start apologizing. They know they're in the wrong. By the time they put the car back together it was 4 a.m.

"And so it happened twice in the same day. It was just the weirdest thing. They didn't find anything and then they kept apologizing because they know I coulda sued 'em.

"So I drive towards where I have to be at court, find a shitty hotel, check in and try to sleep for a few hours before I have to get up and get dressed for court.

"I was there on time, but they're always waiting for something, trying to do something. They tell me it's going to be another 30 days. I'm so pissed."

"The DEA finally comes to court and tells the truth. They're saying there was no informant.

"They testified that it was a setup, that they had a task force of 20 to 30 FBI and DEA agents working the case to get me.

"They said 'Yeah we gave these guys the information' – that the deal I was doing with my nephew was going to go down. And they gave them all the information they needed so they could come in and sweep me up.

"As soon as the DEA came and testified, the head of the DEA told my lawyer 'Your guy's gonna walk.'

"Once they came to court and testified that they turned the information over to Will County, the case should have been dismissed right there; but Will County kept denying it. Clearly the Will County prosecutors were lying.

"I'm thinking my lawyer should ask for a dismissal then and there. He doesn't; *what the fuck!* They've got me all fucked up so I can't do anything.

"The lawyer says 'Take it easy, it's going to get dismissed.'

"But it keeps getting dragged on and on. It really pissed me off. I don't know what his deal was. The fucking lawyer that I paid was supposed to be good. He fucking can't do his job. He's a fucking scumbag.

"During those 3 months I went up to Milwaukee I'm staying in a hotel by my kids so I could be with them every day.

"I'm thinking to myself *What am I going to do now?*

"I wanted to buy a house near my kids. There were several times where I paid large sums of money for my quarterlies; later I found out it went in and came right out. Someone is taking it out and some IRS agent is thinking 'Well he didn't pay it.'

"They had put a lien on me for another seven million dollars. They can only have that lien for 10 years, then it's supposed to come off and they have to notify everyone within six months.

"My credit was zero. I went from having bullets credit to zero.

"Missy called asking for the diamond necklace. She said 'You know that necklace you bought for our first Christmas? *I want that.*'

"I said 'Well *I don't have it.*'"

"My mom passed in 2005. I've had feelings that she's come to me at night in dreams.

"She told me 'Things are going to be good, you're going to be fine. Don't worry.'

"Then I was in Chicago or somewhere, fighting my case when I heard my father was in the hospital. He had a bad heart, emphysema and a pacemaker.

"I went to see him with Douglas.

"My brother's teeth were breaking and rotting out from smoking crack. My uncle's a dentist and he would have helped him for free. But he wouldn't do it; so now he has no teeth.

"We were walking out of the hospital when a very pretty nurse checked me out. Douglas said 'Did you see how she's looking at you?'

"I said 'Next to you I look like Cary Fucking Grant.'

"Our father recovered and went home; but then a week later he had a relapse and had to go back to the hospital. I was on my way to see him but I didn't make it to the hospital before he died."

He remembered his dad's prayer the day he was born; "Dear Lord, please let this kid live."

"He smoked two packs a day, but he carried me. If something had happened to me, he couldn't have lived with himself.

"My parents left my little brother their house and their money; none of the rest of the family needed it.

"Douglas smoked it all up."

"I always thought nothing's ever going to happen to me in spite of the near misses and the warnings.

"A whirlwind was building around me, but I wasn't paying attention. I lost my house. My wife and kids were gone. I lost my mom and dad.

"My nephew was just an idiot. He asked me to bring him product and doesn't do what he's supposed to do. I get in trouble; he blames me.

"I go 'How the fuck you gonna blame me? I told you what to do. If you listened, I wouldn't have been in trouble. We could have gone on from there.'

"I'm bouncing around – it wasn't a good situation. For that I blame myself. I was very stupid; some things I would have never done before in my life, I did.

"My friend Ray in New York said 'You're one of the smartest people I know, but what you did – you kept tempting fate. It finally caught up with you.'"

A.S. empathized. "Everyone I know who's gone too far for too long, when easy money continues to come easily, you get the attitude that you're somewhere above the law; you've escaped the law, it's never going to go down. *And it does.*

"But who knows when to get out?"

He knew I knew he never does.

I said "Yeah, like gambling. Like knowing when to walk away from the table."

A.S. laughed. "I don't want to walk away from the table until I have the title to the casino."

•　•　•

By this time it's nearly ten years since Allen went over the cliff in the Jeep. You don't just *walk away* from sliding off a cliff.

"I couldn't turn off my right in my golf swing, I couldn't walk without a bad limp. I had pain medication, but it hurt inside my groin; it felt torn.

"I saw one of the top surgeons in the country. At first he's telling me it's going to be six months before he can get me in; then he looked at the x-ray and said 'I'll get you in right away.'

"The Super Bowl was in Detroit that year. My surgery was scheduled for the Friday after the game. Me and Ricky, LaMonte and some other people from Arizona planned to go.

"I was already in Chicago, so I drove to Michigan. We arranged a place downtown; I think it was in the GM Building, in the lower level.

"Joe Vicari who owns Andiamo's is like family. He had a bar down there and he fixed it up and got food for me and had big screen TV, all that kind of stuff so we could watch the game and drink and do whatever we wanted.

"I sold some tickets to pay for all of our stuff.

"Ricky went to the game for about a minute. We hung out for a week, we were just partying and we had a great time.

"The week after the game I was admitted to Rush Presbyterian in Chicago.

"I had a hernia, had to have that fixed first. It hurt because they cut through your stomach. They turned it from an outie to an innie, which was weird.

268

"About a month later they did my hip. My doctor said 'You're going to have to manage the pain.'

"I told him 'I don't want to take OxyContin.'"

"At first you're not supposed to get out of bed. You stay in the hospital until you learn to go up and down stairs with your crutches.

"I had got into it with The Rocketman, so after the hospital I went to stay with Peter's brother-in-law in Chicago. Peter's family took good care of me.

"The hospital sends a nurse every day for a couple weeks to make sure everything is going well. You can't even get up to go to the bathroom at night.

"I took the Oxy for a while; then I said 'I'm done with these.' After that I was taking the Percocets – they have acetaminophen and more narcotic. Then I weaned myself off everything.

"The doctor said it would take six months to recover, but I was moving around pretty good in about a month. I could walk. And then they do some light rehab and you go to physical therapy. Stretch your legs, have you work with heavy balls and stand on one foot, then the other.

"My hip felt so much better; I'm a miraculous healer.

"I was planning on going to Mexico and just swimming in the ocean for full rehab; but then I got indicted and I couldn't do that.

"I started coming back to Tucson between court appearances.

"Douglas called the county and told them I was leaving the state. I have no idea why he did that.

"They told me 'You're not supposed to leave the state' – but they told Douglas 'We don't care, as long as he makes his court dates – which he has.'

"I kept going back and forth to court; then that summer I had a 30 day continuance because my attorney was defending the policeman that killed all his wives."

On 4/19/10 Emanuella Grinberg of CNN reported "Former Illinois police officer Drew Peterson has changed up his defense team two months before the murder trial in his third wife's death is scheduled to begin.

"Joining the defense team is Joseph Lopez, a veteran trial attorney nicknamed 'The Shark.' He is known in legal circles and among mafia buffs for representing some of Chicago's most notorious mobsters."

During the continuance, Allen says "There's a guy I got to know, a young kid. I would get him some product once in a while. He'd sell it and give me the money. It was easy. That's how I was living then.

"My friend in Chicago introduced me to him. This was the guy who sold the dope I had brought in. He was one of the people I made very rich.

"So the kid calls me and asks me to set something up for him.

"I told him, I said 'You know what? I can't help you.'

"He pushes.

"I said 'You just gotta wait. I'm not going to do anything.'

"He says 'Please, you've got to. I have this guy; he'll buy 300 pounds *every other day*. You can move probably 5,000 pounds just this summer alone.'

"I said 'No.' I kept telling him 'NO!'

"He said 'I *know* you can go down and get it.' He says 'I'll buy your ticket, pick you up, *anything*.'

"So I go down to Arizona. My cousin picks me up at the airport and we take a drive to where the product is, so I can look at it and make sure it's decent, make sure it's what they want.

"I said 'This will work fine.' They said they're going to send it.

"I told them 'I'll be there in 3 or 4 days' and this guy is supposed to pick me up at the airport when I come in.

"I have drivers to do all this stuff but he no-shows and now I have nowhere to go. I called a friend and he comes and gets me.

"One of my Mexican friends was coming up in a couple days, so I had to get an extended stay place. He was going to hang with me for the summer while we did these few tons. We were going to get a place in Chicago.

"Another friend warned me that the kid got busted and rolled over. I said 'Why would he tell on me? He's going to make money!'

"So he drops off a truck and I'm feeling really freaked out, but at the same time I have one of my friends from Culiacán with me.

"I said 'I don't feel good about this.'

"He was like 'Don't worry about it.'

"The deal was going down in a bad area with a lot of gangs. If I had known that, I would have never went out there.

"I end up going to pick it up. "I get in the truck and it had the 300 pounds in it.

"It's rush hour and you can't tell if somebody's following you.

"Suddenly there are 30 or 40 cop cars, unmarked cars and helicopters. They pull me over. They break the windows out of the truck with their guns and throw me on the ground.

"I had this small Cartier wallet; I kept my credit cards and pictures of my kids in there.

"One of the cops opens it and he says 'You have beautiful kids. It's a shame you're going to be away from them for a while.'

"I said 'This is the first inning of a 9 inning game.'

"They wanted me to get more dope so they could round up more people and then they'd let me go. My guys from Tucson had sent the stuff up there, so I had different places I *could* go get it.

"I said '*Absolutely not*. You can go fuck yourself. Take me to jail.'

"Now I know I'm completely fucked because I'm out on bond from a case that should have been dismissed. Any time you're out on bond and commit the same crime, you're going to get hammered; which I did.

"They had a big file on me when they got me. Now I've got two cases to deal with. I'm going from one court to the other and I can't bond out.

"The friend from Chicago – the friend I made rich – had a watch of mine, a very expensive watch, a Panerai. I asked him to give it back. I said 'I just need to sell it to pay an attorney.'

"He said 'Well, I already bought the watch.'

"I said 'Alright.' That's the kind of cheap prick he was. He wouldn't even give my watch back.

"My Mexicans were going to hit the kid who snitched on me *and* this friend who introduced us. They wanted to kill him, but I told them 'No, please don't. It would make me look bad.'

"One guy had already disappeared and I didn't want it to turn into more of that. I didn't need them having hits out on people for pretty much no reason.

"Well, there *was* a reason but if they took care of them while I'm locked up in Chicago, the feds would know I put the hit on them and I'd be *really* fucked."

"The lawyer from my other case wouldn't drive all the way out there if I didn't give him money and I didn't have any. I used it to pay for everything.

"Joe called Freedom Freddie and told him to take the case.

"Freedom Freddie did me no favors.

"Now I know for sure I'm going to jail for a while. I didn't have good representation. I didn't have enough money to make it a decent fight.

"The key to everything is money. I thought it might be 2 or 3 years and it ended up being 6."

21 Paying the Price

"I was pretty much one of the top guys in the country. The government estimated me at dealing 180,000 tons. How many people sell that kind of weight and don't get caught for 20 years?

"I think that's why I got as big a sentence as I got; they were pissed.

"The difference between jail and prison is in jail you're fighting your case, you can bond out, you have options. Once you go to prison your options are over with. You're serving whatever time you agreed to.

"The sentence was 12 years, but you do 50% of your time and you're supposed to get six months good time.

"Everyone in the federal lockups in Illinois was there fighting their case. I stayed in county for 2 ½ years trying to figure a way out."

The 2 ½ would count toward his total years.

"So now I'm stuck in jail with a bunch of gangbangers.

"You don't look at the time, you just go day by day. I just did my thing. I didn't bother anybody; I didn't make any problems for the guards or anything.

"I had a couple guards that would bring me this special soap I liked. It was no big deal to them, they would just do it."

Allen says "My goal in prison was to keep my health and get out of there no worse than I came in."

Some prisons soak taxpayers $35,000 a year per prisoner. Not much of that goes into *feeding* them. They'd rather make a profit.

"You've got to go to the store and buy food. It's a commissary. You try to spend as little as possible because they marked everything up so much.

"You buy Ramen noodles or dried beans you could mix with hot water and summer sausage. All that food that'll kill you, the salt in the noodles alone. So you try to mix everything up."

A little extra money would have gone a long way.

"The Rocketman never thanked me for not saying anything. He never sent me a dime while I was locked up.

"I've got a cousin who did very, very well. He got into the stock market at the right time.

"His father had a tire store off I-75 and McNichols in a really bad neighborhood. They fixed and sold tires and worked hard; sold a ton of tires and made good money.

"We're related on both sides. His dad and my mom are cousins. And his mother is my brother-in-law's sister.

"We grew up together, we were really close. I stayed at his house; we went to California together and spent the summer with my sister because she was his aunt.

"I got ahold of him one day.

"He says 'Is there is anything I can do?'

"I said '$200 for commissary, something like that?'

"He said 'No problem.'

"But he never answered my phone calls after that."

Prison overcrowding was another problem.

"I was going back and forth to court, from one court to the other. They'd bring me back to Kane County, Illinois, keep me a day or two and ship me out again.

"They sent me to McHenry County because they had a big federal population there. I'd stay until my next court appearance, go and come back, that kind of thing.

"They'd take me in shackles in the back of a van.

"Sometimes I'd get money from my lawyer, like $20 or $30 when I needed real food. He'd hand it to me secretly.

"I'd say 'You know guys, how about something to eat on the way back, my treat?'

"They'd say 'How the fuck do you get money?'

"I said 'Don't worry about it.'

"These guys would stop and get whatever I wanted. KFC was a little slice of heaven. No Taco Bell!

"One of the places they used to send me didn't have any windows. They had small glass skylights way high up. That was the only natural light.

"There was no yard, but actually it wasn't bad because you could do shit, you could do your laundry every day.

"You weren't locked in a cell. The cells were all open and you had three roommates.

"I went there once or twice and they kept sending me to McHenry.

"And then at the end Kane County opened up the gym for inmates that were low risk, guys who were well-behaved and didn't cause problems.

"They let us sleep there and stay up all night watching TV; they gave us the remotes. It was a reward for good behavior.

"The day after they moved me there this guard that didn't like me comes and throws me back in the worst of the worst places in the prison, where they're all murderers in for life sentences. That's where all the high bond guys are."

There was someone who didn't like you?

"There were *a lot* that didn't like me."

He continued. "My bond was $800,000 so he made me move back there and I was there for probably half a day and then they moved me right back. I guess he got in some kind of trouble for doing it."

"They were building a new jail in Kane County. When that opened I stayed there until I went to prison."

"While I was in jail Missy told the girls I abandoned them.

"She was doing every drug. She would get Xanax and take it all day and just be a mess. So her parents put her in rehab and took the kids to live with them. They took care of them, got them everything they wanted or needed; they didn't go without.

"Missy's mom's got her master's in education. She would help the kids with their homework. That's why my kids go to school and get good grades – because of them. I owe them a debt of gratitude for that.

"I know they spent a lot of money on my kids. If I make a lot of money I plan on giving them some.

"Missy was in rehab 6 months, they weren't messing around with her. She came out clean, but blaming me. How the hell can you blame me for your drug addiction? I met her when she was 20; she started doing drugs when she was 15."

Over the course of two years we had become good friends. Allen was the first call on Christmas and a shoulder when things went bad.

He'd been telling me about drug use in prison when – late one night – a friend called crying. Her sister died of heroin mixed with Fentanyl.

I knew it was a national problem, but I went online to learn more; *thefix.com* had an article – *Drug Dealers Are Mixing Fentanyl with Heroin in Potentially Deadly Combo* by May Wilkerson, 8/28/15.

The article said more than 1,000 people died from Fentanyl-heroin overdoses between 2005 and 2007. "The more narcotic you take, the less your body has an urge to breathe," said Dr. J.P. Abenstein, president of the American Society of Anesthesiologists. "And it makes sense that a lot of people are overdosing on it because they aren't sure how much to take."

The following morning I told Allen about it. He explained that Fentanyl is "Like OxyContin, it's a pain medication. It comes in a patch, it's a gooey liquid in the patch. They open the patches and mix it with the heroin."

According to drugabuse.gov, "Fentanyl is a powerful synthetic opioid analgesic that is similar to morphine but is 50 to 100 times more potent. It is a schedule II prescription drug, and it is typically used to treat patients with severe pain or to manage pain after surgery. It is also sometimes used to treat patients with chronic pain who are physically tolerant to other opioids."

That's how Allen knew it on a personal level. He said "I took Fentanyl when I was in pain, when they were trying to wean me off of the OxyContin."

I've heard it's also prescribed in lozenge or lollipop form in hospice units for patients dying of agonizing cancers.

On *thefix.com* I learned that DEA seizures of drugs containing Fentanyl more than tripled between 2013 and 2014, from 942 to 3,334.

Allen added "Special K is a horse tranquilizer. Ketamine. They add that too. People who do Special K can go into the K hole and you can't move for a while. You just sit there and you're out of it.

"I had a friend who sold it. He got 19 years. He sold it but he didn't do it. You see people dying from the stuff you're selling them, you're not going to do it.

"When they were moving me around Chicago, there were these guys, a whole crew of them that was arrested for selling heroin mixed with Fentanyl. A lot of people died."

They were the Mickey Cobras. The Washington Post headline for 6/26/06 read: *Chicago Gang Targeted in Heroin Deaths.*

'Fentanyl-laced heroin has been blamed for more than 200 overdose-related deaths across the eastern half of the country in recent months, at least 70 in the Chicago area…

"Assistant U.S. Attorney Gary Shapiro alleged that the Mickey Cobras gang marketed its drugs to take advantage of the deadly heroin's notoriety, selling products with names such as 'Max Pain,' 'Lethal Injection,' 'Fear Factor,' 'Drop Dead' and 'Final Call.'

"They carry niche marketing to its extreme," Shapiro said. "They sell branded heroin."

The article said 47 members and gang associates were charged; 30 were arrested. Allen met some of them.

"The Mickey Cobras were all locked up where I was. I started talking to the top guy. He said they wanted to give him 25 years to life. He said 'What should I do?'

"I said 'I don't know.' I looked at the rest of the guys with him. They were all gang bangers, hard core street thugs. I said 'They're not going to *not* tell to get a better deal.'

"He said 'How do you know?'

"I said 'I just do. It's the way it is. It's going to come down to you or them. They're going to say you're the leader.'

"He said one guy already made a deal to cooperate. He showed him to me and I never talked to the guy again. I would never talk to him. And he didn't talk to him.

"I said 'He's already told you were the guy. They know he'll testify, you really don't have much of a choice.'

"I said 'Listen to your lawyers, see what they come up with.'"

Allen's next move was traumatic. He didn't like talking about it.

"After 2 ½ years bouncing around Illinois they put me in Stateville, Illinois. When you go to Stateville you're being processed for a penitentiary, unless you did murder or something like that. If you murdered somebody, you go behind the wall."

Stateville Correctional Center

Stateville is a maximum security state prison for men. In 1994 John Wayne Gacy – The Killer Clown who killed 'at least' 33 boys and young men – received a lethal injection there.

It ranked seventh on *inmatesurvival.com's Top 10 Worst, Toughest, Deadliest and Most Dangerous Prisons and County Jails in the United States of America.*

They call it 'Hotel Hell.'

"I'm looking at it and I'm thinking *What the fuck. This is not going to be pleasant.*"

"They put you in a bullpen and you have to fill out a bunch of forms; it takes a whole day.

"They want to know how much money you have and what your assets are because they charge you if you have more than a certain amount; *they charge you rent to be in prison.*

"Then you're standing in a big shower with a bunch of other guys and 15 guards spray and delouse you."

Was that the worst moment of your life?

"*All* of those moments were the worst in my life. I hate having to remember it.

"They use black lights to see if you have any bugs on you. They spray you down with pesticides and shit and give you an itty bitty towel.

"After that you wait in line to see every doctor and dentist to check you for stuff. People had MRSA, a really bad staph infection – all kinds of stuff.

"They said 'You want an AIDS test?'

"I said 'Yeah, might as well.'

"They give you a pair of boxers, socks, a yellow jumpsuit and white canvas shoes. Everything is used, there's nothing new.

"I wear size 11 ½ shoes; they gave me size 13."

Charles Shaw, author of *Exile Nation* was in for 13 days.

"It was 'only' thirteen days, I can tell myself now, four years later. But while it was happening, it was a form of torture that leaves an indelible scar on a person's soul. That is why they call Stateville, 'Hotel Hell.'

"It is a cold and sterilized form of detention, a little taste of a Supermax prison for everyone. Once they process you in, put you in that big powder blue jumpsuit and those slipper-shoes, stuff you into that 6 x 10 cement hole, and slide that automated steel door shut, you don't come out again. You are on 24-hour-a-day lockdown, with your cellmate if you have one, and nothing else. Nothing to read, nothing to see, nothing to do but wait, wait, wait. And once the waiting begins, things start to go all sorts of ways inside your mind."

Allen did more than double Shaw's time.

"I sat there for over 40 days. You don't get out of your cell ever, even in the dead of winter. You get out once a week for 5 or 10 minutes to take a shower and that's it. *No hocus pocus.*

"You're just there until you're going to leave and you don't know when you're going. They pass out bags; you open the bag and it'll have your name and the place you're going. They put you in a jumpsuit to transport you.

"You gotta get up and go to the bus at 4 or 5 in the morning. They start marching people up to the buses, shackle you and you get on and go for your ride.

"There's a bucket in the back of the bus in case you have to pee. Other than that, the bus doesn't usually stop. They don't give a fuck.

"Where I went they had to stop at another prison on the way. They let us get off the bus to walk in a fenced area to stretch our legs, but it was raining and freezing and nobody had a coat. I'm like *this is going to be a long time.*

"Then they talked about sending me to Taylorville in southern Illinois.

"I said 'Do I want to go there?'

"They said 'Yeah.'

"I think that was a little extra bonus. It was one of the nicest facilities there was. They interview you to get to go there. You can't have gang affiliations, certain tattoos and whatnot.

"When you leave Hotel Hell you don't get anything, you leave in their transport clothes; an orange jumpsuit, a t-shirt, underwear and shoes. That's all.

"You take that off for Taylorville."

Taylorville Correctional Center

"I gotta tell you, Taylorville is half a step up from a looney bin. That's where they send all the child molesters, rapists and gays. Those guys are all crazy and I was in a long time. It's almost like dog years; one seems like seven.

"A lot of 'em are young, not educated, and their IQs are so low they don't understand a lot of things.

"There are middle aged people that have been doing shit for so long … men who've been abusing their kids; how do you touch children? There's guys there that screwed animals. *C'mon.*

"We were given blue pants and a light blue shirt. Two pairs of pants, two shirts, a jacket – all the stuff you need. You get an ID you're supposed to wear on your shirt at all times."

"The rooms at Taylorville are small and there's 20 people in a room – 10 bunk beds on each side.

"Every night I watched TV in my bunk. I had my own cable TV. You can't have volume on your TV, you have to wear a headphone.

"I had a mattress; I took off the plastic so it would just be cloth. I put my sheet on that and threw the plastic in the garbage. They came out with a thicker mattress but you couldn't get the plastic off it. I said fuck that, I'm staying with this one.

"In Taylorville they had bath sheets. I'd wash 'em every week but they still get like brownish, so I used to get new ones all the time. I got enough so I could change 'em every month and give the old ones away.

"I couldn't sleep well. Sometimes you have dreams where you're not really there. You think it was just a dream that it happened; and then you wake up and *Oh yeah – I'm here.*

"One guy swore he wasn't gay but he was always staring at me. I'd wake up and he'd be looking at me while I was asleep.

"You have to worry about that. You have to be ready to fight over stupid things. It's the same as you see on TV, but not as bad as Oz.

"Some people you look at and you know they don't belong there. Others, it's like *This mother fucker deserves to be UNDER the jail.*

"People that are fine one day can be totally freaked out the next day. They find out what's happening on the outside and it fucks them up because there's nothing they can do. Like 'Oh my wife is cheating with the neighbor now.'

"There was health care, but we called it 'death care.'

"One guy had cancer and they wouldn't do anything to treat it; it was too expensive, so he died.

"They give you a checkup every year. The doctor was horrible, but she kind of liked me. I never told her about my back problems, but I told her about my hip replacement. She gave me acetaminophen."

"Everyone knew I got popped with over 1,000 pounds. They didn't know the extent of how large I was. You can't tell people, why waste your breath.

"The niggers in that jail used to make me laugh. They'd say 'Give me 1,000 pounds and I'd know what to do.'

"I said 'Yeah, give you 1,000 pounds, you'd fuck it up in one minute you're so stupid.'

"They don't have anybody they know that could buy it or move it. Eights and quarters and all of a sudden they get 1,000 pounds – what are they going to do with it? Absolutely get caught.

"The guys in prison are all small timers, they don't know. I mean you gotta understand I was like one of a kind, the only one that did what I did."

Some of the guards had a sense for who he was.

"The IRS and Department of Treasury came to come see me, so they knew I wasn't just a regular inmate. They came to tell me I owed them a lot of money.

"They asked 'How you gonna pay for this?'

"I said 'I got Ramen Noodles. That's all I have.'"

"You have to have a routine. That's the best thing that you can do is just have some kind of a routine you do every day. It makes the days go faster.

"Ray sent me books and magazines. Every couple months I'd call him and tell him I want this book and that book and he'd send them."

What did you like to read?

"*The Girl with the Dragon Tattoo, Hawaii* ..."

Michener? That's a really long book!

"I had the time." Hours and days and months and years to fill.

"You play dominoes. You work. You figure out what you can eat. You don't have chow halls in your barracks.

"The only thing you have there is hot pots; we rigged them so they could boil and make coffee. We had to hide those."

Prison meals gave the day structure *minus* satisfaction or nutrition.

"You figure out what's on the menu for dinner and decide if you're going to go eat their slop.

"In the Fed they get real bread. Everything in the state penitentiary they process themselves, or have the inmates processing. In Illinois you can never eat the bread, it's all 900 years old. It's white bread and it's shit.

"I never ate a lot of things there; wouldn't eat the boloney."

The web is full of stories about prisons that serve too little food, too old food, green bologna and even maggots.

Alex Friedmann, Managing Editor of *Prison Legal News*, an independent publication of the Human Rights Defense Center, wrote "Everyone should have the right to decent food—adequate, nutritious food. It's not just that the [prison] food is bad, which generally it is. Food is used as a punitive measure."

Allen says "Some guys would be so hungry they'd go through the garbage for tray scrapings.

"I had a few friends who would send me money regularly so I would be alright - Peter, LaMonte, Ricky and Slavik. Slavik would send me $350 to $400 at a time.

"I'd buy peanut butter and snickers bars on commissary and give 'em to my friend that worked in the kitchen at the chow hall.

"He'd make peanut butter snickers cookies and we'd sell 'em for like $5 apiece.

"The only thing was I had to tell the COs what I was doing. Actually all of the COs knew that I was doing it.

"One tried to play a joke on one of the guys in my unit. He calls him and says 'Omigod, your guy just got grabbed up by the fucking warden!

"I told him 'Don't do that!' They can't see out in the yard from where they are. I got the cookies and I left.

"It's like a big square complex with sidewalks. I'm just walking along and the guy from my unit is calling the towers to see what's going on with me."

"When I first got there I cut across the grass in the yard.

"It was cold outside and I was in a hurry to go to the chow hall to get something to eat because I had to see the doctor.

"The sergeant started yelling at me. He said 'We paid a lot of money for these sidewalks, you don't go on my grass!'

"He was a big guy. I said 'Looks like you've been taking some shortcuts yourself there buddy.'

"He couldn't be mad. I made him laugh.

"Yard time starts at 12:30 and goes to 3:00, but your housing unit can only go for half at a time.

"After I was there for a while I could go out on everybody's yard, I knew the guy that was running it. I thought *This is great.* I'd go outside, walk and hang out.

"I gambled every day. I was gambling for money, food, and write outs. Envelopes with stamps are money, that's currency in jail. They're almost 50 cents apiece, two is a dollar.

"There's housing, each unit has 200 – 100 on each side. And there's doors with guards that you have to go through to get to the other side. They knew I had juice, so I could move around. I could say 'I'm going to see so and so.'

"I'd find out who the COs are. If they were newbies, I'd see if they're decent."

He had to be careful.

"Everybody would tell on people. One lieutenant told me 'They have informants on your wing.'

"I never believed they could call in directly to Internal Affairs but one day one of the sergeants I knew really well said to be careful. He goes 'They tell on everything, some *do* have a direct line to IA.'

"I said 'You're kidding? I thought that was an old wives tale or something.'

"He said 'No, it's true.'"

What's the worst that could happen?

"They could land you in the hole. The hole is segregation, you don't get to do anything. You're segregated from the regular prison population, all by yourself in a cell with no TV, no privileges.

"I had met a guy that was really a good guy. Steve was a drunk driver, killed a guy and got 9 years.

"He was with me the whole time I was there. We played poker, bet on sports on TV.

"He was my partner.

"I said 'Whenever you want to play, let me know.'

"The black guys liked to play spades. Not a racial thing, that was their game and they want to gamble on it.

"People would owe money. This one guy, I just kept making him buy me stuff at the commissary until he paid me off.

"Another guy I knew, I was always nice to him even though I knew he was a child molester. I was taking advantage of him.

"He was one of the guys who got arrested and was chained to a radiator for 48 hours because Cook County had nowhere else to put them. There was a bunch of 'em and everybody got paid. He got a $1,300 check.

"He had the money on his books and now he wanted to play poker. He thought he could win.

"I used to tell him 'Don't gamble any more. You're not good at it. You're not going to win, you're *not* going to beat me playing cards.'

"He lost all of his money and went in debt on top of it. He owed me $300 and he was afraid.

"I told him 'Don't worry about it, we'll work it out.'

"But there was no working it out. He got nervous and told on everybody – but he didn't tell on me.

"Then he got himself put in the hole to protect himself."

"I did things to get 'extra good time' towards my release. This stuff is so below you, but you gotta do something. I took a computer class. I was a teacher's aide in a culinary class. I volunteered to teach.

"Taylorville is the most insane place that I've ever been to. The level of education these people have or don't have would astonish. You see the damage that crack does to the children. Their mother was on crack, 'Lo and behold, look at little Johnny – he's retarded.'

"There are third generation crack babies in jail; you see the damage. They can't read or write. Come on – something's wrong with this."

"My girls were 12 and 7 when I went in. Missy wouldn't let them come see me when I was locked up. It was hard. I didn't know what was going on.

"Missy's parents know her shortcomings. They were decent with me.

"I owe a big debt of gratitude because while she wouldn't let the girls see me, they said they'd bring them down to visit. Only she wouldn't let them.

"For six years I didn't see my kids. Almost 6 ½ years. *I cried.*

"I'd call them at least three or four times a week. You put money on your phone account. You have a code, you dial in so they know who's dialing.

"The call quality is pretty shitty. There's a booth and one phone that sits out in the open; it's loud and hard to hear.

"In federal when you punch in your code to make a call, they have discs that will record that call.

"And your mail is always opened unless it's legal mail. The girls would write me and send pictures."

Even that was problematic.

"My youngest sent me a little bracelet she made and I was wearing it.

"One of the lieutenants goes 'What's that?'

"I said 'It's something my daughter made. I got it in the mail.'

"He said 'You shouldn't have got that in the mail.'

"I said 'So? I did.'

"He goes 'Well, I'm going to have to take it. It's contraband.'

"I said 'It's harmless' but he took it anyway. You could count on him being by the book every time."

"Nobody in my family came to see me, nobody I knew except for one friend in Chicago I've known for a long time. He came once the first summer I was there and then I couldn't get him back in.

"I went and begged the lieutenant in IA but he wouldn't let him in. He was the only visit I had.

"Douglas was writing me in jail and I was writing him back. He didn't have any money to send me, but he wrote 'I'll try to send you some next month.'

"Then all of a sudden the letters just stopped.

"The others never wrote even *one time* while I was locked up for 6 years. They're all thinking 'Too bad for him.'

"My niece got married. I was pissed. They could have sent me an invitation. It would have been a nice gesture to be invited even though I couldn't come.

"They could have sent me pictures to make me feel better. Any time you get mail when you're locked up it's a good thing.

"All I got were bills.

"My uncles in Dearborn passed away while I was locked up. Uncle Freddie and Norman. I used to get cars on the A Plan from him."

I told him in 2008 Gary Triano's wife was accused of setting up the hit. He was surprised.

"He owed everybody money. I never suspected her; she was last on my list."

In 2010 Augie Busch made news when a 27-year-old model died of an overdose in his mansion.

Not a surprise.

"I got 12 years, of which I was only supposed to do 5 ½ years, but they took away the good time. I did every minute of my time *plus* some.

"Your 'out' date is your 'out' date, but *they never filed my paperwork to go back to Arizona*; that meant I would have to stay in their jurisdiction until they sorted it out.

"I didn't have a place to stay so they pressured me to go to rehab. It was the only place they could send me. I was told I could just check in and leave."

There was one last hurdle before his release.

"When you get arrested they keep your clothes in case you get out or bond out. They ask where you want them sent. I was wearing shorts and a t-shirt so I said 'Just throw 'em away.'

"Now that I was waiting to leave I called Elaine and asked her to buy me jeans and a shirt so I'd have something to wear when I walked out.

"She told me to go to Salvation Army; like I could ask the guards to take me shopping or something."

Shocked and disappointed, he said "She could have just sent me some of her husband's clothes.

"The prison gave me a tight t-shirt and a pair of sweats with no pockets. They were supposed to give me cash but they didn't; they gave me a check and I had no way of cashing it.

"If they would have given me cash I could have bought my own shit. I had to go from the train station to where this place is, so there was all kinds of stuff."

"I was released from prison to rehab in May, 2013. It was my first time ever having to stay for a long time. Oh, I did not like it. I will not do anything stupid to go back."

What were those first few hours of freedom like?

"It was kind of strange. They drove me to the station because I had to take the train to Chicago.

"You know which people are prisoners because we all had the same shit on. I had to ask a stranger how to get where I was going downtown. He told me which trains to take."

"I was told I could just check in at rehab and leave, but my parole officer said I couldn't. I filled out my paperwork to go home to Arizona – *again* – and gave it to her.

"She said 'It's going to take a while.'

"Getting out of rehab was a cluster fuck. I had to spend more than six months in a halfway house with bed bugs.

"I went and saw the person that does the evaluations. She knew I wasn't a gang banger like most of the people there. She gave me a letter that said I wasn't required to do any rehab stuff.

"I didn't have to go to any classes, but while I'm on the premises I had to attend AA meetings. It depended on who was working. If it was a friend that I knew well, I could say 'I don't want to go that meeting.'

"Otherwise I'd sit there and I'm like *Omigod, these people are really fucked up. They would drink just to get drunk. What's the fun in that?* There *is* no fun in that. Just getting plastered 'til you can't walk – or drive into a tree or crash ... it makes no sense.'

"They tell you not to drink while you're there. I had one or two beers a week; they didn't check on me.

"Everyone there was on heroin, it's cheaper than most other drugs. My roommate OD'd.

"The girl that was my case manager liked me a lot. She always let me do whatever I wanted. I'd walk all around the city, from Navy Pier all the way north to the end of the Red Line.

"Friends were sending me money but I told 'em I had a job. I had a bank account, I had a driver's license.

"I couldn't play cards at all, they felt it caused fights or something; but there was a TV room where we had our meetings.

"On Sundays we'd gather around the TV.

"I'd order pizza and soda and we'd sit there and watch football if I didn't want to go out.

"I volunteered two or three days a week at a food shelter.

"After a while my case manager thought I should work on a political campaign for a guy who wanted to be re-elected state rep. I met the rep's friend Ralph through her. I helped get his guy on the ballot.

"I'd go to the stops where I knew I could get signatures. I dressed nice, I asked nice.

"After I helped with the election, Ralph told the rep how much I had done and put in a good word for me.

"The rep said 'I hear you want to go home.'

"I said 'Yeah.'

"He said 'When?'

"I said 'Right now.'

"He picked up the phone and called the head of Illinois Department of Corrections. They gave me a number and the time and said they would call me and tell me when I got approved.

"About a month later he called and told me, 'You're good to go, you can leave. But I might wait until your parole officer tells you.'

"I said 'I ain't waiting for shit.'

"I went back and told the manager at the rehab center that 'I got approved to leave. I'm getting picked up in the morning, I'm getting on an airplane and I'll check in at the parole place.'

"I came back to Scottsdale and they said I wasn't supposed to be there so soon. They made me wait six hours in the lobby before processing me.

"Then I went to live at my friend Scan's house. I knew him since JNC. He had a million dollar+ condo in a gated community. He told me I could stay there and help him at the restaurant.

"I got back right around Thanksgiving. I went with Scan to his ex's and we had Thanksgiving dinner. It was nice, with his family and his kids; everybody was there. We played beer pong and had a good time.

"I ended up staying there more than six months. It was Scan's friend that knew the people in L.A. that asked for this book.

"My parole officer never came to see me at Scan's. Then they told me I didn't even have to come in and see them anymore. I could just fill out a report and send it in every month.

"I just had to change the date and send it in."

• • •

Over the years things had changed in Detroit. The hard feelings that transpired within The Outfit in the late 60s came to an interesting conclusion.

In 2013 – one month after Allen's release – there was *another* costly dig for Hoffa's remains. A.S. knows people from the demolition company. He says "They were people I knew and had been doing some work with.

"I asked one of them, 'Why are they doing this? They're not going to find anything and if they do what does it all mean?'

"He told me he had asked an FBI agent 'Hoffa has been gone so long, why are you doing it?'

"The agent told him 'Because it's in the budget to try to find Hoffa's body and the case has never been closed. If we don't use it, we lose it.'

"That's $2 million a year trying to solve the disappearance, so they've pursued all leads. Some don't seem to be leads anybody would want to take."

Where did that lead *come* from?

On 6/17/13 Kevin Dietz, Reporter for Click On Detroit wrote *Feds dig in Oakland Township for remains of Jimmy Hoffa* - 'Location comes from aging mobster's tip'

"Mafia underboss Tony Zerilli told WDIV in an exclusive interview earlier this year that Jimmy Hoffa was buried in a shallow grave in this field... The property being searched today was once owned by mafia member Jack Tocco, Tony Zerilli's cousin, and became the head of the Detroit mafia after Hoffa's disappearance."

A.S. believes "That tip was Zerilli's personal vendetta to put some hurt on Jack."

The following year 87-year-old Jack Tocco died of natural causes. The press says he was 'the longest-serving mafia Godfather in the United States.'

Burnstein wrote that Tocco's death signaled "the end of an era – some would say a Golden Age – in the Detroit Mafia."

22 Sorting it Out

"Sometimes I dream that I'm still in prison. I'll jump up and see that I'm not and it'll be OK."

Allen had been out of Taylorville for about six months when we started working together.

He began by telling me about the first girl he met after prison. It was an awkward moment. I didn't know him. I braced myself for too much information.

He said "This girl that I know here, we're friends. We kind of hit it off.

"It's nothing sexual with her. I don't know, I just don't feel that way toward her. It wouldn't have been right because I would have been in it for sex and she would have been in it for the other reason.

"So I just didn't do it. But we're friends and we do things together and stuff.

"She's got an autistic son who's blind. When we go out she says 'Being with you is like having two of him.' She's gotta take care of both of us.

"We go out to the pool and I throw the ball for him.

"She says 'You KNOW he can't see!'

"I said 'I know. But he can feel when it splashes.'"

Life on the outside has been difficult. Despite charisma, education and legitimate business experience "Nobody wants to hire a felon."

"Here in Tucson people that are *in that business* know me on the street. Sometimes I run into the Mexicans. They know I didn't say anything about anybody. They'll see me, come up and kiss me, give me a hug.

"And people who know who these guys are will turn and look. They're like 'What the fuck? Who is this guy?'

"Once I got out my Mexican friends wanted to give me a lot of drugs so I could get back on my feet. I coulda got a ton or tons, but I said 'No thank you!'

"They're like 'If you want two, you can have them for free.' That's $4 million. I couldn't do it. I can't do it. I'd go away forever.

"I don't care how people make money, I really don't.

"Do what you want, do what you can, but I'm not going to do anything that puts me in jail.

"They're still doing it - everyone's always trying to get me to do things. NO. Now I'm afraid to even introduce people."

"Obviously it's a relief that I don't have to worry about dealing with the cartel any more. I don't have to worry about making payments or getting things rounded up.

"I don't have to worry about next week they need $500,000 or something like that.

"I had a friend who some guys owed him money. They went to his house and shot him eight times so they wouldn't have to pay him. They didn't shoot him in the face, but they shot all over his body – torso, legs, everything – as he was trying to get away.

"It was brutal, but he lived. And he says it was like the amount of money was a joke. To us $350,000 wasn't a lot.

"And it's such a relief that I don't know anything; they're not going to come after me. Most of 'em are dead now. Dale told on the rest of 'em, so they're in jail.

"I ran into a friend of mine here that I've known for a long, long time. He was never in the business but he knew what I did. The first thing he says is 'You're not going to kill him are you?'

"I said 'No, that's not in my mind. I don't like the guy, but I have no animosity towards anybody; life's way too short for that shit. It's like taking poison and waiting for the other person to die.

"The guys that told on me, I don't really blame them because they were looking to get out of trouble however they can. I'm not doing anything to anybody. Just live your life.

"What happened was pretty much my own fault. I was really self-destructive."

"The scar under my neck from where I crashed through the window – that's nearly gone.

"The scar from the cast iron fence is in what's left of my hairline; but I'm still in a lot of pain from the accident. There's some times that I can't lay on my back. I can lay on my side with a pillow between my legs for only so long, then I have to roll over.

"Now that I know how addicting drugs like OxyContin are, I won't take them. Even though I'm in pain, I just go through it.

"It's not worth it. I've had so many friends that I know die from opiates. Percocet, Percodan, Oxycodone, OxyContin and Vicodin – they're all opiates.

"When you take opiates like that it sends signals to your brain to block out the pain. What happens is you have to take more and more and more and you just can't get ahead.

"It's a constant struggle all night, but I've learned how to deal with it. I don't take any pain medication except for ibuprofen. And I smoke weed. It helps.

"With medical marijuana there are different strains for different things. It's better quality, it's grown better. Some of it's not grown in dirt, it's grown in water. It's cared for with the perfect amount of light.

"I still take Valium to loosen up because I have back spasms. And last month I got a shot of steroids in my back.

"I've had three surgeries so far because of that accident – with more on the horizon. I had nerve transplant surgery, hernia surgery, hip replacement and now they want to put new discs in my back. My discs are degenerated, almost bone on bone. The nerve's coming out, something's wrong.

"I'm like 'No, you're not operating on my back.' I always still tell everybody 'Don't get your back operated on!' The people I know that have had it, they're all crippled and addicted to pain medication."

"On the bright side, my liver got a 6 year break.

"My friend Charlie from U of A – his grandfather started one of the banks here and his father's loaded. He owns the largest cattle company in the United States.

"Now Charlie works at the bank. In the time that I was away he got married, had a family and quit drinking.

"We went to lunch a couple of times. Charlie said 'I don't know how to put my finger on it, but I've had to go through a lot of therapy.' And he goes 'When I'm with you, I enjoy being with you, but it brings back things I want to do.

"It's hard for me to hang out with you because you're always ready to go, ready to have a drink, have a this or that.'

"He says 'So the feeling bothers me so much I don't want to see you because of it. I'm sorry, but I've just got to take care of myself.'

"I respected him for that. He was being honest with me."

Allen's brothers and sisters are mostly OK.

"Elaine is going to be 80. She works every day as a paralegal, has been with the same law firm for a long time. As busy as she is, her house is always immaculate.

"Nadra is teaching at the school where my mother went, in Dearborn by Dix.

"Cindy's good, she's always good. We always got along. She says Douglas is doing OK, he's working. I haven't seen him for ten years. He doesn't want to talk to me.

"David was working for AAA. Now he owns his own insurance company in Dearborn. Everybody knows the last name, so he's got a big following of insured people that knew the family.

"My nephews – all of those kids ended up with me. All of 'em made money. None wound up in jail.

"Even Rocketman didn't wind up in jail. When he needed something I took the rap for him. Now we don't talk.

"I was on Rush Street in Chicago with my friend Aldo and he offered to take me to Carmine's for dinner. It was a nice day so we sat outside. At some point I went into the restaurant to use the bathroom.

"Later I find out The Rocketman and his mother were in the restaurant. *They ducked and hid from me.*

"I didn't even know that they did that until Midge told my Aunt Josephine. Aunt Jo was pissed and she told Peter.

"I made 'em all rich. I probably made 20 millionaires personally. They spent the money and wanted more. It's greed. Money changed them."

"I went by the arena after I got out and everything was torn down. Everything was gone. It was kinda sad. We used to have some good times there.

"I hadn't talked to George because he was struggling without me; he couldn't make money.

"He got himself in serious trouble with his family, went somewhere in the mountains east of Tucson and killed himself. Someone stumbled across the body. It had been out there for over six months."

"Tiny was living in the U.S.

"He was in jail for 58 ½ years and then he went home to his mom's house when he got out.

"And Whetto puts him right back in.

"When I got out of prison I should have went by his house to see if he's still alive."

"I don't know what's up with Ozzie now, don't know what he's doing. He had a pizza place in Tucson, but it's closed.

"Something happened with him that he knows I know he was in on it the whole time. That's what it feels like to me.

"I know guys he knows, so I hear stuff. If he was innocent in all this, he woulda made some effort to get in touch. He would be calling. We would be talking.

"In the end everybody betrays you for their own good.

"I don't have many friends left. After this book is out, I'll have even less."

"Missy wasn't in the marriage for 'better or worse.' She was only in it for better or better.

"When she found out the dot.com company wasn't going to work, that she wouldn't have millions in the bank, she didn't want to have anything to do with me.

"She was my wife. I didn't think she would ever betray me. She took everything of value and left me with nothing.

"Missy works and makes good money and her parents still give her an allowance.

"Now that I'm out I get a letter from Arizona Department of Economic Security for child support. They say 'Well, you were ordered to pay $5,000 a month in 2003.'

"I said 'Fine, whatever.' So I do the math. And it says I owe $365,000 – half of that's interest. The other half, 14 years at $60,000 a year – it doesn't add up.

"They kept the meter running while I was under indictment. They knew I couldn't work, knew I couldn't do anything.

"In jail I was making $28 a month. At that point in time the child support should have stopped. It should have been abated. How am I supposed to pay?

"Missy's dad likes me but he doesn't.

"He knows I didn't cheat on her or do anything to deserve what I'm getting. But at the same time he's paying for everything.

"I want to repay the money her parents spent."

Allen sees his daughters regularly; that means seeing Missy now and then.

"She seems to be doing well, staying clean. The last time I was with her I asked if it was OK if I had a drink. She said it didn't matter."

How are things between you two now?

"It's hateful on her side. I don't have time to hate anyone. I would have never in a million years got married if I thought I would wind up like this.

"On the other side, I have two beautiful kids. At least I got that out of her.

"My children are the two losers in this whole situation. I can never ever make that up to them. For not being there for certain things. It broke my heart. That is the tragedy of the story."

In 2015 three teenage girls wrote organized crime boss Whitey Bulger in prison as part of their history assignment.

When they asked about the consequences of crime, he responded "I know only one thing for sure; if you want to make crime pay, go to law school."

Several of Allen's attorney 'friends' are proof of that.

"I go from building in a 1.5 million house in Tucson to not having a place to live. Futon Ron kept my house but he never paid me. I didn't think he'd do this in a million years.

"We were in Tucson to see LaMonte and my oldest daughter says 'Can we drive by our old house?' Her little sister didn't remember much because she was so young.

"I thought we were just going to drive by and look at it from the street; not go in the gates or anything. We were sitting out front and the kids were just looking in the gate going 'Wow' when Ron's wife came home.

"She would have known me but she didn't see me because I was sitting in the back seat. She recognized my kids and said 'You guys want to come in and look at the house?'

"I stayed in the car and let the girls go inside.

"They said they changed some things, took the saguaro rib cabinets and herringbone ceilings out and put in whatever they wanted.

"Ron's wife was really nice to them – until she saw me; then she went white as a ghost."

And then there was Stealthy Steve, 'the big time tax attorney.'

"Stealthy Steve would tell me 'Go pay this, go pay that.'

"I paid him 1.9 million at one time. I paid millions in cash. In my records they have my fines at millions and millions of dollars that I paid in to them.

"Probably a year into the IRS investigation – after I paid him a lot of money – Stealthy Steve left the legal firm and opened his own.

"That deal the US Attorney made with me, that I could take my money from before '89, put it in the bank and use it … I never heard anything about it again until 2006 when they came back and said I grossly underestimated my income.

"That couldn't be. They went back to years that were already audited. I had already paid taxes on that money. One year they charged me numbers that exactly coincide with the money I paid in – $1.9 million.

"When I got out I didn't know where my records were. Finally I found out the paperwork was at the law firm in Phoenix.

"I called a woman who was still working there. She told me they were going to send it to my father-in-law, but they didn't because there were so many boxes.

"When I finally got them I went through them with a new friend I met him through a guy who's connected.

"Dale is a government agent. He knows more about tax than just about anyone in the country. He knows all the tax laws, takes seminars almost daily.

"He has access. He's what they call 'an Enrolled Agent in the Department of Justice.' He tells *them*.

"I knew I had to get my taxes in order. I walked into his office and said 'Can you help me?'

"He said 'Yeah, no problem.'

"I gave him a couple grand and he started working on them.

"It's hard to go through 15 boxes of tax records. He looked at my stuff and he knows I got a letter of immunity. I proved all the stuff that I told him was true.

"He's got this new software that enabled him to see how many times they went after someone and trace the money.

"He was looking at how much I was paying and he goes 'Did you get any of your returns?'

"I said 'I got a check one time for $25,000 from the IRS. I thought *Wow this is cool!* I put it in the bank but I never got another one.

"I called my lawyer about it. Stealthy Steve pretended he was happy for me, but I think he was getting the money I should have gotten. He was friends with the prosecutor, so they made a deal I guess.

"I was paying my taxes and I don't know how they were doing it, but they were taking my money in to the IRS and transferring it out to a different bank account.

"Dale goes 'I've fought some of the big cases' – he started laughing – 'I thought they were big but you blow 'em all away. There's an instance here where you pay $1.9 million to the IRS one day, the next day it shows it going in, shows it being paid to the IRS; and the next day shows it going out to a bank account other than the IRS.'

"The next day it shows no action taken. Like I still owed the money.

"This was quarterly I paid. I'd get the money and pay in cashiers' checks. Late fees, interest and penalties; it doesn't even show that I paid my fine. Now where did that money go?'

"Dale says it's the most amazing thing he's ever seen and he's been doing it since he was 18.

"The debt dropped from my files in May of 2016 – and they stopped bothering me. I got out of my tax situation by Stealthy Steve and them stealing my money!

"Dale says 'They stole probably $10 to $15 million from you.'

"He wanted to go after the money because after this long I would have had $30 or $40 million dollars in interest on it. That would have been fine for me.

"The government is the most corrupt people on fucking earth. I hate 'em. No scruples.

"I don't know who was involved. My lawyer had to be in on it, all these guys had to be in on it. Maybe the IRS agent. Looks like they were just stealing as much as they could get.

"I didn't know anything sometimes. It's just a fucking cowboy state.

"A year after I got out I ran into Stealthy Steve at one of my favorite restaurants. He saw me, turned gray as a ghost and was shaking.

"He didn't know that *I didn't know* he ripped me off. If I did, I would have choked him out right there."

During the years Allen was incarcerated – between 2007 and 2013 – six states legalized medical cannabis, Massachusetts decriminalized cannabis and Washington and Colorado legalized recreational marijuana.

On November 8, 2016 the L.A. Times announced that California voters approved Proposition 64, "making California the most populous state in the nation to legalize the recreational use of marijuana. The approval of the ballot measure creates the largest market for marijuana products in the U.S."

Allen told me "Arizona declined; that just means people will continue buying Mexican weed. We live on the border, *wake the fuck up people!* Kids are not going to stop smoking weed, it's just never going to happen.

"If they want to block the kids from getting shitty product, just legalize it and regulate.

"I was ahead of the times. I always knew marijuana was going to be legal; I didn't know how long it would take."

"Living dangerously was a little bit of a rush. I liked the action and dodging the government here and there.

"The IRS spent $60, $70 million investigating me, trying to get me. That's not to mention how much the FBI and the DEA spent; well over 100 million dollars trying to get one guy for selling marijuana.

"The government needs to catch on to the fact that they can make a lot of money *taxing* weed. They can make their money legally; they don't have to steal it.

"My story? It's not over. Not by a long shot."

DEALING WEED

About the Author

I was chosen to write Allen's book because I know a guy who knows a guy. The biggest surprise was the people, places and events we have in common. I've lived much of my life on the cusp of his circle.

Like Allen, I was born with a connection to Detroit's prohibition past. Grandpa ran booze across the Detroit River and met my grandmother at one of the city's legendary dance halls.

In the years following prohibition they built a house, had a family and achieved respectability – until their 15 year old daughter came home pregnant.

My mother raised herself while her parents raised me. There were no bunnies at bedtime, no Little Golden Books. Fortified with warm beer and unfiltered Camels, grandpa told me about the times he flipped his boat and swam for his life.

Who wanted him dead? The Purple Gang? The River Gang? I'll never know. I *do* know he inspired my love of boats, history and gangster stories.

I don't remember the time before my 'father.' An Italian jazz musician married my mother, gave us his name and found a priest who was willing to christen me.

He took me to rehearsals where I played outside with children of all colors. On Sunday mornings, he was my accomplice in skipping church to watch Lassie.

When they split, he grew his reputation in Detroit's jazz scene and my mother became a Watchtower wielding zealot. She had me banging doors before I was tall enough to reach the bells.

A shy, fearful kid, the end of times mentality *nearly* crushed my spirit. I grew to marry an elder's son and accepted that I would dutifully walk three steps behind as he rose in the organization.

When we happened upon the truth of my past, I *ran* – from squeaky clean elder to ultimate badass. My first love was associated with The Outfit.

Those years defined me, from the characters we hung with to the secrecy and surveillance. 'The boys' were masterful storytellers. I enjoyed their gestures, word choices and intonations. It was a rush.

After he dumped me – as is their way – I rebounded with the big man on track; a successful businessman who owned, trained and raced thoroughbreds from Hazel Park and DRC to Hialeah.

I knew of mob influence at the track but paid no attention. I was learning from an entrepreneur who knew how to get what he wanted.

I wanted to become a professional writer. Landing my first full-time job was surprisingly easy and aspiration turned to obsession. I became an award-winning automotive marketing writer, wrote radio and TV commercials for Harley-Davidson dealers, conducted many interviews for print and web and wrote several non-fiction books.

In 2004 I circled back and googled my first love. I was afraid he wouldn't remember me. Turns out he was afraid he'd never see *me* again.

We've been dearest friends ever since. When planets align we hang with the boys in Naples and Detroit. It's always good food, great stories and much laughter.

The Allen Ahee Story

www.ingramcontent.com/pod-product-compliance
Lightning Source LLC
Chambersburg PA
CBHW072112270326
41931CB00010B/1537